Law and the Russian State

The Bloomsbury History of Modern Russia Series

Series Editors: Jonathan D. Smele (Queen Mary, University of London, UK) and Michael Melancon (Auburn University, USA)

This ambitious and unique series offers readers the latest views on aspects of the modern history of what has been and remains one of the most powerful and important countries in the world. In a series of books aimed at students, leading academics and experts from across the world portray, in a thematic manner, a broad variety of aspects of the Russian experience, over extended periods of time, from the reign of Peter the Great in the early eighteenth century to the Putin era at the beginning of the twenty-first.

Published:

Peasants in Russia from Serfdom to Stalin: Accommodation, Survival, Resistance, Boris B. Gorshkov (2018)

Crime and Punishment in Russia: A Comparative History from Peter the Great to Vladimir Putin, Jonathan Daly (2018)

Marx and Russia: The Fate of a Doctrine, James D. White (2018)

Forthcoming:

A Modern History of Russian Childhood: From Imperialism to the End of the Soviet Era, Elizabeth White (2019)

The History of the Russian Worker: Life and Change from Peter the Great to Vladimir Putin, Alice Pate (2019)

Dissidents, Émigrés and Revolutionaries in Russia: Anti-State Activism in International Perspective, 1848–2015, Charlotte Alston (2019)

Law and the Russian State

Russia's Legal Evolution from Peter the Great to Vladimir Putin

William E. Pomeranz

BLOOMSBURY ACADEMIC
LONDON • NEW YORK • OXFORD • NEW DELHI • SYDNEY

BLOOMSBURY ACADEMIC
Bloomsbury Publishing Plc
50 Bedford Square, London, WC1B 3DP, UK
1385 Broadway, New York, NY 10018, USA

BLOOMSBURY, BLOOMSBURY ACADEMIC and the
Diana logo are trademarks of Bloomsbury Publishing Plc

First published in Great Britain 2019

Copyright © William E. Pomeranz, 2019

William E. Pomeranz has asserted his right under the Copyright,
Designs and Patents Act, 1988, to be identified as Author of this work.

For legal purposes the Acknowledgments on p. viii
constitute an extension of this copyright page.

Cover image: The court in session during the trial of British businessman Greville Wynne and Russian scientific worker Oleg Penkovsky, Moscow, 1963. (© Keystone/Getty Images)

All rights reserved. No part of this publication may be reproduced or transmitted in any form or by any means, electronic or mechanical, including photocopying, recording, or any information storage or retrieval system, without prior permission in writing from the publishers.

Bloomsbury Publishing Plc does not have any control over, or responsibility for, any third-party websites referred to or in this book. All internet addresses given in this book were correct at the time of going to press. The author and publisher regret any inconvenience caused if addresses have changed or sites have ceased to exist, but can accept no responsibility for any such changes.

A catalogue record for this book is available from the British Library.

A catalog record for this book is available from the Library of Congress.

ISBN: HB: 978-1-4742-2422-2
ePDF: 978-1-4742-2423-9
eBook: 978-1-4742-2424-6

Series: The Bloomsbury History of Modern Russia Series

Typeset by Integra Software Services Pvt. Ltd.

To find out more about our authors and books visit www.bloomsbury.com
and sign up for our newsletters.

To my parents – Jacqueline Pomeranz and Jerome Pomeranz (1930 – 2010) – who always believed in me.

CONTENTS

Acknowledgments viii

Introduction 1

1 Law and Empire under Peter the Great 9
2 The Expansion of Russian Legality 21
3 The Judicial Reforms of 1864 and the Modernization of Imperial Law 37
4 Law, Politics, and Revolution 57
5 Filling in the Blanks: The Creation of Socialist Law 73
6 Socialist Legality and Illegality 91
7 Russia's Long Constitutional Crisis: 1985–1993 107
8 The 1993 Constitution: A Framework for Reform 123
9 Vladimir Putin and the Restoration of State and Law 143

Conclusion 165

Notes 170
Bibliography 203
Index 219

ACKNOWLEDGMENTS

This book is the result of a career path that has never followed a straight line. I have had the privilege to work in academia, the nonprofit sector, law firms, and think tanks—as well as an early stint as telemarketer for the Cleveland Indians. Because of these personal twists and turns, however, I have arrived rather late at my first book, and so, with the reader's indulgence, I have a long list of acknowledgments to work through.

I am extremely fortunate to have had a series of mentors in high school, college, and graduate school who invested considerable effort to open my eyes and introduce me to Russian history, language, and culture. I will always be indebted to David Chollet, Linda Gerstein, John Gooding, and the Edinburgh University Russian Department for their inspiration and guidance. I spent five years at the School of Slavonic and East European Studies (now a part of University College London) under the supervision of Professor Geoffrey Hosking. It was a remarkable time to be studying Russian and Soviet history, and I will always be indebted to Professor Hosking for his thoughtful critiques and constant encouragement throughout the dissertation process. He still remains my model of what a scholar and mentor should be. As my co-supervisor, Professor William Butler generously shared his extensive knowledge of Russian law while providing an outstanding example as to how one might combine an interest in Russian legal history with the practice of law.

I returned to the United States with plenty of knowledge but no immediate job prospects but soon found myself attending the noon-time discussions at the Kennan Institute, led by its director Blair Ruble. Fortunately for me, Blair was not only an outstanding scholar but also a baseball fan, and he proceeded to open doors for me in Washington, DC. I should add that he showed similar generosity to dozens of other scholars, so I am not alone in saying that Blair Ruble helped make my career. In 1992, I landed at the National Endowment for Democracy (NED), where for seven years I got a front-row seat on all the changes in Russia, Ukraine, and the post-Soviet space. I will always be grateful to Carl Gershman, Barbara Haig, and especially Nadia Diuk for giving me the opportunity to work in such a rewarding environment.

While working at the NED, I managed to find the energy to attend law school at night at American University's Washington College of Law. The highlight of this experience was working with Professor Herman

Schwartz, who supervised two independent research projects on the Russian Constitutional Court. I proceeded to spend the next eight years practicing law, first in Moscow and then in Washington, DC. Once again, several individuals invested considerable time and effort to make me a better lawyer. In particular, I want to thank Carol Patterson, Adrian Moore, Tom McVey, and Jimmie Reyna. A special note of thanks goes to Max Gutbrod, who supervised me when I worked with Baker & McKenzie in Moscow. I often say that I learned Russian civil law in the finest German civil law tradition. Max has remained a valued colleague, coauthor, and friend, and many of the ideas in this book sprung from our discussions over dinner.

I will always be grateful that I had the opportunity to move from the nonprofit to the for-profit sector and to learn how the "real world" worked. Even better was making the transition back to the public sector. It started at Georgetown University, where Professor Angela Stent provided me with an opportunity to teach a course on Russian law at the Center for Eurasian, Russian and East European Studies. Teaching forced me to present my thoughts on Russian law in a coherent manner, and they were tested by an outstanding group of graduate students at every turn. Soon thereafter, Blair Ruble facilitated another critical transition, and for over a decade I have served as the Kennan Institute's deputy director. The Kennan Institute is an integral part of the Woodrow Wilson Center, and I have benefited from the inspired leadership of both Lee Hamilton and Jane Harman. For the past five years, I have had the pleasure to work with the current director of the Kennan Institute, Matt Rojansky, who has provided constant encouragement for this book, as well as fostering an environment that advances the work of all scholars. Finally, I have benefitted from the support of a talented staff and series of hard-working interns, including Andrey Sazonov, Nikolai Rice, Natalia Romanova, Norman Rozenberg, Mikhail Strokan, and Ekaterina Zeveleva. A special note of thanks goes to Alina Strokan, who helped immensely on my research on the Russian procuracy and then voluntarily stayed on and became one of my most enthusiastic readers.

Numerous colleagues have provided assistance and advice along the way. The list is too long to tally without forgetting important names, but it has always been rewarding to work with many colleagues across multiple disciplines. The rule-of-law community is more compact, and I specifically would like to thank the following people for their support: Mikhail Antonov, Sergei Antonov, Suren Avanesyan, Randy Bregman, Jane Burbank, Anton Burkov, Tatiana Borisova, Svetlana Boshno, Ethan Burger, Jonathan Daly, Thomas Firestone, Stephen Frank, Cathy Frierson, Rozaliya Garipova, James Heinzen, Jane Henderson, Susan Heuman, Kathryn Hendley, Eugene Huskey, Pamela Jordan, Jeffrey Kahn, Lauri Malksoo, Lauren McCarthy, Oleksandr Merezhko, Mark Pomar, Aaron Retish, Oleg Rumiantsev, Robert Sharlet, William Simons, Gordon Smith, Stanislav Stanskikh, Peter Solomon, Alexei Trochev, Stephen Williams, William Wagner, and Richard Wortman.

I am grateful to Jonathan Smele and Michael Melancon, the editors of this series, for challenging me to write this book. Rhodri Mogford and Beatriz Lopez at Bloomsbury have been a delight to work with as well. But the greatest source of support as always has come from my family. My late father was sometimes a bit puzzled at my career choices, but he and his wife, Dr. Barbara Barna, never wavered in their support and pride in all of my endeavors. My mother Jacqueline Pomeranz remains my biggest fan, and she always encouraged me to think big, no matter what I do. My brother Russell has kept me grounded as only an older brother can. Finally, my late sister Emily loved asking questions about what I do even if she had trouble pronouncing any Russian word. She sadly passed away during the late stages of this project, but I know she would have been so proud to see this book come to fruition.

My final words of gratitude go to my immediate family. Growing up in a household of two Russian specialists, my daughter Kira has shown great patience with our long-distance travels, Slavic conferences, and obscure dinnertime conversations. She is now off to Georgetown on her own journey of discovery. Finally, my wife Kelly Smith has brought all of her considerable Russian expertise and ruthless editorial judgment to bear on this manuscript. Moreover, she has steadfastly supported all of my personal twists and turns, making major sacrifices of her own along the way. It is no exaggeration to say that this book would not have been possible without her love and encouragement.

Introduction

A trip to the law section of any major Moscow bookstore is always a revelation. In a country often referred to as "lawless" or suffering from "legal nihilism," a visitor will discover a wide collection of textbooks covering virtually every area of Russian law, as well as the country's main legal institutions. These books are not for the casual reader. Most consist of detailed legal commentaries to inform both students and practitioners about the content of the law. Others present comprehensive histories that trace the evolution of Russian legal institutions over several distinct political regimes.

A European lawyer—one steeped in the continental practice of civil law—will feel relatively at home with this legal specialization and the emphasis on statutory law. Alternatively, a lawyer from a common law jurisdiction will recognize that while Russia does not follow the Anglo-American tradition of precedent—hence Russian textbooks do not focus on case law—ample opportunities still exist to investigate Russian law from a comparative perspective.

But both common law and civil law lawyers will be stumped by the wall of books on the theory and the history of state and law. For an American lawyer, the emphasis on the "state" is immediately problematic. The state as a single, unified entity does not exist under the US constitution; indeed, its preamble only contains the aspiration to "a more perfect union," and the constitution proceeds to define a divided government based on the principle of separation of powers. A European civil law lawyer will be more familiar with notions of state and law since for centuries Europeans experienced law as the positivist commands of the sovereign. Yet this theory was gradually diluted during the nineteenth and early twentieth centuries as elected legislatures appropriated the sovereign's law-creating powers for themselves. In 1945, the renowned legal scholar Hans Kelsen reformulated his "pure theory of law" and published *The General Theory of Law and State* in English, a reversal of terms with clear political implications. Henceforth, law, with a specific emphasis on human rights, would limit the power of the state. Indeed, after the Second World War, Western Europe witnessed the rise of both national constitutional courts and European-wide judicial institutions to defend fundamental civil liberties.

Yet despite a convergence in the common and civil law worlds around the concepts of separation of powers and human rights, Russia still upholds the concept of "state and law." The word order is not accidental. The state has served as the dominant administrative, law-creating, and unifying political body throughout Russia's existence, and the legitimacy of every ruler—from Peter the Great to Vladimir Putin—ultimately has relied on the elevated position of the state. Law appears as a secondary actor. It inevitably follows the distinct needs of the state, which is unrestrained by natural law or social contract theory. Yet despite law's subordinate status, Russian law is neither static nor meaningless. At various stages of Russian history, Russia has pursued legal modernization as a necessary accompaniment to economic modernization. Even during its socialist experiment, the Soviet Union invented and exported its own brand of socialist law around the world, only to return to a more conventional understanding of law after 1991.

But while law is firmly linked to the development of the Russian state, its evolution cannot be told as part of a continuous constitutional history. Instead, the chronology of Russian law is best understood through the actions of individual rulers who have added to—or subtracted from—the content of Russian law as part of their broader efforts to maintain control over society. Contemporary books on the history of state and law largely follow this periodization. Yet Russian law is not only a top-down exercise; it is also shaped from below, due to a persistent demand for law that has manifested itself both in the regular adjudication of everyday legal disputes and in highly charged political cases. Indeed, looking around the bookstore, visitors will see collections of great political speeches by members of the pre-1917 legal profession (the *advokatura*), including Spasovich, Plevako, and Karabchevskii. These landmarks in legal rhetoric are now more than a century old, yet they still have not lost their eloquence or their relevance in today's world. And so they still occupy a prominent space on the bookshelf, a testament to the idealism that can accompany Russian law.

A tour around the bookstore raises other questions as well. The store will have a section on constitutional law that includes detailed commentaries on Russia's most recent 1993 constitution, complete with references to the major decisions issued by the Russian Constitutional Court. While Russia possessed no constitution prior to 1906, it made up for lost time and produced no less than seven constitutions during the twentieth century. Admittedly, the early Soviet constitutions were largely for show, with only the 1977 constitution acknowledging upfront the dominant role played by the Communist Party. Nevertheless, the Soviet constitutions have largely disappeared from the bookshelves, even though they all addressed the relationship between state and law and therefore shed considerable light on Russia's legal history.

While the number of books on constitutional law appears rather modest, the section on the prosecutor's office (*prokuratura*) looms surprisingly large. Founded by Peter the Great in 1722, the procuracy stands out as Russia's longest-running legal institution. Moreover, one of the core missions assigned to the procuracy, encapsulated in the unique Russian notion of *nadzor* (supervision), has now lasted almost 300 years and remains an essential part of the procuracy's powers today. No continental European legal system retains such a concept, and when the European Court of Human Rights first confronted this concept of supervision and supervisory review in the 1990s, it ruled this power in clear violation of the European Convention on Human Rights. Yet *nadzor*—albeit in different forms—persists to the present day, and the modern procuracy continues to insert itself into the administration of justice. Moreover, from a practical standpoint, the procuracy remains far more powerful than the judiciary and the bar, thereby posing a distinct conundrum to Western commentators trying to describe the inner workings of the Russian legal system.

A quick tour around the Russian bookstore identifies just some of the pertinent issues for an investigation into the history of Russian law. Such an analysis requires not only an understanding of the law as written but the complex political, social, and economic environment in which Russian law has operated. As the legal historian Harold Berman notes, a legal system is more than the laws in force:

> Law is a monument of history, constructed over many centuries, not simply out of words and documents but out of human actions and human lives. Law is more than rules; it is the legal profession, the law schools, the technique and tradition of judging, administering and legislating. Law is also the sense of law, the law-consciousness of the people.[1]

This book follows Berman's basic instruction and traces the history of Russian law from the imperial period through to the present day. The book analyzes the competing policy options confronting a multinational state and global power and how these choices have been translated into law. The book further addresses how law enters everyday life without ultimately binding the ruler or the state, thereby permitting both parties to operate outside formal legal parameters when necessary. Finally, this book traces the development of state and law not just as a means of administration but as the default ruling ideology. Russia has turned to numerous ideologies over the centuries—the imperial triumvirate of autocracy, orthodoxy, and nationality; the Soviet pursuit of international socialism; Putin's sovereign democracy and conservative patriotism. This book contends that in absence of a single overarching ideology that covers over 300 years of Russian history, the theory of state and law represents Russia's most enduring governing philosophy.

Yet it is the "autocratic and unlimited" ruler (to borrow tsarist terminology) who has consistently set both the tempo and the tone of Russian law. Therefore, the chronology of this book follows the policies of tsars, general secretaries, and presidents as the primary instigators and enforcers of Russian law. The book further focuses on specific branches of law (primarily civil, criminal, and when applicable, constitutional) as well as the three main institutional pillars of law (procuracy, judiciary, and the bar) to analyze how the Russian legal system works in practice. The book does not attempt to analyze every important statute or each procedural rule, nor does it describe every internal bureaucratic debate and major political trial; instead, it seeks to integrate law into the broader narrative of Russian history. In so doing, the book builds upon the work of historians, political scientists, law professors, legal practitioners, journalists, and other commentators who have examined specific aspects and periods of Russian law. This survey of Russian law would not be possible without these exemplary and thought-provoking studies addressing legal topics from medieval *Rus'* to the present.

Chapter 1 begins with Imperial Russia's first law code, the *Ulozhenie* of 1649, and Peter the Great's creation of a modern secular state at the beginning of the eighteenth century. Peter never replaced the *Ulozhenie* of 1649—legal reform played second fiddle to imperial expansion—but he sought to update Russian law as part of his state-building activities. Yet Peter's legal modernization was accompanied by increased supervision of state institutions, thereby setting the two extremes of Russian law that have never been fully reconciled.

Peter's vision of law would guide Russia for more than a century as subsequent rulers struggled to codify Russian law and to transmit the empire's central commands to what was an increasingly diverse and multinational population. Chapter 2 discusses how three major successors to Peter the Great attempted to expand the domain of Russian law; Catherine the Great focused on property rights and administrative reform; Alexander I toyed with constitutional change; Nicholas I collected Russian law into one source while rapidly expanding Russian legal education and the cadre of professionally trained jurists. Yet throughout this period, law and justice remained a component of state administration. It was not until Alexander II and the Judicial Reforms of 1864 that law became a truly independent factor within Russian government and society, with both top-down and bottom-up challenges to the autocracy's monopoly of law-creating powers.

As Chapter 3 reveals, the Judicial Reforms of 1864 were not as all-encompassing as often remembered, since they did not address Russia's underlying substantive law. Nevertheless, the Judicial Reforms launched a series of processes that transformed Russia's legal institutions while increasing the role of law in governance, commerce, and everyday life. For all these positive developments, however, the autocracy never embraced the full possibilities of a law-based state; instead, it maintained a highly compartmentalized vision of law that broached no limits of its extensive public law powers. Thus, law became a source of conflict, and Chapter 4 examines the evolution of this struggle by looking at the political trials of the late tsarist period, the drafting of Russia's first constitution in 1906, and finally the 1917 revolution itself.

In February 1917, the Provisional Government put forward its own progressive vision of law based on a more advanced understanding of civil rights and the rule of law, but it did so at a time of economic, social, and military collapse. The Provisional Government ultimately lacked the minimum force necessary to enforce the law and hold the empire together. Therefore, in October 1917 it lost power to the Bolshevik Party and Vladimir Lenin, who dismissed law as an inherently bourgeois preoccupation and source of oppression. Thus began a twenty-year cycle of dismantling and then reestablishing the legal system as the Soviet Union lurched from the pursuit of revolutionary consciousness to the need for basic stability.

Between 1918 and 1936, the Soviet Union wrote three constitutions that, while never formally observed, nevertheless elucidated the evolving relationship between the Soviet state and law. Chapter 5 examines these constitutions as a critical window on how law emerged in the Soviet Union, even as the excesses of Soviet rule—most notably Stalin's terror—undermined the very notion of law as an independent force in Soviet society. Stalin's successors sought to limit the extremes of Soviet law without fundamentally changing the Stalinist system and the monopoly of power enjoyed by the Communist Party. Chapter 6 explores Khrushchev's and Brezhnev's attempts to reform Soviet law and the legal challenge posed by various groups—nationalists, religious believers, economic speculators, dissidents—that fell outside the socialist system.

The elevation of Mikhail Gorbachev as general secretary in 1985 ushered in a new era of fundamental legal change. Yet law turned out not to be the savior of a revived Soviet Union but rather a critical catalyst in its ultimate demise. Thus, for the second time in the twentieth century, liberals assumed power in Russia. And for the second time, they inherited a bankrupt, disintegrating state. Chapter 7 covers Russia's long constitutional crisis that stretches from Gorbachev's legal reforms through Boris Yeltsin's 1993 confrontation with the Supreme Soviet. Yeltsin ultimately survived, but only because he was willing to violate the law and dissolve (and fire upon) the legislature in order to defend his democratic mandate. Yeltsin subsequently presided over some of the most far-reaching legal reforms in Russian history, including the adoption of the country's most liberal constitution.

Chapter 8 provides a detailed analysis of the 1993 constitution and argues that while Yeltsin moved Russia closer to the Western consensus positions on separation of powers and human rights, his constitution retained the principle of state power—with its broad historical overtones and discretionary authorities. Yeltsin's chosen successor Vladimir Putin would seize on these statist principles and use them to his maximum political advantage. The final chapter of the book focuses on Putin's restoration of top-down legality and explains how the legal system works in present-day Russia.

This book largely takes a chronological approach in examining the development of Russian law and its legal institutions. Several common themes, however, run through the manuscript as well, and they require particular attention in understanding the evolution of Russian law over the centuries. The first recurring issue involves the question of sources of law, or put more bluntly, where do Russian lawyers and citizens go to find the relevant statute or rule? Common law and civil law lawyers approach this essential task in very different ways, fundamentally disagreeing over the relative law-creating powers of the legislature and judiciary, respectively. To summarize, common law jurisdictions allow judges to make law, while in civil law countries, this task falls almost exclusively on the legislative branch. In the case of Russia, which has no long-standing tradition of an independent legislature or judiciary, both the ruler and the bureaucracy have filled the law-creating void and produced all types of regulations—codes, statutes, decrees, rulings—that carried the force of law but were not necessarily presented in a systematic or transparent fashion. Indeed, the tsarist and the Soviet regimes often failed to even publish their legislation, making it impossible to determine what the law actually was on a given subject. So as one traces the history of Russian law, one must appreciate its general opaqueness and how such uncertainty influenced public perceptions of the law.

A second frequent theme in this book concerns the geography of Russian law. Imperial Russia gathered numerous territories during the eighteenth and nineteenth centuries, but its rulers did not necessarily insist that these regions adopt the actual substance of Russian law. Instead, they only demanded recognition of Russia's sovereignty over the territory. Thus, a significant degree of legal pluralism existed within the boundaries of the Russian empire, and it was not until the late nineteenth century—in the aftermath of the 1864 Judicial Reforms and the creation of more vigorous legal institutions and court procedures—that the autocracy actively began to pursue uniformity in Russian law. The Soviet Union was much more centralized, but it too endowed the republics with their own constitutions and legal codes. This grant lacked real political significance until the late Gorbachev period, but it ultimately led to the passage of legislation that openly defied Soviet law while exposing the weakness of the central governing institutions. The question of the geography of law also dominated the presidency of Boris Yeltsin. In a bid to keep the Russian Federation together, he signed numerous bilateral treaties with individual regions, even though these agreements undermined the country's unified legal and economic space.

A final theme that repeats itself throughout the book is what Professor Kathryn Hendley refers to as the duality of Russian law.[2] Hendley's research focuses on modern-day justice, and while she fully recognizes that Russian courts can be highly politicized, she balances this observation with a detailed description of everyday law that operates independently and in a highly transparent manner. She finds a persistent demand for law that would be irrational if Russian justice were as corrupt and dysfunctional as often described by journalists and commentators. Rather, Hendley portrays Russian litigants as savvy consumers of the courts. In fact, everyday law has existed in one form or another throughout most of Russian history, as has, one should hasten to add, the ability of the Russian state to engage in selective, and highly coercive, punishment. The duality of law remains a consistent feature of the Russian legal system, with major implications for how people engage with the law.

All of which leads to one last question: by what yardstick does one measure the development of Russian law? The most conventional reference point is the Western notion of the "rule of law," a concept that defies a single definition but when interpreted most broadly incorporates such fundamental ideas as equality, uniformity, procedural regularity, transparency, and accountability—plus an appeal to natural law principles as the ultimate philosophical check on man-made laws. The "rule of law" exists as an ideal type that is not met in practice by its most ardent Western advocates. Thus, the danger always exists that Western commentators will impose a "rule of law" standard that has eluded even the most advanced legal traditions at various points in their history. The "rule of law" model is even more problematic when applied to Russia. Hendley, for example, argues that it is too "all or nothing" and fails to take into account the dualistic nature of Russian law.[3] Moreover, the difficulty of applying the rule-of-law ideal to Russia is only compounded by the fact that not one but two words—*pravo* and *zakon*—are used to approximate the English word for law. While the terms are sometimes used interchangeably, they can, in certain contexts, imply vastly different meanings. *Pravo* incorporates a more philosophical understanding of law to suggest notions of justice, individual rights, and limited government, while *zakon* focuses on the written statute without making any broader normative judgment. This distinction becomes critical, however, when one seeks to apply such Western concepts as the "rule of law" to Russia, since its understanding varies depending on whether one is referring to *pravo* or *zakon*.

This book proposes an alternative benchmark, the Russian notion of *zakonnost'* (legality), by which to gauge the evolution of Russian law. Like other Russian legal terms, *zakonnost'* has multiple meanings. The idea of *zakonnost'* can, in certain circumstances, be expanded to approximate the notion of the supremacy of law. It also, however, can be understood more narrowly. The historian Marc Szeftel defined *zakonnost'* as "law abidingness," while Russian commentators have recognized that the term carries a more functional component that simply demands the strict observance of all laws.[4] This requirement applies not just to citizens but also to government institutions. As the historian Richard Wortman has noted, the autocracy pursued notions of legality "as means to induce officials to implement the legislative enactments of the supreme power."[5] Thus, at various points in Russian history, the state and its rulers have emphasized the need for legality and law abidingness without necessarily recognizing the rule of law as the ultimate objective.

The use of *zakonnost'*—and other Russian terminology—is not intended to gloss over or diminish the problems associated with Russian law and its legal system. These shortcomings can be found throughout Russian history, and this book addresses them both within the specific Russian context and in comparative perspective. These established weaknesses, however, should not be used to relegate law to the margins of Russian history. On the contrary, law is intimately related to the notion of Russian statehood. It also stands at the crossroads of centuries of political, economic, and social change. Therefore, this book takes Russian law out of the periphery and places it front and center in the historical narrative. Moreover, by seeking to understand Russian law on its own terms—and through the prism of state and law—this book analyzes the distinctive aspects of the Russian legal tradition while simultaneously revealing the continuities between Imperial, Soviet, and post-Soviet law.

1

Law and Empire under Peter the Great

Peter the Great's transformation of the Russian state at the beginning of the eighteenth century marks Russia's entry onto the world stage. Peter relied on his personal law-creating powers to modernize the state, in the process restructuring the military, economy, church, and legal system. His unrestricted view of state power, however, was accompanied by a narrow vision of legality, a belief that if everyone—bureaucrats and subjects alike—simply followed the letter of the law, the state would operate like a smooth running machine.

Yet no legal system ever starts from scratch. Peter inherited a relatively new law code and a distinct legal tradition from Muscovy that would influence developments for centuries to come. Of particular importance was the Law Code (*Ulozhenie*) of 1649. Rooted in the laws of Moscow, Pskov, Novgorod, and Kiev, the Law Code of 1649 holds a special place in Russian history in large part due to its longevity. It remained Russia's governing law for some 180 years, by far the longest serving source of law in Russian history. This chapter examines Peter's legal inheritance from Muscovy and his attempts to update and expand Russian law to meet the needs of a rapidly expanding empire. In the process, foreign law and practices entered into Russia, but they remained fully subordinated to the goals of the Russian state.

The Muscovite legacy

The Law Code of 1649 was born of crisis. In June 1648, nineteen-year-old Tsar Alexei faced an internal revolt sparked by the corrupt rule of Boris Morozov, Alexei's former mentor and *de facto* ruler since Alexei had assumed the throne three years earlier. The growing social unrest led to calls for a new founding law, and a special Assembly of the Land (*zemskii sobor*) was summoned to prepare and ratify the Law Code. This marked the last time that Russian autocrats would seek the formal approval of legislation by their subjects for another 250 years.

The speed with which the Law Code was drafted confirms that a significant body of substantive Russian law predated its proclamation. Many of the individual statutes came from the government chancery offices and consisted of highly specific rules and regulations, as opposed to more general norms. Thus, the Law Code possessed limited potential for interpretation but instead imposed narrow, specific requirements. Moreover, not all of the law in this new code was necessarily Russian law. Approximately 20 percent of the Law Code of 1649 came from the Lithuanian Statute of 1588 and Byzantine law.[1] From the Lithuanian Statute, the Law Code of 1649 borrowed contract law, legislation protecting the sovereign, and some of the more heinous laws on torture. From Byzantium, Russian law incorporated new crimes against faith and the person, as well as the rights of the family. What the Law Code specifically omitted was the Lithuanian Statute's notion of a law-based state (*Rechtsstaat*), the legal concept that all citizens, including the ruler, are subject to the law. Furthermore, Muscovite law made no concession to the notion of separation of powers. As the historian Richard Hellie notes, "The executive essentially ran everything; it served (with the rarest of exceptions) as its own legislative arm, and also was its own judiciary."[2]

The codification process in any country requires the gathering and restating of law by subject. The 1649 code consisted of twenty-five chapters, covering the tsar and his court, the church, and different social groups (townsmen, guardsmen [*streltsy*], Cossacks, slaves), thereby reinforcing its established social hierarchies. The code further distinguished between civil and criminal laws. It addressed such standard civil law subjects as property, inheritance, and contracts. Criminal law covered crimes against the state, the church, property, morality, and the individual (i.e., murder, assault, slander, etc.). Most importantly, the state retained exclusive jurisdiction over all high crimes, thereby maintaining a monopoly on violence essential to running a continental, and still expanding, empire.[3] Violence inevitably meant torture and executions, which were also sanctioned under the Law Code. Russian law also recognized a distinctive form of punishment: exile. Indeed, the death penalty was used increasingly sparingly in Muscovy; instead, criminals were regularly sent to Siberia where rather than being imprisoned (the state lacked the resources to maintain such facilities), exiles worked as garrison guards, artisans, and peasants, among other occupations. Thus, Muscovy criminal law played a unique role in the colonization of the Russian empire.[4]

The Law Code of 1649 has been praised as "one of the most important documents of Russian history and one of the major monuments of legal history."[5] It codified an ongoing shift that would shape the practice of Russian law for centuries to come—the choice of inquisitorial procedures over the accusatorial (adversarial) system of justice, the primacy of written over oral evidence, and the focus on statutes over common (i.e., judge-made) law. Muscovy clearly diverged from the Anglo-Saxon model, but it remained consistent with other continental legal developments, and the creation of a single, unified source of law in the middle of the seventeenth century marked a significant achievement in governance.

The Law Code of 1649 was not just a legal document, however. It possessed broader implications for Muscovite society as well. In particular, two groups—the peasantry and the Church—saw their social standing decline significantly in the aftermath of its adoption. For Russian peasants, defeat was total: the code legally enserfed just over half the peasantry by creating an unlimited statute of limitations for the recovery of fugitive peasants who attempted to flee their landlords. The Church was semi-secularized through the creation of a new government office (the Monastery Chancellery), which was assigned responsibility for administering church lands and the people who lived on those properties. The Monastery Chancellery proved short-lived, but the reform paved the way for full secularization of the Orthodox Church by Peter the Great in 1721.[6]

Townsmen did better under the Law Code in which they received near-monopolies on trade and manufacturing. Yet they too found their personal mobility sharply circumscribed, restricted to the town in which they presently resided. Thus, the new legislation codified a highly stratified, caste-like society, yet it also provided all subjects—no matter what their nationality, religion, or social standing—access to the legal system.[7]

The Law Code of 1649 was quickly recognized as the main source of law for Muscovy with broad acceptance among the people.[8] The historian Nancy Shields Kollmann's innovative examination of both Russian criminal law as well as defamation suits during the Muscovy period reveals a regularity of practice and readiness among the parties to settle the cases themselves.[9] Kollmann also demonstrates a willingness of all layers of Russian society to turn to the courts to resolve their problems, especially in slander cases. Valerie Kivelson identifies a similar phenomenon in property disputes during the seventeenth century. She found that Russian courts "gave people of all ranks a venue in which they could engage with each other and the state, in the person of its local officials, would pay attention."[10]

Yet while historians identify a persistent demand for law in seventeenth-century Muscovy, they also recognize the shortcomings of the prevailing legal system. Property disputes, Kivelson argues, were bogged down by conflicting evidence and a glaring lack of truthfulness among the parties, leading to protracted litigation that dragged on for years.[11] The Law Code's ability to evolve and serve as a forward-looking, norm-creating document also was limited. According to Richard Hellie, the Law Code demonstrated "an inability to combine ideas, to generalize, to pick out the general and subordinate the particular."[12] Muscovy further lacked the basic legal institutions and people—law faculties, independent judges, trained lawyers—who could contribute to the growth of law as a broader governing or philosophical principle. Instead, it was state secretaries, chancery officials, clerks, and other bureaucrats who initially shaped Russian law and relied on it to solve practical, everyday problems. These bureaucrats and scribes actually held an empire together with limited administrative resources, but they lacked the formal legal knowledge and expertise to expand the domain of law beyond certain technical functions. Finally, Kollmann highlights the persistent problem of corruption that infected law enforcement and court officials.[13] The Law Code of 1649 did not prevent law from primarily being a local matter, open to personal rule and favoritism. The prevalence of corruption furthermore was a manifestation of a lack of bureaucratic manpower—and a weak state—that invariably affected Muscovy's ability to administer justice.

Muscovy's internal constraints, however, did not impede its pursuit of greater imperial glory. Just five years after the adoption of the Law Code of 1649, Muscovy signed one of the most important treaties in Russian history: the Pereiaslav agreement of 1654. The Ukrainian Cossack state and its leader, Hetman Bohdan Khmelnytsky, were engaged in a conflict with the Polish-Lithuanian Commonwealth and in desperate need of allies, so Khmelnytsky turned to Moscow for protection. The tsar's envoy agreed to provide such protection but refused to negotiate over the exact terms of the agreement. The envoy even refused to swear to abide by the treaty's promises, stating the tsar swore no oath to his subjects. In desperation, however, Khmelnytsky signed the agreement.

The historian Serhii Plokhy argues that a fundamental misunderstanding stands at the root of the Pereiaslav agreement. The Cossacks thought of the treaty "as a contract with binding obligations on both sides," while the tsar "perceived the Cossacks as new subjects toward whom he would have no obligations after granting them certain rights and privileges."[14] In other words, although there were still many battles to be fought, the Pereiaslav agreement began the process whereby Muscovy gradually assumed sovereignty over Kiev and other parts of the Cossack state. Yet in extending control, there appears to have been no expectation that the Law Code of 1649 was about to become the law of the conquered region. On the contrary, Cossack chroniclers in the 1700s extolled the Pereiaslav agreement as the Magna Carta of Ukrainian liberties in the Russian empire.[15] The Pereiaslav agreement embodied an essential feature of imperial policy that would dominate Russian law until the advent of the Russification policies of the late nineteenth century; namely as long as a region accepted the tsar's ultimate sovereignty, it could retain both its legal traditions and its underlying customs and laws.

Thus, to speak of one Russian law on the eve of Peter the Great's reign would be to mischaracterize its inherent flexibility and pluralism. Moreover, while many foreign visitors would castigate Muscovy as lawless and deeply corrupt, Russians regularly turned to the courts to litigate all kinds of cases. Recognizing the Muscovy legal system's profound weaknesses, which were both prevalent and hampered further development, Kollmann nonetheless concludes that it was functional and consistent "with contemporary strategies of state-building and governance."[16] Peter would take this inheritance and forge a great and powerful state.

Law and the creation of the Russian empire

Peter the Great's vision of a modern Russia began with his elevation of the state. The state went from merely providing personal service to the tsar to representing the common good and the fatherland.[17] Peter further pursued a separation of ruler and state. For example, he distinguished between the state's property and his own. Upon joining the army, soldiers now swore loyalty to both the sovereign and the state. Finally, he ascribed the empire's highest law-creating powers to the state. As the historian V. O. Kliuchevskii later noted, Peter's decrees claimed that the state's interests represented the "highest and unconditional norm of state order" and that the state was the "supreme carrier of law and the keeper of the common good."[18]

Thus, the impersonal but all-powerful state moved to the center of Russian governance and law. Peter would subsequently revamp Russia's administrative system and social order to maximize the rendering of state service. The renowned table of ranks, which defined a career ladder and created a merit-based aristocracy, was grounded on the notion of service to the state. The state, however, stood for more than just central administration; it served as the primary symbol—and designated defender—of national unity in an expanding multinational empire. The state further did not recognize any abstract, philosophical constraints; there was no concept of natural law that somehow existed outside of—or higher than—the state to check its authority. No founding social contract existed either; on the contrary, as the legal theorist N. M. Korkunov later argued, the essential relationship between the Russian state and its subjects was that of dependency.[19] Indeed, under Peter the Great's system, there were no "free" people other than the indigent and the mentally ill, and Peter made sure that these groups were rounded up by the state.[20]

The rise of the impersonal state, however, did not lead to a corresponding diminution in Peter's actual power. In reality, the separation of state and ruler was a legal fiction. Peter remained an absolute monarch in the truest sense of the word, evident in his personal law-creating powers. Peter was by no means the first monarch whose word literally was law. Nevertheless, the tsar's ability to issue decrees (*ukazy*) that carried the force of law served as an essential feature of Russian law. Peter's legislative output was prodigious—he issued thousands of decrees, showing a degree of personal engagement and attention to detail that would help define his historical legacy. His decrees in St. Petersburg, for example, covered not only where one could build but also the dimensions of chimneys, the form of roofs, and the order of digging ponds.[21] Peter did create a pseudo legislature—the Ruling Senate—that also possessed certain law-creating powers, but it was the sovereign's pen that remained the primary source of law in Russia.

What Peter's flurry of decrees most directly upset was Russia's prevailing legal code. The Law Code of 1649 remained the primary source of law, but Peter's own voluminous output somehow needed to be incorporated into a legal code that was current, comprehensive, and assessable. Peter convened several commissions to address the codification question, yet no revised code ever emerged during his reign. Therefore, the law remained a combination of statutes, regulations, and decrees—some published, others never publicly announced or distributed—that formed a confusing and often contradictory legislative base. The ambiguous nature of Russian law was exacerbated by the fact that Peter rejected any idea of an independent judiciary that could fill in the gaps and interpret the law.

Peter's reliance on the majesty of the state and personal rule served as two essential pillars of Russian law and autocratic rule. Two other developments—empire and modernization—infused a significant degree of flexibility into Russian law and led to major structural reforms. It must be remembered that Peter's search for foreign conquest and military glory overrode his domestic agenda at all times, including any efforts to rationalize Russia's administrative and legal systems. His own extensive foreign travels had a profound impact on Russian law, since he discovered European models and institutions that he admired and later tried to transplant, albeit with his personal modifications, to Russia. Most famously, his administrative reforms relied heavily on Swedish law and led to the creation of collegiate boards (i.e., departments of justice, finance, etc.).[22] Peter also learned what he did not like during his travels abroad. During his trip to London in 1698, he came upon some wig-wearing barristers. When informed of their profession, Peter proclaimed: "Lawyers! What is the use of so many? I have only two in my whole empire, and I mean to hang one of them as soon as I return."[23]

But Peter's foreign military victories raised serious dilemmas for Russian law. As he annexed the Baltic States and moved south to the Black Sea, he acquired not only new peoples but new, and sometimes more advanced, legal institutions and cultures. Peter further lacked the bureaucratic manpower to impose Russian law on these newly acquired territories, so he did what his predecessors (and all great empires) did—he decentralized. Thus, the subsequent agreements incorporating the Baltic States into Imperial Russia, culminating with the peace treaty between Russia and Sweden (the Treaty of Nystad) in 1721, allowed these regions to retain their established noble privileges and legal traditions—particularly in civil matters—while militarily and administratively binding them into a larger common enterprise known as the Russian empire. Peter did not treat every national group with restraint; he openly threatened Muslim Volga Tatars and Buddhist Kalmyk nomads if they did not accept Orthodoxy.[24] Nevertheless, Russian national unity—an essential element of statehood—was not found in an overarching imperial theory of law but in the pragmatic implementation of centralized bureaucratic control and decentralized legality.

The urgent need to modernize represented a second critical factor in Peter's approach to Russian law. Peter pursued the modernization of Russia's military, administrative, and economic practices in direct pursuit of greater imperial glory. But such ambitious goals inevitably required the passage of laws (or more accurately, the introduction of decrees) and a more robust legal system. Thus, legal modernization became an integral part of Peter's overall modernization efforts. For example, to spur economic development, he broke the distinction between private (*votchina*) and state (*pomest'e*) land and instead established the notion of immovable property that could be entailed to a sole successor and only sold under extreme need.[25] This decree not only updated Russia's long-standing inheritance rules and prevented the fragmentation of wealthy landed estates. It also indirectly pushed other sons into military and state service, since they henceforth would be deprived of any livelihood related to working the land.[26] Peter further created state monopolies and ordered that certain goods (hemp, raw leather, potash) be sent to St. Petersburg for export in order to raise state revenues to buy ships, arms, and needed raw materials.[27]

Yet in many ways, prevailing Russian law worked against economic modernization. Peter's patrimonial state remained openly suspicious of property rights, which were still linked to the provision of state service and could be arbitrarily revoked by the ruler at any time.[28] While Peter significantly increased his public law powers over the state and the bureaucracy, he paid considerably less attention to expanding a system of private law that could defend property rights and more broadly promote economic growth and civil society.[29] Russian civil law further lost its significance the farther one moved into the empire's hinterland. The historian Lindsey Hughes argues that:

> away from the center, the monarch's command was diluted. Nobles literally "took the law into their own hands". In the provinces, landowners had legal jurisdiction over their serfs. They often disregarded laws on property and inheritance. What they wanted was not a strong judiciary, but rather officials sympathetic to their particular needs.[30]

Such local realities pushed the pursuit of a unified and comprehensive system of civil justice to the back of Peter's reform agenda.

Peter's modernization plans also entailed secularization, and one of his most dramatic reforms would be establishing a lay person (ober-procurator) over the Orthodox Church. Henceforth, the Church would be part of the state, not a distinct legal entity that could challenge the state, as had occurred in medieval Europe with the secession of the Catholic Church from the Holy Roman Empire in 1075.[31] The Church retained its own system of courts, but as with so many other of Peter's reforms, significant overlap existed with secular courts that only led to confusion. State officials regularly subjected members of Russian clergy to state courts even though, in theory, clergymen could only be tried in church courts. Alternatively, laymen continued to be subject to church courts for a series of crimes (blasphemy, heresy, illegal marriage, divorce). Thus, despite Peter's secular push, the separation of the two jurisdictions remained incomplete during his lifetime.[32]

Peter's attempt at legal modernization also came face-to-face with custom, which itself had remained a critical source of law for both the monarch and his subjects. Custom in the village meant that the relationships between lord and peasant—and among the peasants themselves—were governed by informal, unwritten rules, not national legislation. Peter never attempted to regulate these local relationships, other than to grant the lord unlimited control over his serfs. Nevertheless, Peter clearly viewed himself as a transformative leader who was not going to be obstructed by tradition. Most notably, in the aftermath of his son Tsarevich Alexei's death (itself largely precipitated by Peter's investigation into Alexei's alleged betrayal), Peter rejected the custom of male primogeniture and via decree established new rules of succession that allowed the tsar to designate his successor. In so doing, Peter initiated a broader debate that would last until 1917 over what role custom should play as a source of law in the Russian empire.

A final element of Peter's legal modernization program concerned his efforts at the rationalization of justice. Peter devoted significant attention to the inner-workings of Russia's judicial system, struggling to impose a legal hierarchy where none previously had existed. In this regard, he achieved some modest successes. The Ruling Senate served as Russia's highest judicial instance for some (but not necessarily all) appeals. In 1717, a collegiate system of government was established that included a justice college that served as an appellate instance for lower regional courts. Finally, between 1719 and 1722, Peter introduced various reforms in the local court system that culminated in 1722 with the establishment of provincial courts headed by a military official (*voevoda*) and lay assessor.

Historians have recognized that Peter's efforts to create a more rational system of justice held out some promise. Nancy Shields Kollmann, for example, emphasizes the dramatic improvement in court documents during the Petrine period.[33] She also highlights the establishment of appellate review in major capital crimes cases, and the further institutionalization of the inquisitorial process, which relied on the exchange of a highly formalized system of written proofs all conducted behind closed doors. Judges in criminal cases provided detailed explanations of their determinations and used sanctioned violence (i.e., torture) as proscribed under law.[34] Kollmann also shows that defense of honor and defamation cases relied on established legal procedures with a subtle shift during Peter's reign from a collective to an individual concept of honor.[35]

Yet despite such advancements, Peter's court reforms still faced serious obstacles. Most notably, Peter failed to lay the groundwork for a genuine independent, professionally trained judiciary. Since there was no corpus of lawyers, judges came largely from the military, assisted by chancery bureaucrats who provided the critical practical knowledge to administer justice.[36] Moreover, judicial power was not separated from state administration. The Senate remained both a judicial and an administrative organ; it not only reviewed cases but also published decrees that possessed the force of law and were mandatory for other state bodies.[37] Governors also doubled as judges, thereby further blurring the distinction between state administration and the judiciary.[38]

Peter's other main effort of updating Russia's legal machinery—the creation of an appeals court (the justice college) based on the Swedish model—further failed as a central judicial body. Several social categories (townspeople, merchants, entrepreneurs, workers, military personnel) were subject to different colleges and therefore fell out of the justice college's jurisdiction. Thus, the caste-based court system, as established in the Law Code of 1649, continued during Peter's reign, meaning that different laws applied depending on one's social standing.[39] Finally, at the summit of Russia's judicial hierarchy remained Peter himself. He allowed for direct appeals to the emperor all the while complaining bitterly about the overwhelming number of petitions that he had to resolve.[40] This culture of complaint suggests that instead of turning to Peter's revamped court system for a legal determination, Russians still relied on administrative procedures to resolve their personal grievances.

The urgent need to modernize—to catch up to Russia's European competitors both militarily and economically—meant that Peter did not have the luxury of waiting to see whether Russian law could evolve and support his grandiose ambitions. Thus, Peter required some alternative means to provide oversight and impose his will on the existing state structures, and that process can be summarized in one word: *nadzor* (supervision). Supervision existed everywhere in Peter's legal system. It began in the confessional, where the priest was required to report any intended criminal act (especially one directed against the tsar) to the appropriate authorities. Police surveillance also expanded and became an essential feature of Peter's political system. It covered one's personal appearance—to enforce Peter's order requiring the shaving of beards—the construction of buildings, the catching and return of fugitive serfs, the introduction of an internal passport system, and the investigation of all acts of treason, both real and imagined. The police so dominated the enforcement of Russian law that the Russian historian Evgenii Anisimov has described Peter's system as a "state inspired by the police."[41]

The need for supervision, however, eventually compelled Peter to introduce a new legal institution to watch over Russia's fledgling legal and administrative apparatus: the prosecutor's office (procuracy). In many ways, the procuracy was misnamed from the start. Peter evidently was impressed by French prosecutors during his visit to Paris in 1717 and simply assigned this title to his new creation in 1722. However, the roots of the procuracy primarily can be found in Russia. In 1711, Peter had established the office of the fiscal, which was responsible for supervising government bodies and, if necessary, initiating proceedings against officials in the Ruling Senate.[42] The fiscal and other structures of oversight, however, had failed to achieve more routine compliance with tsarist legislation. Hence, Peter established the procuracy in 1722 with the primary goal of supervising Russia's highest governing body.

According to the original decree creating the procuracy, the procurator-general's main assignment was to sit in the Senate and watch.[43] His responsibilities further included taking notes and ensuring that existing legislation was followed to the letter. Indeed, the founding decree specifically required the procurator-general to maintain a book indicating which regulations had been followed and, if not fulfilled, identifying why such orders had not been observed. Thus, the procuracy performed an executive, not legal, function in which its primary task was to oversee the observance of laws by state bodies.

Procurators were also assigned to supervise other major governmental institutions and mid-level appellate courts (*nadvornye sudy*). Yet the procuracy's powers were primarily preventative; it could suspend Senate decisions, but it could not reverse them.[44] Moreover, the above supervisory function was mainly administrative, not legal, in the sense that the procuracy did not represent the state's interest in court but instead simply oversaw the execution of existing legislation.[45] The procuracy was granted one significant legal privilege, however, namely the right to initiate legislation in the Ruling Senate.[46] Therefore, it was a law-proposing institution, further blurring the distinction between administrator, legislator, and judicial official. Finally, the procuracy existed as a top-down organization with its lower ranks attached to various government bodies that reported directly to the procurator-general who, in turn, was directly subordinate to the emperor. As a result, it famously acquired the nickname "the eyes of the sovereign" and became the primary agent in Peter's quest to centralize, and maintain unity within, Russia's legal and administrative structures.

Conclusion

Peter was always a man in a hurry, and his ability to implement his legal reforms never matched what existed on paper. Historians who have looked at aspects of everyday law under Peter have identified positive changes from the Muscovite period, although Russian criminal law was not for the faint of heart. As Kollmann notes, Peter raised the level of violence over his Muscovy predecessors, most notably by producing highly brutal and theatrical public executions.[47] Nevertheless, Kollmann identifies strong pockets of procedural regularity and professionalism within Peter's court system, essential features of law and growing state legitimacy. She particularly highlights the growing regularity of criminal law practice: Peter's reforms "were institutionalizing the principle that deviance was punished, that the law was transparent and that it was wielded knowledgeably and equitably."[48]

Even taking into account such realities, however, the legal system forged by Peter the Great still faced significant hurdles going forward. Many of the obstacles were left over from the Muscovy period, most notably, the absence of law faculties and the ability to train jurists. Moreover, Russian law remained without a clear division of functions; there was no prosecutor's office focused on criminal prosecution, no defense bar, and perhaps most significantly, no independent judiciary. Instead, judicial responsibilities were performed primarily by administrative and military officials, depriving the judiciary of any notion of independence.

The administration of the law was corrupt and highly bureaucratic. Indeed, while the impersonal Russian state symbolized unity and the common good, local administration consisted of real people whose personal interests remained paramount. Bureaucrats supplemented their low salaries by extracting money from the local population, a practice known as *kormlenie* (literally "feeding").[49] Peter did attempt to establish a more hierarchical court structure, but jurisdiction remained a fluid concept that significantly undermined efforts to rationalize Russia's system of justice. Peter further failed to clean up Russia's diverse sources of laws. Thus, Russian law still rested on the Law Code of 1649 and a series of decrees issued by Peter that were neither codified nor readily accessible.

Modern-day commentators looking backward naturally criticize the absence of an accessible, comprehensive law code, although most early eighteenth-century legal systems suffered from similar defects. Peter, however, remained suspicious of independent explanations of law. According to Peter, "laws and decrees should be written clearly so that they cannot be reinterpreted. There is little justice in people but much perfidy."[50] Peter never went beyond this narrow, functional understanding of *zakonnost'*, where laws were issued by the ruler as a set of instructions for state institutions and their officials.[51] Peter further was not interested in promoting secure property rights and other private law principles that could potentially challenge his centralized state. Instead, supervision and surveillance became essential features of Russian legality during Peter's reign, culminating with the creation of the procuracy in 1722. Finally, while formal law was primarily pursued top-down, a vast bottom-up system of both non-Russian and informal (i.e., customary) law existed within the borders of this expanding empire. Thus, Peter's capacity to deliver legality and strict obedience to the law was limited in such a vast and under-managed state.

The restrictions on Peter's legal authority primarily were informal. He still felt obliged to engage in politics—if only to maintain elite support and promote state service—but he faced no constitutional or defined legal limits to his absolute rule. Peter further wrapped himself in Roman symbols and even appropriated the title of emperor. Yet conspicuously absent among the Roman imagery was Roman law, the essential building block of every Western legal system. Instead, two competing policies—modernization and supervision—produced a functional but limited system of legality. Russian law supported Peter's immediate state-building objectives, but it still lacked the intellectual and institutional resources to establish itself as an independent, mediating force within society. Peter may have opened a window on Europe, but Russia remained on its own distinct legal trajectory.

2

The Expansion of Russian Legality

The next major stage in Russia's legal development coincided with the ascension of Catherine the Great to the throne in 1762. For the next century, she—followed by Alexander I (1801–1825) and Nicholas I (1825–1855)—would articulate a vision of law and legality that addressed the specific needs of a growing empire. The stature of law grew significantly with universities and elite secondary schools producing Russia's first cadre of home-grown jurists. Moreover, two distinct strands of law emerged—a top-down bureaucratic form of legality that was designed to deliver the autocrat's central commands to the regions, as well as a court system theoretically divided by estate (i.e., class) that provided citizens with a forum to resolve basic civil disputes. In 1832, Russia finally replaced the Law Code of 1649 with a complete compilation of acting laws, a monumental accomplishment that presented Russian laws in a more coherent and accessible manner.

But as Russian law gradually extended its internal reach within the empire—to Ukraine and the Caucasus—other regions remained outside Russia's formal legal structures, exacerbating the problem of legal pluralism and the unequal application of law within the empire's borders. Imperial expansion raised philosophical questions as well; as Russia moved westward, it consistently bumped up against alternative legal theories and practices. Although Russia borrowed selectively from these Western principles, it never embraced them. Instead, the state retained its unlimited monopoly on force even as it turned to the law as a means to impose a minimal degree of order across two continents and a highly diverse population.

Catherine the Great and enlightened legality

Catherine the Great fancied herself as an "enlightened" monarch whose rule would incorporate more Western legal principles. Thus, she toyed with an alternative understanding of law and invited the Russian nobility in 1767 to assist in the drafting of such legislation. Before convening the Legislative Commission, Catherine issued her *Nakaz* (Instruction) to the group, outlining what she believed should constitute the essential features of Russian law. The *Nakaz* admittedly makes no claim of originality; 294 of the 526 articles in Part I of the instructions came from Montesquieu's *Spirit of Laws* (*De l'esprit des lois*). Another 108 came from Cesare Beccaria's *On Crimes and Punishments* (*Dei delitti e delle pene*).[1]

What is revealing about the *Nakaz* is how Catherine adopted the above works and other liberal treatises to suit her specific political circumstances. Most noticeably, Catherine sidestepped Montesquieu's assertion that any large empire invariably comes under the category of despotism. Instead, she self-classified Russia as a monarchy—a much more progressive category under Montesquieu's legal theory—and proceeded to articulate a heightened role for the judiciary within the Russian political system. Article 21 permitted the courts to declare a law in violation of existing legal codes, while Article 24 allowed a high court to examine the laws of the sovereign and to protest if it found those laws objectionable. Catherine further proposed elevating the Ruling Senate as the main depository of law and equated its powers with the French *parlements*, although the former's right to postpone a legal act far outstripped the Senate's right to hear mere legal representations.[2]

But while flirting with constitutional limitations on the autocrat's powers, the *Nakaz* also served to highlight the divergence between Catherine's idealistic vision of law and Russia's underlying legal reality. Despite brushing aside Montesquieu's categories of despotism, Catherine left no doubt as to the centrality and the unlimited power of the Russian autocrat. According to Article 9 of the *Nakaz*, "The Sovereign is absolute; for there is no other Authority but that which centers in his single Person, that can act with a Vigour proportionate to the Extent of such a vast Dominion."[3] Moreover, the *Nakaz*'s assertion of the existence of fundamental laws implied a normative content to law that was largely absent from the Russian legal vocabulary. The Law Code of 1649 had codified specific statutes and decrees, not general principles of law. Montesquieu's *Spirit of Laws* also required the establishment of certain intermediary bodies to exercise power in a legal manner. Montesquieu identified the nobility as the appropriate intermediary; Catherine in her *Nakaz* chose to rely on the courts, even though the imperial court system was notoriously corrupt and underdeveloped. Indeed Catherine herself remained highly skeptical of an independent judiciary and the powers of judicial interpretation. Article 153 began by stating that nothing was more dangerous than the expression: "The Spirit of the Law ought to be considered, and not the Letter." Instead, a judge should only be responsible for "ascertaining the Fact."[4]

The Legislative Commission subsequently met and debated the legal questions raised within the *Nakaz* (local administration, the rights of the nobility, serfdom), although not the fundamental principles of autocratic rule.[5]

The Legislative Commission never produced any final recommendations—events, most notably the Russo-Turkish War of 1868–1874, intervened. Catherine's original *Nakaz* still stands out as articulating an aspirational notion of law that pushed Russia in a western direction. Catherine had even declared in Article 6 that Russia was a European state. But while Europe remained the ideal, Catherine would not return to the general constitutional principles expressed in the *Nakaz* during her reign. Instead, the gap between Russia and Europe was narrowed through a more practical measure, namely by providing greater protections for the institution of private property.

As previously noted, Peter the Great originally broke the distinction between state and non-state land and created "immovable" property that could be entailed to a single heir. Yet even after his reform, an underlying service obligation remained for the Russian nobility and the rest of the Russian people. It was Catherine's husband, Peter III, who during his brief seven-month reign ended the service requirement for the nobility, thereby establishing more secure ownership rights. Catherine not only upheld this new property right, she expanded it. In 1782, in what can only be described as an overly generous gesture that future rulers and bureaucrats would deeply regret, she granted by manifesto all subsoil rights to property owners as well.[6] Various explanations exist as to why Catherine bestowed such a substantial legacy on the Russian nobility. She had come to power in a palace coup—and was not Russian herself—and so needed to mobilize support among the aristocracy for her rule. The historian Ekaterina Pravilova, however, sees this decision as Catherine's recognition of a weak state, that the Russian state lacked the resources to oversee these vast land holdings and therefore repackaged an act of necessity into a "benevolent gift."[7]

Yet Catherine was in the process of transforming the perennially "weak" Russian state by increasing its ability to deliver law and legality to the regions. Her landmark legislation, the Administrative Reforms of 1775, replaced Peter's provincial chief officer (the *voevoda*) with the provincial governor whose primary function was to enforce the law in his respective territory. Such an assignment, however, was narrowly construed and mandated that the governor limit himself to the strict letter of the law.[8] The 1775 administrative reforms further redrew Russia's internal boundaries and divided the empire into new administrative units that contained roughly equal numbers of inhabitants. In addition to rationalizing state administration, this reorganization, according to Marc Raeff, "helped spread the network of state institutions, facilitating the penetration of administration and its policy aims to the provincial and district levels."[9] Thus, a top-down legality finally infiltrated the regions of the empire, creating the first truly viable "power vertical" in Russian history.

Catherine's major judicial reforms were introduced as part of the 1775 administrative legislation. Most importantly, she attempted to establish a more independent court system, albeit one that retained the estate-based features of the Law Code of 1649. For members of the noble estate, new land courts and district (*uezd*) courts were established; judges were appointed in the former, assisted by assessors elected by the nobility. In the district courts, however, judges and assessors were all elected by the nobility, thereby introducing a partial but nevertheless substantive break in the long-standing link between administrative and judicial officials. A similar situation applied for townspeople, where magistrates were appointed on the provincial (*guberniia*) level but elected on the town level. Decisions from the lower courts could be appealed to regional civil and criminal courts and then ultimately up to the Senate.[10] Only in the countryside was the traditional merging of judicial and administrative functions fully maintained in law, although the historian John LeDonne insists that administrative influences and patronage politics continued to permeate all levels of the Russian judiciary after the 1775 reforms.[11]

The estate-based nature of Russian justice was reinforced in 1785 with Catherine's respective charters to the nobility and the towns. These charters assigned specific civil and personal rights to each estate. The Charter to the Nobility, for example, confirmed the nobility's exemption from state service as well as their right not to be deprived of life, title, or property except by the judgment of their peers. According to the historian Richard Pipes, "the thirty six articles of the first part of the Noble Charter were a veritable bill of rights which created, for the first time in Russia, a class of persons whose life, personal liberty, and properties were guaranteed."[12] The Charter to the Towns relied significantly on foreign sources of law from the Baltics, Sweden, Lithuania, and Prussia. Towns (as opposed to the individual town dwellers) received certain tax privileges while the rights of individual town residents varied significantly depending on their ranking within the various merchant guilds; members of the first guild, for example, were allowed to drive in a carriage; members of the third guild could not.[13]

The clear loser in Catherine's designation of rights once again was the peasantry. Catherine prepared a specific charter for the peasantry, but it was never published. Instead, in the process of granting the nobility ownership of land, Catherine also gave the nobility almost unlimited power over those serfs who were tied to the land.[14] Yet the autocracy also had an incentive to maintain certain minimum living standards among the peasantry, so that the state could maintain an army, raise tax revenues, and cultivate the land. As a result, some administrative responsibilities were transferred down to the village level, where peasant patriarchs (the heads of households) ensured that serfs met their service obligations both to their landlord and the state. As part of this informal devolution of authority, the patriarchs also adjudicated disputes among serfs based on local custom. Thus, according to the historian David Moon, the village society developed "mechanisms to mediate between the conflicting interests of member households."[15] Peasants pursued alternative legal remedies as well, such as the opportunity to appeal both criminal and civil disputes to the manor authorities for resolution.[16]

The major exception to the maintenance of the estate-based judicial system under Catherine was the introduction of the "conscience" courts. These tribunals broadly followed the example of the English equity courts, providing for greater flexibility and leniency when reviewing cases. Any subject could file an appeal to the conscience court no matter what one's social standing. In civil cases, judges not only followed the law but also possessed discretionary powers based on their requirement to uphold personal security. In criminal cases, the conscience court created a right of habeas corpus if no charges were filed within three days.[17] The dockets of the conscience courts varied from region to region, but they generally were known for their relative speediness, flexible procedures, and willingness to consider mitigating circumstances to limit the severity of Russia's harsh criminal penalties.[18]

Nevertheless, while experimenting with some court structures, Catherine largely retained an estate-based legal system, revealing an essential underlying feature of Imperial Russian law; it was never associated the idea of equality. A defined system of rights emerged in tsarist Russia, but one's ability to exercise these rights depended on one's position within the prevailing social hierarchy.[19] Such a differentiated system of rights was perfectly compatible with the running of a multinational empire—the British empire, for example, never promised equal rights to all of its subjects. Nevertheless, Russia would spend centuries addressing how to reconcile principles of universality and uniformity of law to a prevailing system of differentiated rights.

Catherine presided over other important innovations as well, most notably, the establishment of law as a recognized academic discipline. Semen Desnitskii studied law at Glasgow University before returning to Moscow to occupy the first Chair of Russian Jurisprudence at Moscow University and to become one of the first professors of law to lecture in the Russian language. Desnitskii encouraged Russian noblemen to study law and to move into positions of administrative responsibility, yet his major work on establishing a more independent judiciary—which included arguments for jury trials and the lifetime appointment of judges—would only be published in 1905.[20]

Yet as Catherine expanded the jurisdiction of law—and its area of competence—within the Russian empire, she still relied on the traditional notions of surveillance and supervision to enforce the law. In 1782, she issued the Police Ordinance, which tasked the police, in addition to its daily activities of combatting crime, with responsibility for supervising all public assemblies and entertainments, overseeing government spending, inspecting buildings and public baths, and monitoring the activities of foreigners. It was the procuracy, however, that rose to the top of the supervisory ladder during Catherine the Great's reign. She invited the procuracy to participate in the drafting of new law codes, and the procurator-general's duties gradually expanded to include the managing of state finances, currency transactions, internal affairs, and even the post office.[21] All these new functions were in addition to the procuracy's original responsibility to supervise the major government institutions, both nationally and regionally. As the procurator-general's authority increased, he began to take on the appearance of a full-blown minister as opposed to a mere supervisor of legality within government institutions.[22]

The procuracy assumed one more role during the reign of Catherine the Great, namely as indirect legal participant. The administrative reform of 1775 created the position of regional and district *striapchie* (state attorneys) who were subordinated to the regional prosecutor and served as his assistants. The *striapchie* participated in criminal and civil proceedings, primarily ensuring that certain procedural formalities were observed. Thus, during Catherine's reign a "state *advokatura*" arose that technically was under the procuracy's wing, although, according to the historian S. M. Kazantsev, one should not exaggerate the involvement of these low-level state attorneys. The "functions of procurators and their assistants [were] insignificant," he argues, "because of the purely inquisitional system of investigation (procurators and *striapchie* could not appear in court), and the prevailing theory of formal proofs."[23]

How everyday law functioned during the reign of Catherine the Great remains largely unexamined by historians. Russians still turned to the court—and found themselves in the dock—as had been the case since the Law Code of 1649 and before. A government inspection tour of six provinces in 1780 was particularly impressed by the small number of unexamined cases, suggesting that the courts were handling their caseload in an efficient and expedited manner.[24] The historian John LeDonne examined civil suits in Nizhnii Novgorod in 1787, where he found an active court with a low number of appeals. Catherine's reforms, he concluded, represented a considerable improvement in the Russian legal system, making "justice more accessible and more responsive to the needs of the parties."[25]

There is one last area of reform that must be considered in any assessment of Catherine's legal legacy. As discussed in Chapter 1, in Peter's rush to expand the empire, he tolerated the persistence of regional legal institutions and traditions in the borderlands. Catherine did not, and as she expanded the empire's borders, she focused on asserting centralized administrative control over these territories. In the Caucasus, for example, she established clan and "frontier" courts that included local representation but left the ultimate decision up to Russian authorities, alienating local religious and secular elites in the process.[26] Catherine moved even more aggressively in Ukraine when, in 1764, she abolished the Hetmanate and later introduced her administrative reforms into the region. From a legal standpoint, this meant eliminating the traditional rights and privileges of the local nobility and assimilating them into the Russian order of service. She further introduced the Russian court system into Ukraine, where Cossacks—who had possessed their own unique legal status within the Hetmanate—suddenly found themselves downgraded to appear in the same courts as Ukrainian peasants.[27]

Yet even as Catherine transformed the system of governance of Ukraine, the substance of law did not necessarily change after these reforms. Some Ukrainian cities continued to be governed by Magdeburg law, and only in 1843 did the Russian *Digest of Laws* officially become the law of the land in Ukraine.[28] A similar pattern could be found in the Baltic States, where Catherine broke the traditional rights and privileges of the Livonian and Estonian nobility but felt no immediate pressure to replace local civil law with Russian law. In reality, the Russian empire had no detailed, comprehensive civil law to export. Moreover, what united the territory of the Russian empire was its military and administrative prowess, not the substance of its economic and commercial laws. Therefore, although Catherine had changed Peter's imperial legal agenda from benign neglect to increased centralized control, she still tolerated a significant degree of legal pluralism that served as an essential feature of Russian law.

To a certain degree, Catherine deserves consideration for the title of legal modernizer. Her reforms distinguished between civil and criminal laws, advanced property rights, established new courts based on elective principles, separated judicial and administrative functions, and otherwise sought to rationalize the administration of justice both at the center and at the periphery of the empire. Yet despite the ambitious nature of these legal reforms, they did not reach the level of "enlightened," as originally expressed in the *Nakaz*. Administrative bodies—most notably the procuracy and the local governor—retained significant levers of control over the judicial system through their broad powers of supervision and surveillance. Moreover, while legal specialists began to be trained during Catherine's reign, Russia still lacked a larger professional cadre of lawyers who could populate and transform the legal system. The proliferation of new judicial institutions caused confusion when confronting practical questions of jurisdiction. Finally, Catherine never succeeded in producing an updated legal code, meaning that the Law Code of 1649 remained the single comprehensive source of Russian law despite Catherine signing more than 5,000 legislative acts during her reign.[29]

Thus, Catherine's legal reforms, while substantial, remained incomplete and only partly pushed Russia down the road of "enlightenment," as Catherine had used the term. In one area, however, her contribution was decisive; she expanded the nobility's property rights, invariably increasing the demand for greater civil law protections for this newly established entitlement. Private law principles already existed in tsarist Russia; Catherine the Great made them a necessity. Property rights henceforth would play a significant role in Russia's legal evolution as the nobility would demand legal protections for their land and possessions. Yet the natural evolution of property rights to civil rights and the liberal state had also been disrupted by Catherine's actions, for while the nobility received their property rights, the peasantry—the largest segment of the population—obviously did not. Instead, over half of the Russian peasantry remained property themselves, and they would never accept—or recognize—the property rights granted to the nobility as just. The top-down introduction of private property by Catherine would influence Russian law and domestic politics until the very last days of the tsarist regime.

Alexander I and the false start of Russian constitutionalism

Like Catherine the Great, Alexander I came to power in 1801 following a violent coup that left his father, Tsar Paul I, assassinated. Alexander would flirt with major legal reform throughout his reign. He solicited and discussed several draft constitutions, as well as seeking out advice from Thomas Jefferson and Jeremy Bentham. Yet Alexander recoiled when directly confronted with any theoretical limitation of power, and no Russian constitution emerged during his reign. Alexander's fickle attitude toward legal reform further applied to his top legal advisor Mikhail Speranskii, who played a critical role in drafting Alexander's reform agenda but was summarily dismissed and exiled in 1812, a "prisoner of the state," as one official described his fate.[30] Speranskii was not done—he would reappear as the great gatherer of Russian law under Nicholas I. For Alexander I, however, as with other Russian leaders, legal reform invariably gave way to military necessity, the preservation of the empire, and his own personal understanding of what it meant to be an autocrat. Alexander ultimately did grant constitutions, but the beneficiaries were the Poles and the Finns, not the Russians.

The various constitutional drafts of Alexander's reign appear to have been rather standard attempts by the nobility to demand certain consultative powers and the full protection of their rights and privileges.[31] Alexander I, however, was no less an autocrat than his predecessors. He rejected any legal restrictions that would intrude on the relationship between ruler and the state. Thus, as the historian Marc Raeff notes, Alexander I's notion of constitutionalism did not include a system of checks and balances; he "meant only the mechanical division of functions of government for the sake of more efficient and orderly administration."[32]

But while Alexander never composed a constitution, he did leave his own distinctive mark on Russia's system of government by introducing ministries with specific areas of competency. The transition to ministerial government stretched out almost a decade, starting with the Manifesto of September 8, 1802, and culminating with the Manifesto of June 25, 1811. The 1802 Manifesto established eight ministries, including a new Ministry of Justice, all of which, in the absence of a formal legislative process, were granted the right of legislative initiative.[33] Furthermore, in 1810 Alexander established the State Council to provide final recommendations on laws proposed by the ministries. On paper, the State Council represented the first step in the creation of a genuine legislature. In true autocratic fashion, however, Alexander avoided the State Council and continued to introduce laws via decree, thereby undermining any nascent legislative authority that the Council might have possessed.[34] The rise of the State Council also saw a change in the status of the Ruling Senate from a quasi-administrative/judicial branch to a strictly judicial body. The Senate's designation as the highest court of the land partly compensated for its diminished political power.

In the process of establishing ministries and attempting to regularize the legislative process, however, Alexander demoted the procuracy. The 1802 Manifesto merged the procuracy within the Ministry of Justice but said little about its duties, other than it was responsible for presiding over all cases within the judicial department.[35] Yet after repeated clashes with the first Minister of Justice/Procurator-General Gavriil Derzhavin, Alexander I ultimately decided to downgrade the Ministry of Justice and the prosecutor's office, limiting the ministry's supervisory powers to judicial institutions and local administration. As political power drifted away from the Senate to the Committee of Ministers and to the State Council, the procuracy's influence further decreased.[36] Local supervision migrated to the newly created Ministry of Internal Affairs, which assumed responsibility for local administration and enforced the law on the regional level. Governors ignored the protests of local prosecutors and failed to send them documents for review as required.[37] No single law defined the procuracy's structure and activities, and the procuracy became increasingly seen as bureaucratic and corrupt.[38] Even the Minister of Justice/Procurator-General V. N. Panin felt compelled to resort to bribery, allegedly paying 50 rubles to speed up the examination of his daughter's claim in a local St. Petersburg court.[39]

The re-classification of the procuracy's legal responsibilities would continue through the end of the tsarist period. The creation of ministerial government, however, definitively altered the law-creating process. The tsar's word was still law, but in the absence of a true legislature, the ministries now gained the specific right of proposing legislation. How often the ministries submitted legislation or published decrees remains unclear. The Ministry of Justice appears to have rarely exercised this right, instead focusing on case management issues before the Senate.[40] The Ministry of Internal Affairs, however, became a regulatory powerhouse; between 1826 and 1853, it issued annually on average 180 circulars and instructions, which possessed the force of law.[41] As the historian Daniel Orlovsky notes, this concentration of administrative power within the bureaucracy represented "one of the primary factors inhibiting the development of separation of powers or the rule of law."[42]

The great irony of Alexander's reign was that while Russia remained without a constitution, Finland and Poland did not. Two major military victories (over Sweden and Napoleon) were followed up by a series of pronouncements, manifestos, and international agreements—the Treaty of Fredrikshamn (1809) and the Final Act of the Congress of Vienna (1815)—that incorporated the Duchy of Finland and the Kingdom of Poland into the Russian empire with special legal status. Finland's constitution technically was just an acknowledgment of the status quo that had previously existed under Swedish rule. Nevertheless, Finland retained its rights, privileges, representative institutions, and fundamental laws, with Alexander I assuming the title of Grand Duke of Finland in 1809.[43] In 1815, Alexander added the title of King of Poland to his portfolio and granted Poland a constitution, which included a popularly elected lower house (the Sejm), freedom of religion, freedom of the press, habeas corpus, and the inviolability of property rights. Alexander, however, retained a degree of personal leverage; under the Polish constitution, he still possessed critical appointment and veto powers, as well as the right to serve as the highest court of appeal at law.[44]

Alexander's motivations varied in terms of his decision to grant constitutional rule within specific parts of the empire. The historian Janet Hartley argues that in the Finnish case, Alexander was primarily driven by practical reasons, namely the need to provide stability quickly and to ward off any counter-claims from Sweden. For Poland, he appears to have been more idealistic, and he even considered the possibility of introducing a similar constitution in Russia.[45] Alexander was not so generous in upholding agreements and recognizing the laws of other conquered territories, most notably in the Caucasus, although customary law continued to function throughout the region.[46] Nevertheless, through the treaty-making process, two sources of foreign law and legal practice now received significant recognition within the Russian empire, an uncomfortable reality that the tsarist state would have to address at a later date.

Nicholas I and the codification of Russian law

Alexander I's death under mysterious circumstances in 1825 prompted yet another moment of political instability and intrigue surrounding the succession process. Instead of a lingering coup, however, the new tsar, Nicholas I, faced an open rebellion. Nicholas only assumed the throne when his older brother Constantine renounced his claim, but Nicholas was immediately met by the Decembrist revolt. The Decembrists, many of whom had spent time in Europe, broadly wanted a constitution (and associated civil liberties), the end of serfdom, and a republic, but they lacked internal cohesion and were easily defeated. Nicholas thus emerged shaken but resolute in his role as defender of the status quo, both in Russia and in international relations. But even though he brought a highly conservative attitude toward the state—and accepted no limits on his powers of personal rule—he also proved to be a modernizer of Russian law, even if that was not his primary goal.

Nicholas brought a narrow approach to the role of law in Russian society, one that corresponded to traditional notions of legality: "Do what the law requires of you; I do not want anything else."[47] Yet before the law could accomplish this function, the rules themselves needed to be collected and presented in a coherent order. At least ten previous attempts at codification—starting with Peter the Great—had ended in total failure. Therefore, in order to accomplish such a herculean task, Nicholas brought back Mikhail Speranskii to head up the Second Section of His Imperial Majesty's Own State Chancellery.

Historians remain divided over Speranskii's political intentions during Alexander I's reign and whether he sought merely to update absolutism or to pursue a more progressive liberal agenda.[48] What Speranskii truly possessed in abundance was legal drafting experience; in 1809, he had prepared a new Russian civil code for adoption that borrowed significantly from French legal principles. He also understood the importance of law and introduced in 1809 an educational requirement for the upper levels of bureaucracy that included a basic knowledge of Roman law and civil law. This prerequisite, however, was quickly disparaged by the nobility and eventually withdrawn.[49] Ultimately, it was Speranskii's reliance on foreign law—at the expense of Russian law and tradition—that doomed his initial codification project and contributed to his political downfall. Thus, by the time Speranskii returned to government in 1826 to begin yet another attempt at gathering Russia's laws, he was, above all else, a political realist, although this did not stop him from pushing the boundaries of his assignment.

Speranskii proposed to Nicholas a three-stage plan of systematization and codification: (1) the creation of a full collection of the laws of the Russian empire from 1649 onward, (2) the preparation of a digest of laws that would include only those laws currently in force within the Russian empire, and (3) the writing of new law codes (*ulozhenie*) that would update Russian law and incorporate it into everyday practice. Nicholas, however, summarily rejected the last stage; instead, he emphasized the need to put the new laws in order but not to create new ones.

Thus, Speranskii's assignment stopped short of actually preparing new codes for the Russian empire. With these marching orders, Speranskii produced the complete collection of laws (*Polnoe sobranie zakonov*) of the Russian empire in 1830 and released the *Digest of Laws* in 1832. The one well-documented example where Speranskii seemed to deviate from his instructions was in drafting volume ten of the *Digest* dealing with civil law. In 1895, Maksim Vinaver, a leading civil lawyer and later a prominent member of the Kadet Party, demonstrated that Speranskii had, in fact, borrowed heavily from French and Austrian civil law principles in preparing this volume. According to Vinaver, Speranskii further manipulated the drafting of the complete collection of laws to ensure that these foreign provisions looked like a preexisting part of Russian law, thereby enabling him to incorporate them within the *Digest* as current law.[50] Such a sleight of hand makes the civil law volume a clear outlier within the *Digest of Laws*, since it was more of a code and less of a compilation.

One should not underestimate the magnitude of Speranskii's accomplishment. According to William E. Butler, "The grand systematization and codification of the 1825–32 period is by scale and result the single best laboratory for revision of the statute-book that Russia has ever experienced."[51] A body of imperial legislation emerged that could be consulted to determine not only the laws currently in force but also their legislative history. The relationship between the *Digest* and the complete collection of laws may have been obtuse, if not outright contradictory, at times, but a centralized and accessible collection of laws came into being where none had existed before.[52]

Nicholas was not finished with legal reform. The *Digest of Laws* theoretically granted the State Council a more formal consultative role in the approval of legislation, although bypassing the Council remained standard practice in the tsar's promulgation of laws and decrees.[53] Nicholas I further introduced a new criminal code in 1845 that defined crimes and their accompanying penalties while retaining distinctions in punishment based on one's estate. New legislation on commercial law was introduced in 1836, thereby establishing a stronger legislative base for corporations seeking limited liability and the right to raise working capital. Russia followed the concession system of incorporation, where the parties applied to the state for a corporate charter in exchange for special economic privileges (i.e., the control over a commodity or service).[54] Nicholas also established commercial courts in Moscow, St. Petersburg, and other cities that relied on more informal court procedures to resolve business and contract disputes.

Yet the modernization of Russian law could not proceed without increased supervision as well. In 1826, Nicholas founded the Third Section of His Imperial Majesty's Own Chancellery in charge of the preservation of state security. The "Third Section" acquired the broad supervisory and surveillance duties that previously had been a part of the procuracy's general responsibilities. Not only did it oversee the government ministers and ministries, the Third Section also obtained the extra-judicial right to receive petitions from Russian subjects who asked that it use its special authority to overcome bureaucratic red tape.[55] Thus, the security services took on an advocacy role that substituted for going to court, thereby creating a specific bureaucratic remedy for dispute resolution. Finally, the provincial reforms of 1837 extended the territorial reach of the Ministry of Internal Affairs and enabled it to transmit central decisions down to the provincial level, forging what in the modern vernacular would become known as a unified system of state power.[56]

Yet despite significant legal and institutional reforms, no body of law, no matter what its claims to comprehensiveness, can necessarily address all questions or keep pace with the rapid changes of daily life. The *Digest* and complete collection of laws were no exceptions to this rule. Speranskii faced numerous technical challenges in compiling these compendiums: he had to track down original copies of laws that were often not readily available. He also had to deal with the secrecy surrounding some decrees that precluded their publication in any collected volume. The decision to include certain administrative orders in the *Digest* further complicated matters because they elevated bureaucratic regulations to the level of actual legislation.

Speranskii also had to confront the question of non-Russian national law. His commission applied the same rigor to collecting local laws as it did to gathering Russian laws, yet with the exception of the Baltic provinces, this regional legislation received no official sanction or recognition by the Russian state.[57] Indeed, while Speranskii was busy collecting these regional laws, Nicholas I was putting down the Polish rebellion of 1830–1831 and abolishing the Polish constitution. Speranskii may have believed that Russian law gradually would triumph over local law, and in cities like Kiev, that assumption largely tuned out to be correct.[58] However, on the empire's periphery, such as among the Middle Horde Kazakhs, local custom and Islamic law still resolved most disputes with little administrative oversight.[59] Thus, despite the gradual expansion of Russian law into new territories, legal pluralism remained an essential feature of the empire, as Speranskii's unpublished compilations of non-Russian law confirmed.

Speranskii's *Digest of Laws* also ran headlong into other practical challenges that were compounded by a ruler who viewed any independent law-creating sources with suspicion and as a threat to his personal rule. Thus, the process of updating the law required the complicated placement of all new laws within the *Digest* and the removal of all out-of-date references. Legislators basically punted on this responsibility, not only sacrificing legal clarity but also putting the onus on the codifier to address inconsistencies.[60] Since Nicholas rejected all judicial interpretation, the law became increasingly bureaucratic, with the codifiers—and not the tsar or his legislators and judges—ultimately deciding its meaning within the *Digest of Laws*. The historian Tatiana Borisova suggests that Nicholas may have preferred this underlying legal uncertainty, since it "preserved an advantageous position for the monarch 'above the law'; it was only he who could restrain the vices of state agents."[61] Borisova further argues that as time went on, jurists turned to the Senate's collected volume of edicts and regulations, as opposed to the actual *Digest*, to learn about and to understand new legislation.[62]

Speranskii may have pulled off the impossible by compiling Russia's laws, but like any legislator, he had left behind ambiguous provisions that required further clarification. Since Nicholas refused to sanction any notion of judicial interpretation, however, it would take much longer to determine what certain provisions actually meant. The historian Ekaterina Pravilova, for example, notes that Speranskii gave the right of ownership over land, rivers, lakes, and roads both to the respective landowner and to the state. According to Pravilova, this provision would spark significant controversy as the autocracy struggled with the question as to what constituted publicly owned property necessary for promoting economic development and the public good.[63]

Nevertheless, Nicholas clearly had addressed one gap in Russian law by at least compiling existing laws in a systematic fashion. Nicholas closed a second major gap as well, namely the lack of trained Russian jurists. Occasional lectures on law had been read at Russian universities since the time of Catherine the Great, but it was only with the University Statute of 1835 that the teaching of law became a recognized course of study at Russian universities.[64] Nicholas wanted narrow practitioners, not enlightened jurists, so he excluded courses on natural law and instead demanded that students focus on the minutiae of law. Yet this did not stop professors from introducing broader legal principles and promoting a new ideal of legality that would inspire a generation of students.[65] This cadre of university-trained jurists was supplemented by students from the elite School of Jurisprudence, which provided a legal education to secondary school students, many of whom came from the ranks of the nobility. Ironically, School of Jurisprudence graduates entered the Russian bureaucracy at a higher level than their university counterparts, even though the latter had been exposed to a more rigorous and demanding legal curriculum. Russia's social structure still favored the traditional elite over the best-educated, and higher legal education was no exception.

The reminiscences of Nicholas's court system often repeat the litany of criticisms that had dogged Russian law since Peter the Great. Justice under Nicholas I was inquisitorial, excessively reliant on written proofs, class-based, understaffed, overly administrative, slow, corrupt, and non-transparent. The best evidence in criminal cases remained either confession or the testimony of two eyewitnesses, thereby encouraging the authorities to resort to torture in order to obtain convictions.[66] Civil disputes were known to drag on for decades, while the collection of any judgment depended on the arbitrary enforcement powers of the police.[67]

Yet change was working its way through Russian law, and the historian Sergei Antonov has presented an alternative view of Nicholas's legal system based on his study of criminal cases involving fraud and the abuse of credit. While not rejecting the above criticisms out of hand, Antonov argues that the nature of administrative interference was not as disruptive as often portrayed; governors were not allowed to overturn a court ruling on their own authority but could only petition the Senate for additional review if they disagreed with a particular decision.[68] Antonov further describes a fluid, as opposed to a rigid, class-based court system that regularly met in joint session to handle cases involving litigants from different estates.[69] There was, according to Antonov, more procedural regularity in pre-reform Russian courts than originally believed, accompanied by the emergence of legal representatives who could successfully shepherd a case through Russia's less-than transparent legal system. Therefore, Nicholas's considerable investment in updating Russian law appears to have paid dividends during his own reign, and not just after his death with the drafting of the Judicial Reforms of 1864.

Other long-term historical studies of Russian law during the eighteenth and early nineteenth centuries reach similar conclusions. Michelle Lamarche Marrese's study of the property rights of noblewomen from 1700 to 1861 found that women possessed greater control over the disposition of their personal assets under Russian law than their European counterparts.[70] Thus, the reigns of Catherine the Great, Alexander I, and Nicholas I had expanded notions of Russian legality. These changes included the rise of more secure property rights, the establishment of ministerial government with explicit law-creating powers, and the emergence of a cadre of university-trained jurists. Additional inroads were made in distinguishing between civil and criminal laws, as well as between judicial and administrative institutions. The recognition of foreign law and differentiated system of rights persisted under Russian law, but that made Imperial Russia no different than any other empire.

Russia further did not suffer from the absence of law by the middle of the nineteenth century. Indeed, the complete collection of laws demonstrates a state that was pumping out legislation at a consistent rate, both in the form of decrees and more comprehensive, normative statutes. Moreover, law, at times, truly limited the state's ability to act. Tsarist bureaucrats and entrepreneurs would struggle for decades to obtain access to subsoil rights, which Catherine, in her infinite wisdom, had transferred to landowners as part of her generous grant of private property. The Russian state also performed one of its essential functions by providing a means of civil adjudication and criminal punishment. Historians who have examined individual case files have discovered an unexpected degree of procedural regularity in the review of disputes, a sign of a more efficient legal system and far greater acceptance of prevailing inquisitorial practices, at least as they related to civil litigation.[71]

Yet such positive examples of justice rendered—while significant—should not be extrapolated so far as to define Russian law or to elevate its place within Russian society. Measuring the level of corruption remains a difficult task in the twenty-first century; it is impossible to do so retroactively to the eighteenth and nineteenth centuries. Nevertheless, the repeated accounts of corruption, bribery, and arbitrary criminal procedures (not to mention the abuses of serfdom and the exile system) could have only undermined public confidence in the Russian legal system. Expanded property rights further did not follow the Western example and lead to increased political demands by the aristocracy to check the autocracy's power.[72] Russia still lacked advanced civil law procedures and a theory of private law—the backbone of civil society—that could limit the expansive public law powers of the state. And while individual pieces of legislation carried different designations (code, charter, instruction, decree), they all emanated from within the bureaucracy and were imposed on the people with no public participation.

The historian George Yaney later referred to this system as the legal-administrative state, where the bureaucracy believed that "the state had to usurp (and create) law in accordance with its necessities."[73] But who would oversee the bureaucracy? The Russian state was not monolithic; bureaucratic infighting existed within different ministries in St. Petersburg, between the capital and the regions, as well as among the provincial governors and the local nobility. These internal debates, however, did not rise to the level of a nascent division of powers. Despite considerable reforms, Imperial Russia still lacked a definitive separation between administrative and judicial functions, as well as between executive and legislative responsibilities. Therefore, in order to check the growing power of the bureaucracy, the autocracy pursued a policy of "supervision" of both public administration as well as the general population, thereby making surveillance an essential feature of Russian governance and law.[74]

The autocracy, as it turns out, could not bring itself to trust the bureaucracy as an independent source of legal authority, since it potentially impinged on the tsar's unique legal privileges. In particular, the autocrat enjoyed considerable law-creating powers through the right to issue decrees. Some decrees rose to the level of laws, others were considered administrative acts, and still others remained secret and were never published. Nevertheless, they collectively demonstrated the tsar's ability to legislate all by himself/herself. Speranskii went so far as to tutor Alexander II in the 1820s that the tsar's conscience served as a fundamental source of Russian law.[75] Thus, while the bureaucracy assumed more legislative functions, the law remained highly personalized in Imperial Russia. It originated from the tsar's pen with no broader restraints—either legislative or philosophical—on the ruler. Indeed, the fictional division of state and tsar served the same purpose under Nicholas I as under Peter the Great: the state served as the primary law-giving body but in practice placed no limits on the autocrat's personal rule.

Nicholas I's world of law and order, conservative values, and international stability would fall apart in the aftermath of Russia's defeat in the Crimean War in 1855. Yet as would occur at several major inflection points in Russian history, the reactionary ruler ironically had prepared a new generation of liberal thinkers and jurists who possessed the expertise to re-imagine how Russia might be governed. The path ahead was by no means clear, and the state still retained significant resources to block and disrupt such reforms. Yet in the aftermath of Crimea and the death of Nicholas I, the opportunity presented itself for dramatic change, and in rapid succession, Alexander II would free the serfs, establish institutions of local self-government, and introduce the Judicial Reforms of 1864.

3

The Judicial Reforms of 1864 and the Modernization of Imperial Law

Liberal evolutionary change has always eluded Russia. As the previous chapter demonstrated, Catherine the Great, Alexander I, and Nicholas I each assumed the throne under contentious and violent circumstances that left them favoring traditional notions of Russian absolutism and statehood over liberal rule-of-law principles. Russia's twentieth century would be marked by revolution, terror, and national upheaval—hardly auspicious ground for moderate liberal thought. Thus, historians are left with only one, highly imperfect period—starting from Alexander II's great reforms of the early 1860s and ending with the outbreak of the First World War in 1914— to explore what gradual liberalization might have looked like in Russia and what obstacles stood in its way.

The Judicial Reforms of 1864 stand at the center of such an inquiry. The major innovations included the establishment of an independent judiciary, autonomous regional bar associations, and the jury system. All three institutions created new opportunities to both interpret and defend the law as an independent force in Russian society. The Judicial Reforms further created favorable conditions for the expansion of private law— the essential legal foundation for property rights and economic growth. Finally, in the aftermath of the Judicial Reforms, a diverse group of Russian legal theorists emerged who countered established notions of Russian law with a more modern vision of the law-based state. Yet even as new legal institutions and court procedures pushed Russia in a more liberal direction, the administrative state remained firmly entrenched.

This chapter examines all of these liberal trends—institutional, practical, and theoretical—and how the Judicial Reforms changed, and did not change, Russian law. Indeed, while the autocracy never overturned the Judicial

Reforms, it found numerous ways to obstruct their development and to defend Russian legality. The autocracy also possessed its own intellectual champions who challenged the liberal notion of the rule of law. In particular, the late nineteenth-century legal philosopher Nikolai Korkunov reinforced basic state and law principles while justifying the autocracy's significant flexibility in governing a multinational empire. Therefore, this chapter will explain the decidedly mixed results brought by evolutionary change over the fifty-year lifespan of the Judicial Reforms. It will demonstrate that law remained a highly elastic and conventional tool in the hands of the autocracy, even as the liberal tendencies unleashed by the Judicial Reforms gradually transformed the meaning and daily practice of Russian law.

The Judicial Reforms and their uneven reception

A bureaucratic maze—as well as a crucial and unexpected change of mind by Tsar Alexander II—surrounds the drafting of the Judicial Reforms. The process began with a modest proposal from Count Dmitrii Bludov who, as the head of the Second Section, supervised the codification process. He wanted to improve Russia's system of civil procedure without altering the fundamental characteristics of Russian justice (i.e., the inquisitorial system, the emphasis on written proofs, administrative control, etc.). Alexander II shared this limited objective and initially did not see the need for a fundamental transformation of the legal system. Alexander II was forced to reconsider his position, however, as he contemplated major reforms on other fronts. Most notably, the liberation of the serfs accelerated the debate on the need for the strict legal protection of property rights. The nobility insisted on strong legal guarantees so that they could defend their personal property from administrative abuse as well as compete economically in a post-emancipation world.[1]

Therefore, the property rights granted by Catherine the Great ultimately culminated in the demand for fundamental legal reform. Moreover, the legal expertise that was so noticeably absent when Speranskii gathered Russia's laws thirty years previously now existed in abundance and played a vital role in the drafting of the Judicial Reforms. The State Chancellery prepared the outlines of the reforms in the 1862 *Basic Principles for the Reform of the Courts*. As throughout Russian history, the proposed changes were borrowed from Western countries (notably France and Belgium).[2] Even if not distinctly original, however, the results were truly groundbreaking. *The Basic Principles* proposed several new institutions, including an independent judiciary and autonomous regional bar associations, as well as jury trials. In addition, the procuracy, Russia's longest-running legal institution, was to be transformed. While certain residual elements of supervision would remain, procurators would turn into prosecutors, whose new responsibilities primarily revolved around representing the state's interests in criminal court proceedings.

These new institutions were to be accompanied by new procedural rules, including the introduction of the adversarial process, oral proceedings, public hearings, and the acceptance of judicial discretion in resolving cases. The principles further represented a definitive break between judicial and administrative institutions, with judges receiving lifetime tenure to ensure their independence from state interference. Finally, the new judicial institutions possessed a unique public education element; in particular, the drafters believed that the jury system would play a significant role in teaching Russian subjects about the law and the new court system.[3]

The Basic Principles served as the basis of the reforms that were promulgated on November 30, 1864. The idealism surrounding the Judicial Reforms of 1864, however, concealed a significant lack of appreciation of how these legal institutions worked in practice, as the establishment of an independent bar association illustrates. A defense lawyer's primary responsibility, wrote one commentator in 1861, was to serve as a mediator between the state and the people while popularizing the new legal system. A genuine adversarial relationship between the state and an attorney was not envisioned: "The actual advantage for the state of this [profession] can only be in those cases when lawyers understand their sublime responsibilities to preserve peace and tranquility between citizens and the state, prevent all superfluous lawsuits, [and be] defenders of positive rights, not petty, temporary personal interests."[4] With such an idealistic outlook, it is not surprising that in the eyes of many critics, the Russian bar ultimately failed to live up to expectations.

The Judicial Reforms also created a streamlined, hierarchal court system that, in sharp distinction to the previous estate-based system, was open to all subjects. It would take decades to fully implement these changes—Siberia, for instance, did not come under the Judicial Reforms until 1897. The initial dividing line between the regular and lower courts depended on the potential severity of the sentence in criminal cases or the value of the dispute in civil cases. The justice of the peace courts, which were headed by judges elected by local government institutions (the *zemstva*), handled civil suits below 500 rubles as well as minor criminal cases.[5] All other cases came under the jurisdiction of the circuit courts, with appeals possible to the regional Judicial Chamber (*Sudebnaia palata*) and then to the Ruling Senate, which was divided into two bodies: the Civil Cassation Department and the Criminal Cassation Department. Certain exceptions existed to this process; state crimes, for example, were tried in the Judicial Chamber as the court of first instance and included both judges and class representatives.[6] Moreover, the Church retained jurisdiction over many family-related issues, most notably divorce.

Overall, the Judicial Reforms struck a major blow against Russia's established estate-based system of justice with one critical exception. The newly emancipated peasants—who made up approximately 80 percent of the population—were deemed ill-prepared to defend their interests in regular civil courts. Therefore, small civil claims were relegated to local township (*volost'*) courts that were allowed to rely on local custom, rather than formal written law, to reach a verdict. The decision to separate peasants from the reformed courts also reflected a weak state that lacked the resources to extend the new judicial system down to the rural township level. The peasantry, however, was not walled off completely from Russian statutory law. Peasants remained subject to 1839 Rural Judicial Code in criminal matters.[7] Moreover, peasant litigants and higher appellate bodies regularly cited Russian statutes in reviewing peasant appeals in civil cases.[8] Thus, while the Judicial Reforms perpetuated an estate-based bias and informal sources of law, peasants still gained access to the new court system.

Yet no sooner were the Judicial Reforms enacted then the traditional administrative forces began to reassert themselves and demand that the independent judiciary and accompanying legal institutions be reined in. Officials at all levels of government—ministers, governors, and local police—felt threatened by the Judicial Reforms and argued that they would not be able to maintain law and order under the new legal system.[9] Thus began the process of chipping away at the new institutions, at first within the bureaucracy but then through a series of major counter-reforms. The opening of new regional bar associations was suspended in 1874 and did not resume for almost thirty years. Defense attorneys, therefore, were deprived of their own self-governing bodies and instead found themselves under the supervision of the judiciary and (indirectly) the state. A series of unexpected acquittals in the 1870s in trials involving revolutionaries and terrorists led to the creation of special closed legal tribunals that were separate from the regular courts. In 1889, the autocracy denied Jews admission to the bar, which up until that point had been the only legal institution where entry was based solely on merit. Finally, the elected justice of the peace was replaced in 1889 by an appointed administrative official (the land captain), thereby undermining one of the hallmarks of the 1864 reforms: judicial independence.

As the above indicates, the administrative state did not disappear after the Judicial Reforms. On the contrary, the power of the Ministry of Interior, which housed the Police Department, retained enormous supervisory and intelligence-gathering capabilities to ensure domestic security. Moreover, the process of promulgating laws, either within the bureaucracy or through the tsar's personal decrees, remained unchanged, often resulting in confusion rather than clarity. According to one commentator, anyone who researched legislation had to sift through "a series of administrative orders which in essence were temporary and disagreed with each other."[10] Thus, the tsar's word remained law, even as more regulations emerged from the state bureaucracy.

Leading government officials and government commissions repeatedly called to unify the state administration and coordinate policymaking to ensure that central pronouncements were translated into law on a local level. As a result, a unified bureaucracy, instead of the new judicial system, increasingly came to be seen by the state as the answer to Russia's legal problems. M. T. Loris-Melikov, the last Minister of Interior under Alexander II, is best remembered for his 1881 proposal to create a bureaucratic quasi-parliament, yet this plan was most definitely in place of, and not in conjunction with, the Judicial Reforms. Loris-Melikov strongly objected to the new legal institutions and practices spawned by the Judicial Reforms. He saw the judiciary as too isolated from the state structures. He further accused prominent criminal defense attorneys of undermining state legitimacy by making statements in court "that had gone unspoken before."[11] What Loris-Melikov desired was strict state legality: the governors-general had to "appear as the highest representative of legality and restorer of violated legality wherever, and in whatever sphere, such violated legality appears."[12]

Top-down legality had been pursued since Peter the Great and therefore represented a continuation of past policy objectives. Other links between the pre- and post-reform periods existed as well. The primary sources of law remained the *Digest of Laws* and the underlying complete collection of laws, even as economic and social conditions demanded that individual laws be revised and updated to keep up with changing times. While the Judicial Reforms called for the establishment of administrative justice to hold state officials accountable for their actions, sufficient legal procedures were never put into place to punish government misconduct.[13] The Security Law of 1881, introduced by Alexander III in the aftermath of his father's assassination, further consolidated the state's discretionary powers, especially its use of extra-judicial exile and administrative banishment.

The tsarist system of exile stood as an enduring symbol of the unrestricted and repressive power of the state. For example, in the aftermath of the Polish uprising of 1863, some 35,000 Poles—politicians, journalists, Catholic priests, students—were banished administratively or extra-judicially across Russia.[14] Yet between 1881 and 1904, the number of political exiles remained relatively low. Instead, administrative exiles, expelled by their own communities in non-legal proceedings, constituted the largest group of deportees. The exile system strained under this surplus of arrivals, but instead of deterring crime, Siberia ironically became a hotbed of sedition, especially as the number of political exiles grew after the 1905 Revolution. The historian Daniel Beer notes that whereas Siberia served "as a realm of political quarantine" when Nicholas II assumed the throne, by the start of the First World War Siberia "had come to resemble a giant laboratory of revolution."[15]

The politicized nature of Russian criminal law—as well as the unrelenting severity of the law on the books—has led some Russian historians to conclude that Russia possessed the hallmarks of a police state. Richard Pipes highlights the legal foundation of an emerging police state in Nicholas I's legislation, which was subsequently expanded by Alexander II in response to Russia's first wave of terrorism. After 1881, Pipes argues, the political police (the Corps of Gendarmes) was completely outside judicial supervision; instead, it only was subject to bureaucratic control, and "its members had the right to search, imprison and exile citizens on its own authority, without consulting the Public Prosecutor."[16] Yet even Pipes concludes that the tsarist police state was a prototype at best that "fell far short of its full potential" since the empire retained open borders and upheld private property rights.[17] The historian Jonathan Daly further contends that the Security Law of 1881 actually curtailed administrative abuse, since it included defined limits to the police's authority. Daly recognizes, however, that this emergency legislation allowed the police and other state officials to circumvent the legal guarantees set forth in the Judicial Reforms.[18]

But if Russia was not a full-blown police state, it still favored administrative solutions over all other strategies. Indeed, the state's search for administrative uniformity stretched to the fringes of the empire and became a central component in the autocracy's Russification policies. The autocracy abolished Polish legal institutions in the aftermath of the 1863 uprising while making Russian the official language of court documents and proceedings. The autocracy also introduced the Judicial Reforms wholesale in the Baltic States in 1889, replacing local judicial institutions with Russian courts and procedures while attaching the Baltic States to the St. Petersburg judicial district. Finally, in 1899 the Russian state launched a major assault on Finland's legal and political autonomy that lasted until the end of the tsarist period. Prime Minister Petr Stolypin would introduce new legislation in 1909 that identified specific subjects and laws that were outside the jurisdiction of the Finnish parliament, and in a rare moment of legislative harmony, the Duma overwhelmingly approved the law.[19]

Thus, the administrative state, which so often disdained law as an intrusive check on its authority, nevertheless relied on Russian law as a means to expand its control in those areas that had still managed to retain their distinctive local legal institutions, legislation, and practices.[20] Indeed, in the eyes of the Russian state, "equality" meant the equalization of laws within the empire.[21] Russian law further served as an equalizing and unifying force in terms of funding the state. As the historian Yanni Kotsonis demonstrates in his comprehensive study of tsarist tax policy, the state introduced taxes on state corporations in 1885 and then moved on to other firms, eventually raising over half of its revenue from taxes on the private sector.[22]

Yet even at the height of the Russification policy, Russian law was still unable to serve as a source of overarching imperial law, especially in regulating basic commercial activities. Russia's *Digest* on civil law remained a hodgepodge of foreign borrowings and confusing references that was inferior to the existing civil codes in the western provinces. Therefore, Poland kept its Napoleonic Code, the Baltic States retained their own private law, complete with references to Roman law principles, and Finland kept its civil law based on the Swedish Civil Code of 1734. Moreover, unlike the British empire, which was predicated on the transfer of English commercial law and property rights around the globe, Imperial Russia exported law primarily as a means to extend administrative and military control. This was especially true in the western provinces, since Russian civil law could not compete with the region's more advanced civil law systems.[23]

One can argue that in theory, the essence of Russian law, and in particular its statutory base, remained remarkably stable in the aftermath of the Judicial Reforms of 1864. The reforms transformed the rules of procedure and created new institutions but produced little change in the underlying substantive civil and criminal laws. Moreover, the supremacy of the Russian state and personal rule—two pillars of Russian law since Peter the Great—survived the Judicial Reforms largely intact. The Judicial Reforms did introduce new adversarial principles in court proceedings. Nevertheless, the inquisitorial nature of Russian criminal procedure remained, especially in the pretrial investigation process, where the charges were formulated without any participation of defense counsel.[24] Finally, the Russian state continued to rely on custom as a critical source of law, and while court procedures became more uniform, the autocracy still tolerated a significant degree of legal pluralism to govern a continent-wide empire. Yet as we will now see, while not necessarily transcending existing practices, the Judicial Reforms nevertheless radically transformed them.

Judges, juries, and new interpretations of Russian law

The distinguishing feature of a continental European legal system, as opposed to a common law jurisdiction, is where one searches to find the law. From a theoretical standpoint, court decisions in the Anglo-American system represent a primary source of law—to understand how statutes have been interpreted and what they mean in everyday practice. In contrast, in a civil law system, the written code should both be sufficiently accessible and detailed so that there is no need to refer to court decisions for additional guidance. Imperial Russia belonged to the civil law tradition, but as previously noted, its codes lacked the detail and uniformity to serve as a source of national law, especially when it came to civil and commercial disputes. Moreover, on a broader level, law merely reflected the positivist pronouncements of the state, as set forth in personal decrees and tsarist legislation. Thus, courts enforced the law but were not legally empowered to provide interpretations of the law, although some explanations inevitably accompanied the determinations in individual disputes.

The autocracy's failure over the better part of thirty-five years to adopt a new civil code created an opening for Russian courts—and particularly its highest civil court, the Supreme Civil Cassation Department—to become a source of law. William Wagner's path breaking study of family, inheritance, and property law identifies numerous decisions where the Civil Cassation Department used its implied powers of judicial review to advance Russian property rights and more broadly to support social change in the absence of specific legislation. For example, the court expanded an owner's testamentary power to dispose of property, thereby providing substance to an unclear branch of tsarist law while granting individuals greater freedom to transfer their property at death through a will.[25] The Civil Cassation Department revised other civil law practices as well, not only allowing for marital separation but further recognizing the right of the separated spouse to receive financial support from her husband.[26]

Compilations of high court decisions served as essential guidance for jurists engaged in litigation. Court decisions (known as "judicial practice" [sudebnaia praktika]) further became a recognized source of law in tsarist textbooks. One should not underestimate just how radical a transformation had occurred. Independent judges—basing their opinions on the arguments of professional lawyers—were directly engaged in law-creating activities, thereby breaking the monopoly previously enjoyed by the tsar and the bureaucracy. Such a groundbreaking shift, however, stopped well short of absolute acceptance of precedent as a legally binding set of rules. Russian jurists shared the civil law system's long-standing prejudice against judge-made law, as opposed to simply following the law as written. This inherent suspicion of independent judges was compounded by a centralized bureaucracy that historically had exerted control over the court system. Thus, while the Russian judiciary may have found new reservoirs of "professional dignity" and purpose in the aftermath of the Judicial Reforms, it still had not vanquished the administrative state.[27]

If top-down law changed, so too did bottom-up. The establishment of jury trials for major crimes sought to educate the Russian people, from the nobility to the peasants, about the law. Therefore, although certain property requirements limited participation, a broad cross-section of the population (with the notable exception of women) participated on the jury. As with much of Alexander II's reforms, however, initial idealism faded in the face of practical realities. Many jurors found the experience extremely unpleasant, from cold uncomfortable courthouses to long, tedious, and at times gruesome proceedings. The historian Alexander Afanas'ev quotes one commentator describing the public response to the call for jury duty: "A veritable epidemic of different illnesses would befall the rich merchants and noblemen who had been selected for jury service; rich landowners would be overrun with unexpected misfortunes on their estates, and civil servants would become suddenly imbued with an exceptional desire to carry out their official assignments."[28]

The pool of peasant jurors was also less than inspiring. The Judicial Reforms designated two potential sources of peasant jurors: those who met the property requirement and those who occupied specific positions within the village society. The peasant jurors came overwhelming from the latter category and were distinguished by their illiteracy and extreme poverty.[29] This problem was less pronounced in the major cities—peasants made up less than 10 percent of the juries in St. Petersburg and Moscow—but in the provinces, peasants constituted more than 50 percent of the jurors.[30]

Questions of whether jury trials were appropriate for Russia, given its underlying social and educational differences, divided contemporary tsarist legal commentators, and they continue to be a subject of debate among historians.[31] From a strictly legal standpoint, however, the jury brought several critical issues to a head that could not be avoided if Russian law was to change. To begin with, the jury deliberation process tested the consensus as to what constituted individual guilt under Russian law. The jury was asked three questions when rendering a verdict: 1. Had a crime been committed? 2. Had sufficient proof been presented that the accused, in fact, had committed the crime? And 3. Did the accused possess the appropriate criminal responsibility to be held responsible for the crime? The last question opened up the jury deliberations to the defendant's state of mind and degree of culpability. Defense attorneys skillfully played on the subjectivity surrounding the broad question of intent, raising a host of social and moral issues to provide grounds for acquittal.

Jury nullification—where jurors put aside matters of law and render a decision based on other extenuating circumstances—represented a significant problem in tsarist courts. Although Russia was by no means the only country to confront this issue, Russian juries were notoriously lenient and forgiving, with a particular soft spot for women defendants.[32] Moreover, since Russians were excluded from the law-creating process, the jury became one of the few public institutions where they could voice their opinion, and increasingly their displeasure, both about the laws themselves and the underlying factual representations put forward by the state. By deciding the issue of guilt or innocence, therefore, the jury provided Russian subjects with the opportunity to object to, or at least mitigate, the law as written. Jurors also managed to articulate standards of guilt that did not match those of the state, although the procuracy reserved the right to appeal sentences to the Ruling Senate on procedural grounds if it disagreed with the verdict.[33]

The jury served as the forum for an additional cultural clash, namely between the state, as the defender of Russian statutory law as written, and the peasantry, whose primary experience with law was though local custom. Historian Jörg Baberowski describes this meeting as two worlds colliding: "Public prosecutors, lawyers, and judges spoke a language which the rural jury did not understand. They understood nothing, and yet were to decide everything: not only the question of whether the defendant had committed the deed, but also whether he was to be found guilty as charged."[34] But even if the parties were speaking different languages, the clash between two legal cultures arguably carried certain benefits for Russia's long-term legal development. Every national law code—the bedrock of statutory law—requires that the drafters take into account local custom so that law can reflect the lived experience of its subjects. Such an accounting was particularly daunting in Russia since it contained so much legal diversity within its borders. Nevertheless, this process had to begin somewhere if Russian law was to reflect the actual interactions and experiences of daily life, and in the absence of other public institutions, the jury became the vehicle for this assessment.

The jury made one additional substantive contribution to Russian law, namely by reinforcing the independence of the judiciary. The pre-1864 legal system followed the inquisitorial model with the judge acting as both the primary interrogator and the ultimate finder of fact. The jury placed the judge in a different position as the neutral party mediating between the state and the defense in an open courtroom. Thus, instead of the final verdict, the judge's instructions to the jury became the yardstick for measuring his impartiality and underlying commitment to the law. It was Judge Anatolii Koni, after all, who asked the jury in Russia's most famous criminal proceeding—the trial of the terrorist Vera Zasulich charged with attempting to murder the St. Petersburg governor-general in cold blood—to resolve the case based on the evidence and their consciences. The jury took Koni's instructions to heart and acquitted Zasulich, to the deep displeasure of the state. Therefore, as the ultimate finder of facts, the jury relieved the judiciary of the responsibility of rendering a decision, thereby enabling judges to assume a more independent position both in the courtroom and vis-à-vis the state.

So despite all the excesses—including the theatrical speeches of defense attorneys, the social drama attached to high-profile crimes, the outsized sense of morality among jurors, and the bewildering acquittals of seemingly premeditated acts of violence—the jury represented one of the first attempts to turn Russian subjects into citizens empowered to provide critical feedback on public perceptions of prevailing laws. At various times, critics would call for the reining in the juries, and the autocracy would legislate around the jury in the major political trials. Nevertheless, the legal community—including the highest judicial body, the Ruling Senate—remained strong defenders of the jury and its right to take into consideration the extenuating circumstances surrounding a given defendant. As the historian Louise McReynolds concludes, the autocracy decided that "it could not dispense with what functioned as an effective mediator between state and society."[35]

Lawyers, everyday practice, and the advancement of Russian civil law

The consequences of legal reform ran wide as well as deep. The demand for everyday law—as expressed in terms of the number of civil actions both before the regular courts and the peasant courts—increased exponentially from 1864 onward. For example, the annual number of civil cases in Russia's justice of the peace courts increased from 237,176 in 1886 to 1,725,343 in 1914. Meanwhile, the number of civil cases in the district courts during this time period more than doubled.[36] Similar dramatic jumps occurred in the peasant township courts, reflecting a highly litigious rural population as well.[37] The end result was the emergence of a genuine system of private law as well as a fundamental reinterpretation of the role that advocates, judges, and prosecutors played in the tsarist civil law system.

The growing demand for legal advice was met by both licensed attorneys and unlicensed lawyers—the so-called underground advocates—and the quality of service varied dramatically across the different levels of expertise. At the top of the profession stood the sworn attorney and his assistant, the attorney-in-training.[38] Admission to the bar required a university degree as well as the completion of a five-year apprenticeship. Sworn attorneys elected (where allowed) their own independent corporate leadership and were governed by a strict code of ethics. The legal practices of sworn attorneys reflect the rise of everyday law in tsarist Russia. The best attorneys represented Russia's economic elite: banks, railroads, insurance companies, major corporations, and wealthy individuals, all of whom needed assistance in navigating the Russian legal system. Leading civil lawyers further contested major cases before Russia's highest courts, contributing legal arguments that ultimately formed the basis of final decisions. The potential client pool for mid-level sworn attorneys was much less attractive. An average legal practice revolved around bankruptcies, the search for debtors, evictions from apartments, and preparing technical documents. This constant pressure to find business led to growing criticism in the press of sworn attorneys for being overly mercenary and not living up to their ethical standards.[39]

The "underground" and mostly untrained lawyers posed a different challenge. They lacked any sort of corporate oversight or professional ethics to regulate their activities. Practicing both in the cities and in the countryside, they took advantage of Russia's less-educated and poorer segments of the population. Their practices also reflected everyday law in action; underground advocates dealt with issues of inheritance, land disputes, divorce, personal injury, and bankruptcy. However, because of their unofficial status, these non-licensed practitioners rarely appeared in court; instead, they specialized in written petitions. But since they were not trained lawyers, their appeals often contained inaccurate legal references (or none at all). Newspapers frequently reported on how these "street" advocates raised expectations and then took financial advantage of their unsuspecting clients. Unlicensed "lawyers" also flooded the courts with unfounded complaints that clearly placed an additional burden on the courts. Underground advocates undoubtedly filled a niche in the market—Russia's lower strata could not afford consulting with a licensed sworn attorney—but they also raised legitimate questions about the quality of service and how people gained access to the legal system.[40]

The bar fought back against these "pettifoggers" and "scriveners," unsuccessfully demanding that their professional monopoly rights, as called for in the Judicial Reforms, be enforced. Sworn attorneys further represented indigent clients free of charge via an established appointment process, but such *pro bono* work never met the growing demand for law among the population. At the turn of twentieth century, young lawyers began to address this demand issue by going directly to the people and establishing public interest legal aid centers in cities across the empire. These consultation bureaus provided legal advice to thousands of visitors annually and therefore represent yet another window on everyday law. In St. Petersburg, for example, workers and other urban residents brought their own distinct legal problems—work-related injuries, salary and rent disputes, requests for financial support from separated spouses, and questions about how to maintain the proper documentation to work in the city. After the 1906 Stolypin land reforms, workers peppered the consultation bureaus with inquiries about their property rights back in the village. And following Russia's declaration of war in 1914, many visitors turned to the bureaus with queries about military service.[41]

But while consultation bureaus represented a positive symbol of civic engagement, they often did not provide the answer that an injured factory worker or an indigent spouse wanted to hear, thereby limiting a bureau's ability to change negative public perceptions of the law. They also ran afoul of the Russian state. In St. Petersburg, the bureaus helped with voter registration prior to the third Duma elections. The state not only objected to this assistance but concluded in 1909 that these legal aid societies had no right to exist under prevailing Russian law and therefore ordered their closure. The bar fought this ruling, and the bureaus continued to operate until 1917, but the controversy demonstrated the state's innate hostility to independent institutions that promoted the individual and social rights of citizens.[42]

As the above indicates, law filtered down to all layers of society, from the upper reaches of the aristocracy to the lowest peasant village. The peasant township courts provide one last snapshot of everyday law in action. These courts only covered certain low-value (less than 100 rubles) cases and were heard by judges elected by the village assembly.[43] Sworn attorneys were disinclined to take on such low-paying disputes to begin with, but the autocracy later forbade licensed advocates from appearing in township courts. This created opportunities for underground advocates, but most peasants simply represented themselves before the village court.[44] The judges followed custom when resolving inheritance cases but were also allowed to rule "by conscience" to encourage settlements in civil cases.[45] The state included these flexible procedures because it assumed that the peasantry was not ready for advanced court procedures. Yet peasants turned out to be highly litigious and actively engaged in inheritance, contract, defamation, land, and other disputes.

Many tsarist commentators viewed these peasant courts as backward and perpetuating a legal segregation that undermined Russia's legal development. Historians, however, have produced a more nuanced evaluation. Jane Burbank argues that township courts served as a unique laboratory for legal change; by using the courts, she contends, "peasants demonstrated that they had a legal culture; they regarded township court decisions as a means to settle problems with their neighbors, laborers, employers, renters, buyers, sellers, and family members."[46] Stefan Kirmse identifies an "intermediate terrain" that encouraged Muslim Tatars in Kazan and Crimea to engage with reformed judicial institutions when perceived as beneficial, while maintaining traditional dispute mechanisms as well.[47] Burbank concludes that peasants willingly sought peaceful resolution of local economic disputes, thereby highlighting the township courts' ability to promote gradual legal change in Russia.[48] Other historians, however, see the reliance on customary law as promoting legal uncertainty within the Russian judicial system, especially with its informal procedures as well as a willingness by peasants to go outside established criminal procedure and resort to self-justice (*samosud*) in punishing local criminal acts.[49]

The historian Cathy Frierson concludes that the township court at the beginning of the twentieth century was "neither a purely peasant institution nor yet an institution of national, formal legality."[50] Such a statement accurately reflects a legal system in transition, not fully unified or integrated, but nevertheless holding out the prospect for positive evolutionary change. Thus, on the one hand, the everyday practice of law in tsarist Russia should not be over-idealized. The bar possessed both high-end, well-educated advocates and bottom-feeding, ethically challenged petitioners. Judges also appear to have been selected based on their overall political reliability as well as their competence.[51] Yet for all their internal shortcomings, the judiciary and the *advokatura* presided over one of the great advancements of the Judicial Reforms, namely the emergence of a viable system of private law. Private law within the civil law system covers those disputes among individuals where the state is not a party, such as contracts, torts, property, and family law. Private law further serves as the crucial legal restraint on the state's public law powers and has long been recognized as an essential building block of civil society, since it reinforces notions of judicial independence, property rights, individual rights, and the adversarial process.[52]

Private law in tsarist Russia started from a low legislative base. As previously noted, numerous commissions were appointed to update the 1832 *Digest* on civil law, and while a new civil code was prepared in 1913, it was never formally adopted. Commercial law also remained largely unchanged from 1836 onward, even as Western countries transitioned from the concession system and state approval of corporations to the registration system and the rapid growth of private corporate activity. The corporation was gradually assimilated into private law in the modernizing part of the world but not so in Russia. The state remained too suspicious of private capital and non-Russian economic activity—it banned Poles and Jews from owning corporations—and therefore Russia retained the state concession system through the end of the tsarist period.[53]

Yet even taking into account these limits, Russian civil and commercial law still presided over a period of steady economic growth at the end of the tsarist period, indicating that Russian law did not represent a fatal impediment to economic development. The daily practices of attorneys, with their diverse clientele and caseloads, along with the Civil Cassation Department's major rulings in inheritance and property cases, further testify to an expanding private law sector that defended both individual and commercial interests while promoting the overall advancement of civil society. Even the township courts—in their review of small civil disputes—supported the broad development of private law principles, albeit relying on custom, and not statutory law, to do so.

Private law's ability to challenge the state's prerogative power should not be exaggerated. As the historian Yanni Kotsonis has shown, the state introduced a modern system of taxation from 1885 onward without ever feeling constrained by the economic or individual rights associated with property ownership.[54] The state also played an outsized role in directing Russia's economic development, and lawyers felt themselves at a distinct disadvantage when going against major corporations backed by the state.[55] Meanwhile, Russian liberals and intellectuals sought to move certain literary works and scientific translations into the expanding realm of public property rights, undermining—or depending on one's perspective, modernizing—Russian intellectual property law along the way.[56]

But even as state and liberal understandings of property rights evolved in tsarist Russia, the growing relevance of private law was tangible. It was not only reflected in the increasing litigiousness of Russian society and the willingness to defend one's legal rights in court. The impact of private law was felt beyond the courtroom as well. The lawyer and politician Maksim Vinaver insisted in 1905 that the unsung civil law practitioner had injected basic civil law principles into the bloodstream of the Russian legal system, in the process making a critical and underappreciated contribution to Russia's political development. "Haven't we directed efforts so that in all spheres of confrontation between the state (*vlast'*) and the individual, the state was reduced to a role of a party, arguing, as the accuser or the accused, in an equal, open judicial process?" Vinaver reminded his fellow civil practitioners.[57] In his eyes, the civil process had become the very embodiment "of the multiple guarantees of freedom of the individual against the unlimited dominion of the administration."[58]

Vinaver's optimism in 1905 regarding the political influence of civil law practices no doubt would be tested in the coming years. Nevertheless, the Judicial Reforms and the rise of private law presided over an essential change in how Russian citizens understood and used the law in their everyday interactions. The Judicial Reforms and the civil process facilitated a second major transformation as well, namely a fundamental realignment of Russia's legal institutions. As we have seen, an independent judiciary emerged that engaged in its own interpretive activities, updating Russian civil law in the process. An advanced legal profession also appeared that, while facing serious internal corporate challenges, nevertheless served as an essential intermediary between state and society in resolving civil disputes. The most overlooked institutional change after 1864, however, occurred in the procuracy. The Judicial Reforms converted a procurator into a prosecutor, with a particular emphasis on representing the state in criminal proceedings.[59] Residual pockets of supervisory authority remained. In criminal law, for example, the procuracy still supervised the preliminary investigation.[60] The procuracy also retained certain supervisory powers over the civil process, although prosecutors proved to be indifferent practitioners of civil law and rarely intervened in private disputes. This withdrawal essentially allowed Russia's sworn attorneys and other practitioners to play the dominant role in the civil process.[61]

The procuracy's assumption of a more conventional role in the adversarial process, however, did not mean that it ceased to be the "eyes of the sovereign." The autocracy's use of regular courts, closed proceedings, and military tribunals to put its political opponents on trial naturally enlisted the procuracy as well. Prosecutors became the public face in a permanent legal struggle that compelled the state to go after violent revolutionaries and peaceful protestors alike. But while the procuracy remained a highly politicized institution, the Judicial Reforms endowed the procuracy with a more regular, and narrow, legal function. The historian S. M. Kazantsev concludes that the years after the Judicial Reforms were the most "fruitful and effectual" period in the history of the tsarist procuracy and asserts that the names of Russia's leading prosecutors were as well known as the most prominent defense lawyers.[62]

Thus, although numerous exceptions and qualifications applied, the Judicial Reforms established the basic institutional building blocks that held out the possibility of future legal modernization right up to October 1917. Yet as we will now see, Russian law was not only evolving on a practical, day-to-day level. The Judicial Reforms further produced a generation of distinguished legal scholars that possessed both national and international reputations. Some of these thinkers would directly challenge the autocracy with innovative liberal and sociological theories of law, yet the most consequential theory, authored by Nikolai Korkunov, would be written in defense of the state.

The golden age of Russian legal philosophy

The law faculty was only formally established by the University Statute of 1835, yet by the beginning of the twentieth century, law attracted the largest number of students at Russian universities. The growth in legal education was accompanied by a dramatic expansion of legal scholarship, with leading experts addressing contemporary issues of civil, criminal, administrative, and international law. Moreover, legal societies sprouted up in Moscow, St. Petersburg, Kiev, Odessa, and numerous other cities. These groups presided over the interaction between scholars and practitioners to propose practical solutions to everyday problems. The societies published major journals and organized meetings of jurists from every professional branch, all in a very collegial atmosphere. According to G. B. Sliozberg, a prominent Jewish sworn attorney, "to work in the [St. Petersburg] Law Society was especially pleasant, because the work took place in a purely scholarly atmosphere, amongst people who had been educated in the shadow of the Judicial Reforms of 1864."[63]

Russia also produced its fair share of major legal theorists whose works challenged Russia's autocratic legal tradition from multiple perspectives. Boris Chicherin represented the standard liberal approach to law, emphasizing the crucial role that private law (i.e., property, contracts, individual rights) played in the construction of civil society and the expression of human freedom. For Chicherin, civil law—and not mass democracy—served as the primary restraint on the state.[64] Alternatively, Pavel Novgorodtsev confronted the tsarist tradition by promoting the natural law tradition and emphasizing that certain legal principles stood above the state.[65] One of the most innovative scholars was Leon Petrazycki, who introduced a psychological theory of law. Petrazycki focused on the inner individual and his relation to others as the primary expression of law rather than external forces such as nature, reason, or the state.[66]

The Russian state possessed its philosophical champions as well. In his book *Russian State Law*, Professor Nikolai Korkunov soundly rejected any notion of social contract or the transfer of natural rights by citizens to the state.[67] According to Korkunov, Russia's social system had been created by the state. Therefore, Russia's individual estate categories (nobility, merchants, peasantry, clergy) did not represent distinct classes that could impose their will on the state.[68] Instead, the state was created by "free" individuals out of their awareness of their absolute dependence on the state, thereby making the state the precondition for any meaningful social interaction and personal freedom. The central attribute of the state was compulsion, that is, the force necessary to hold a continental empire together while allowing subjects to form the relationships that reinforced their mutual dependence on each other and the state.[69] Korkunov referred to this ruling force as "state power (*gosudarstvennaia vlast'*)," which served as the highest level of administrative and legislative authority.[70] The Russian notion of autocracy further concentrated state power in the hands of the monarch, but since an individual ruler could not do everything by himself, the monarch required "organs of power" to administer the state. These bodies implemented the ruler's orders and at all times remained subordinated to his commands as expressed in law. If the organs of power were granted freedom to act on their own initiative, argued Korkunov, the inevitable result would be anarchy.[71]

State power, however, was not only concerned with administrative and governance issues. It was also intertwined with the critical issue of legality. Korkunov devoted a whole section in *Russian State Law* to *zakonnost'*, which he divided into two camps: subjective and objective. Subjective law was that which was imposed on the state by different estates, localities, or citizens, thereby creating a lawful limitation on state power. The West followed this pattern, noted Korkunov, but Russia did not. It was governed by objective law, where the state pronounced its laws on its own initiative in pursuit of a single goal: order. Thus, according to Korkunov, legality in Russia had nothing to do with political rights. Instead, legality was the state's own creation, and, while state power generally was subordinated to law in the sense that it strove to act within established legal boundaries, state power itself was not limited by any particular law.[72]

The final essential element of Korkunov's system was state unity. Russia, Korkunov argued, was a unified state (*edinoe gosudarstvo*), as opposed to a union of states (such as Austria-Hungary) or commonwealth of multiple states. To prove this point, he reviewed the various bilateral treaties with Ukraine (Malorossiia), Poland, and Finland and concluded that none of the above regions possessed equal status to that of the imperial state and therefore could not challenge the supremacy of Russian state power.[73] He also referred to a unified system of state power that was not necessarily restricted by notions of legality but could act extra-judicially to address specific questions unanticipated by prevailing law. "Not in working out general abstract rules, but in deciding concrete questions, put forward by everyday life, [that is] the particular advantage of unified power, since it is the living personification of the state idea."[74] Thus, legality under Korkunov's theory was an inherently flexible concept, based on established rules but also permitting the breaking of those rules when confronted with unforeseen issues.

A short synopsis does not do justice to Korkunov's wide-ranging, and at times, contradictory theory of law. Despite Korkunov's notion of an unlimited state, for example, he nevertheless believed that state power should recognize certain basic civil liberties as the best means to consolidate state authority and limit opposition. Korkunov further discussed the Russian state's persistent failure to protect these fundamental liberties.[75] Yet despite such inconsistencies, Korkunov's theory explained—and justified—the dominant role of the state and its bureaucracy in Russia's top-down legal development. His writings ultimately would resonate across historical periods and be picked up by scholars and present-day politicians alike.[76]

The golden age of Russian law produced other original, world-class legal thinkers as well. Sergei Muromtsev brought the sociological school of law to Russia. This approach looked at the everyday social interaction, as opposed to the historical pronouncements of the state, to find the meaning of law.[77] Fyodor Martens authored the famous Martens clause of the 1899 Hague Convention Respecting the Laws and Customs of War on Land, which provided protections to individuals in times of war based on international law, the laws of humanity, and public conscience.[78] Martens helped place Russia at the forefront of international law—a development that makes sense when one remembers that the state serves as the primary actor in international law. Finally, Bogdan Kistiakovskii synthesized various legal arguments to promote the rule-of-law state that incorporated such basic principles as human rights, federalism, and socialism.[79]

Kistiakovskii, however, would be best remembered not for his theory of law but for his essay explaining Russia's—and more specifically the Russian intelligentsia's—rejection of law as a guiding governing principle. In 1909, Kistiakovskii published his article "In Defense of Law" in *Vekhi* (Landmarks), a collection of essays that sought to explain the political disillusionment that had occurred in the aftermath of the 1905 Revolution and the attempt to impose constitutional limits on the autocracy. Kistiakovskii criticized all of the post-1864 judicial institutions, including the judiciary and the bar, but his strongest words of opprobrium were directed against the left-wing intelligentsia. The Russian intelligentsia, he argued, "never respected law and never saw any value in it."[80] Instead, according to Kistiakovskii, they focused on the "social nature of constitutional government" without addressing its legal character, namely the "protection of the individual's inviolability and freedom."[81] Kistiakovskii went on to criticize the intelligentsia's failure to advance any ideal of the legal individual. "Both sides of this ideal, the individual disciplined by law and by a stable legal order and the individual accorded all rights and making free use of them, are alien to our intelligentsia's consciousness."[82]

As discussed in the following chapter, several of the above legal scholars would become political actors in their own right. But although a wide variety of liberal and innovative legal theories existed, neither the Russian state nor the intelligentsia seemed anxious to embrace them. The philosophical gap between these two political rivals remained wide, perhaps best seen in their different approaches to the theoretical lynchpin of private law and the liberal state, namely property rights. One of the distinctive aspects of Russian property rights was that it never evolved into a broader conception of civil rights and therefore never served as the foundation for a fully modernized Russia. According to the historian Richard Wortman, the autocracy, the leading promoter of property rights, showed scant interest in defending a more extensive system of civil rights (i.e., freedom of speech, assembly, religion, etc.), while the Russian intelligentsia consistently failed to list property rights among its demands for greater civil liberties. As Wortman notes, "The word 'property' conveyed the sense of oppression and exploitation, of an illegitimate usurpation of the possession of all, under the auspices of arbitrary and brutal political authority."[83]

Thus, property rights and accompanying notions of private law remained both polarizing in theory and highly compartmentalized in practice, and Russia's legal thinkers never succeeded in reconciling the deep philosophical divide between the autocracy and the intelligentsia. Instead, it was Korkunov's theory that best explained existing legal principles and realities. While Korkunov died in 1904 and never witnessed the political changes brought by the 1905 Revolution, his terminology—the unified state, state power, organs of power, legality—would eventually become the unofficial vocabulary of twentieth-century Soviet and Russian constitutionalism.

Conclusion

The Judicial Reforms posed an unprecedented challenge to the autocracy's understanding of law. Scholars, judges, and lawyers proposed new legal theories and further engaged with the law in practical ways that strained traditional notions of Russian legality. All sectors of the population, including workers and peasants, gained access to the legal system, and on close examination, late Imperial Russia turned out to be a highly litigious society. Yet despite certain encouraging trends, the evolutionary potential of the Judicial Reforms should not be overstated. The choice confronting the autocracy was not between liberal reform and conservative counterreform, narrowly defined. Instead, the state had to select among seemingly irreconcilable policy options. Therefore, by necessity, tsarist law remained pluralistic, dualistic, and autocratic at the same time. The Judicial Reforms both supplemented and challenged Russian law, sometimes in profound and unexpected ways, but they never overrode these three basic characteristics.

Thus, Russian law retained a high degree of diversity throughout the reform period. The Russian empire incorporated several sources of foreign law as it expanded westward, as well as relied on a kaleidoscope of customary law traditions that stretched from the Russian heartland to the Caucasus, Central Asia, and Siberia. As a result, the rights of a Russian subject depended on multiple variables—estate, nationality, religion, place of birth—which formed a highly differentiated system of rights that, while fully compatible with the running of a multiethnic empire, posed long-term problems in any transition to a more united nation-state. The autocracy tried to use law as a means of political and social integration, yet its Russification policies remained far from complete at the time of the empire's demise.

The law-creating powers asserted by the Russian judiciary also promoted more unified interpretations of law, although the judiciary did so distinctly outside traditional—and trusted—administrative structures. But despite certain centralizing tendencies, legal pluralism remained an essential feature of Russian law until the very end of tsarist rule.

Russian law also was dualistic. The Judicial Reforms established the prerequisite institutions and legal space that allowed for a dramatic expansion of private law after 1864 and the resolution of civil disputes without state involvement. The growth of private law was primarily an urban phenomenon, but the use of custom in township courts also contributed to increased reliance on judicial procedures (however informal) to resolve civil cases. Yet as will be discussed in Chapter 4, the development of everyday law coexisted with a highly politicized system of justice, where the courtroom was used to punish the autocracy's political rivals, both radical and peaceful. Ironically, the legal profession, which played such a crucial role in the advancement of private law principles, also served as an intractable opponent of the tsar's repressive policies. The state ultimately directed both civil and political cases to the courts for resolution and saw no contradiction in doing so, since at all times it believed that private law principles—and the broader assertion of property rights—posed no absolute limits on the state's public law powers.

Finally, Russian law was autocratic. As Korkunov argued, the unified state served as the highest political objective, and law and legality never got in the way of defending the integrity of the Russian state. On the contrary, law remained subject to the individual discretion of the tsar and his bureaucratic representatives, with the ultimate goal of ensuring that the declarations of the center were transmitted down and enforced in the regions. Supervision further served as an essential feature of Russian law—of the court system, the growing revolutionary movement and the prevailing multiethnic population—and a decrease in the procuracy's supervisory powers was more than compensated by the growing oversight authority of the police. New interpretations of law—found in both judicial decisions and jury verdicts—spoke to a growing vitality within the Russian legal system, but they did not fundamentally reverse the autocracy's long-standing law-creating powers.

Thus, law in late tsarist Russia remained decidedly administrative, diverse, flexible, highly politicized, and asymmetrical, even as pockets of law were modernizing and pursuing more liberal and national goals. Historians who have studied specific branches of prerevolutionary Russian law—divorce, citizenship, religious freedom—invariably come up against the state's competing policy objectives.[84] The contradictions within Russian law ultimately could not be maintained within the legal system itself and ended up spilling over into the realm of politics. As we will now see, the courtroom would serve as the initial platform for fighting Russia's political battles, and when the legal system proved insufficient, Russia would seek its answer in constitutional change and finally in revolution.

4

Law, Politics, and Revolution

Political trials have always played a major role in the telling of Russian legal history. The Judicial Reforms created a unique platform—the courtroom—that allowed lawyers to deliver stirring speeches in defense of individual rights and basic rule-of-law principles. The actions of Russia's famous defense lawyers, however, cannot be viewed in isolation. They were part of a larger political effort to transform Russia into the *sine qua non* of Russian liberalism, the law-based state *(pravovoe gosudarstvo)*. This term is often equated with the Anglo-Saxon notion of the rule of law but, as the legal historian Harold Berman notes, the terms are not necessarily synonymous. The rule of law invariably incorporates certain natural law principles and fundamental civil rights that cannot be infringed upon by a nation's highest legal authority. The law-based state instead correlates to the German principle of *Rechtsstaat*, where the state (and more specifically, the legislature) serves as the highest source of law while being bound by its own legislation.[1]

This chapter analyzes tsarist's Russia's pursuit of the law-based state by focusing on three distinct processes: the role of advocates at political trials, the writing of Russia's first constitution in 1906, and the Provisional Government's legal policies during the Russian revolution. The Judicial Reforms created the initial opening for politics to enter the legal system. It divided executive and judicial functions while enabling the bar to challenge the legal foundations of autocratic rule in open court. This chapter explores the role of sworn attorneys at the major political trials and how two distinct generations of advocates viewed their professional responsibilities before the law and their clients. These prominent courtroom proceedings further illuminate how the *advokatura* attempted to use the law to challenge the state's public law powers and hold it accountable for its actions. That such proceedings even occurred—and had political resonance—testifies to the potential of Russian law during the late tsarist period.

Yet courtroom speeches, no matter how powerful and eloquent, could not by themselves transform Russia's political system. The law-based state required the further separation of the executive and legislative branches to be realized in practice. This division unexpectedly occurred in the aftermath of the 1905 Revolution, when under severe political pressure the tsar finally agreed to a constitution. Therefore, this chapter also examines the main provisions of the 1906 Fundamental Laws and their attempt to establish a legal hierarchy and genuine legal restraints on the autocratic state. Imperial Russia's constitutional experiment would be short-lived, however, as evolutionary change suddenly gave way to revolution in February 1917. The Provisional Government pursued an ambitious program of legal reform and transitional justice during its eight months in power, but as this chapter concludes, Russian law ultimately failed to keep pace with the growing social and economic demands of the Russian people. The Bolsheviks and their anti-legalist policies would ultimately triumph in October 1917, and it would be another seventy years before Russia would rejoin the debate on the law-based state.

The knights of the living word

The full consequences of the Judicial Reforms of 1864 were revealed for the first time in the autocracy's decision to prosecute its political opponents in public trials. These controversial proceedings can be divided into two halves: the first period (1866–1878) witnessed the trials of terrorists (Nechaev and his co-conspirators, Vera Zasulich) as well as populists associated with the "going to the people" movement. The results of these trials, from the state's prospective, proved so disappointing that in 1878 it decided to remove such controversial proceedings from the regular courts. It was not until the early twentieth century that a second round of public political trials occurred, targeting workers, peasants, religious dissenters, and the free press, as well as terrorists and revolutionaries.

From the first political trial in 1866, three parties fought for center stage: the government, the defendants, and the defense attorneys. An overconfident procuracy approached political trials with the assumption that judges would go along with the prosecution's case, no matter how flimsy the evidence. Prominent defendants, in turn, used the proceedings as their own personal platforms, making speeches that denounced the autocracy and Russia's numerous social iniquities. It was the defense attorneys—drawn from a small select group within the profession—who emerged as the stars of these proceedings. They used these trials to highlight the improper and illegal actions of the autocracy while promoting a more liberal vision of the rule of law. Thus, in the absence of a genuine legislature (until 1906), the autocracy met its greatest legal challenge in the courtroom.

One lawyer stood out above the rest at these early political trials—Vladimir Spasovich—the king of the Russian bar, as he was affectionately known, although he was, in fact, Polish. If there was a central tenet of Spasovich's personal philosophy, it was his unquestioned belief in personal freedom and the need to protect the individual from the oppressiveness of the state. In one of his famous "after-dinner" speeches, he toasted "to the human personality, for its inviolability from the state, for its distinctiveness and originality, serving as the source of all human creativity, for its natural crooked line as well as its linear geometry."[2] In 1873, Spasovich optimistically referred to sworn attorneys as the "knights of the living word," but his belief in the basic right of defense eventually exposed him to a blistering attack from Fyodor Dostoevskii in the aftermath of his representation (via court appointment) of an alleged child beater.[3] In Spasovich's eyes, the enemies of personal freedom were the state, the church, nationalism, and socialism. But although Spasovich advocated for change, he believed that it must come gradually. In one of his last letters written in 1906, Spasovich confirmed that for his entire lifetime, he had been "for all progress, but legal, for all evolution, but not revolution, for the establishment of an order according to all parties, in the arena of parliament, but without bloodletting and killing."[4]

Spasovich may have favored gradual change, but the growing radicalization of Russian society could not be slowed down. In 1878, the 29-year-old anarchist Vera Zasulich patiently waited to meet with the St. Petersburg governor during his calling hours. She then shot and wounded him in cold blood as revenge for his ordering of a vicious beating of Arkhip Bogoliubov, a political prisoner. In what was thought to be an open and shut case, the government brought criminal charges against Zasulich in a jury trial.[5] But the defense attorney Petr Aleksandrov delivered an impassioned closing argument in which he highlighted Zasulich's difficult youth and the excessive nature of the punishment inflicted on Bogoliubov for refusing to doff his cap to the governor. Aleksandrov then described Zasulich's state of mind upon learning of the beating: "Who will stand for the insulted honor of the defenseless political convict? Where is the guarantee that such an abomination will not be repeated?"[6] If justice required that Zasulich be punished, Aleksandrov concluded, then "let your chastising of justice take place! Indeed, she may leave the court condemned, but not disgraced, and one may only wish that circumstances which provoked such actions and generate such culprits should not be repeated."[7]

The jury quickly found Zasulich not guilty, forcing the autocracy to reevaluate its legal strategy for handling controversial cases going forward. It had already made one attempt to detach such cases from the regular courts. In the aftermath of the 1871 trial of the Nechaev terrorist group, the autocracy created a special division within the Senate to hear political cases. From the government's perspective, however, these separate proceedings were not only cumbersome to organize, but the Senate quickly proved to be too lenient in its judgments.[8] The Zasulich verdict provided additional confirmation that the regular courts were too unpredictable for such politically sensitive cases. Therefore, the autocracy pursued a third option. After the Zasulich acquittal, major political trials were transferred to military courts where civilians found themselves being tried under the rules of war so as to increase the severity of their sentences.[9]

Thus, from 1878 until the beginning of the twentieth century, the duality of Russian law was absolute; the autocracy pursued political justice with no significant restraint while private law continued to evolve and expand. It was not until 1901 that some (but not all) politically sensitive criminal cases began to be heard in the regular courts. The government may have thought that public proceedings somehow provided a cover of legality that mitigated their repressive policies, but the courtroom came closest to representing an even playing field in tsarist Russia, and lawyers used the law to press for political change.

Two groups of lawyers emerged at the beginning of the twentieth century. Veteran sworn attorneys largely followed the tradition of the 1870s, rallying around the defense of individual rights while generally avoiding any direct involvement in politics. They were now joined by younger, more activist group of attorneys. The legal commentator I. V. Gessen originally highlighted the emergence of this "young" generation of lawyers to emphasize the critical role they played in revitalizing the profession at the beginning of the twentieth century.[10] This generational split subsequently has been cited by the historian Jörg Baberowski to describe the rise of a more radical, and even extremist, cohort of sworn attorneys.[11] But despite possessing different long-term political objectives, sworn attorneys from both generations used these trials to issue a profound indictment against the Russian legal system and the autocratic principles that sustained it.

The veteran sworn attorney Nikolai Karabchevskii serves as the leading example of the older cohort of advocates. He participated as a junior attorney in the trial of the populists in 1877. After 1900, he featured in several prominent cases, culminating in his participation in the Beilis trial of 1913. The defense of individual and civil rights remained central to Karabchevskii's personal philosophy and courtroom speeches, as evident in his 1904 defense of E. V. Anchinkov, who was accused of smuggling the newspaper *Osvobozhdenie* (Liberation) into Russia. Having described how a critical piece of evidence regarding the defendant's alleged anti-government activities had been removed from the garbage, Karabchevskii noted that while always reconciled to the lack of free speech in Russia, he had at least been confident that we had "freedom of thought. I can put anything I want on paper. No one can take this away from a man, just as it is impossible to take away his right to breathe."[12]

Yet while Karabchevskii may have been no radical, his fundamental belief in the adversarial process—and the right for every person to conduct a defense—enabled him to make some of the most heated courtroom speeches in tsarist Russia.[13] He displayed all of his brilliant oratorical skills and his combative nature in the 1904 trial of Egor Sazonov, the assassin of Minister of Internal Affairs V. K. Pleve. In a stirring closing statement, Karabchevskii refused to condemn Sazonov's actions, stating that he sacrificed his youth by taking away "the life of another man, a life which he considered dangerous and disastrous for his fatherland."[14] When the bomb detonated, Karabchevskii concluded, Sazonov smashed the chains that had ensnarled the Russian people, which was why after the blast Sazonov cried out: "Long live liberty!"[15]

Sazonov was convicted, but as the above speech demonstrates, Karabchevskii was capable of the most inflammatory speech despite his membership in the so-designated older generation of Russian lawyers. But notwithstanding the public recognition that accompanied these famous trials, Karabchevskii believed that the calling of an advocate was "higher than politics," and in order to maintain his professional integrity, he refused to join any political party.[16] What truly distinguished Karabchevskii as a political defender of the old school, therefore, was his personal independence and the fact that although he often did not share the personal convictions of his client, he was always willing to defend the rights of the accused. Ironically, this was most clearly illustrated after the February 1917 Revolution in a conversation with Aleksandr Kerenskii, the head of the Provisional Government. Kerenskii offered Karabchevskii the opportunity to become a senator and serve on Russia's highest criminal court. Karabchevskii declined, saying he preferred to remain an advocate. But who are you going to defend, asked Kerenskii, Nicholas II? "Oh I would most willingly defend him," Karabchevskii replied, "if you decide to prosecute him."[17]

Karabchevskii's approach to political trials in many ways contrasted with that of the new generation of lawyers who emerged at the turn of the twentieth century. These "young" lawyers undoubtedly were more engaged in politics. They openly admired the people they defended and sometimes belonged to the same political party as their clients. A steady stream of political trials—involving strikes, peasant uprisings, banned political parties, illegal printing presses, religious sectarians, and random acts of terror—filled the docket of these young political defenders. Both the legal and illegal press published reports of these trials, and the renown of these lawyers grew so much that they were feted when they traveled to the provinces.

The Moscow sworn attorney Nikolai Murav'ev stands out as a leading member of this new generation of lawyers. He participated in more than 100 political cases in both open and closed court hearings between 1899 and 1916.[18] He also helped establish one of the first circles of political defenders whose membership ultimately included such diverse figures as V. A. Maklakov, the future Kadet leader, and D. I. Kurskii, the future Bolshevik Commissar of Justice. The young lawyers regularly worked as a team at the big political trials, collectively representing all of the defendants and coordinating their strategy.[19] Like Karabchevskii, however, Murav'ev never formally joined a political party, although he was elected to the Moscow City Duma in 1916 as an independent socialist.[20]

The young advocates utilized various schemes—from strict statutory analysis to highly publicized and dramatic walkouts—as part of their courtroom tactics. Integral to their strategy was the defense of civil rights, although this concept expanded to include certain social and economic rights as well (i.e., the right to work, the right to strike, etc.).[21] Murav'ev's closing arguments included a combination of political, economic, and social arguments. In one particularly egregious case, where workers received their salaries in company scrip instead of cash, Murav'ev defended the protesting workers. Everyone had the right to work and be paid for that work, Murav'ev argued, yet in this instance, the workers essentially had been advised to work and wait. The workers, Murav'ev concluded, "wanted to work and live … For this they were prosecuted?!"[22] Murav'ev's sharp legal reasoning was also regularly on display at these trials. In one case, Murav'ev disputed the procurator's attempt to punish individual defendants for the unruly behavior of the crowd. "Everyone answers for themselves," argued Murav'ev, and "if it is only known that a crowd misbehaved, that from the crowd a stone was thrown, but one cannot say that this was done by the defendants, then they must be acquitted" under the prevailing law.[23] Finally, following in the tradition of Karabchevskii, Aleksandrov, and other famous Russian defense counsel, Murav'ev took the most violent acts and somehow turned them into an indictment of the tsarist political and economic system.[24]

Some tension undoubtedly existed between the "fathers" and the "sons" of the Russian *advokatura*, most notably during the 1905 Revolution, when the young lawyers demanded that the bar take a much more aggressive political stance in opposition to the autocracy. But despite certain strains, there were several instances when these two generations worked together; Murav'ev noted that the reputation of the Moscow circle of political defenders was greatly enhanced when the veteran advocate F. N. Plevako joined forces with them.[25] Individual advocates undoubtedly disagreed over whether they were supporting evolutionary, as opposed to revolutionary, change through their participation at these political trials. Nevertheless, in their common role as defense counsel, two generations of sworn attorneys—through a combination of strict legal analysis, harsh political and social commentary, and strong moral appeals—used the platform provided by the courtroom to advocate for legal reform and fundamental civil rights. Such actions did not necessarily make them radicals; it made them good lawyers.

The spirited defense put on by Russian lawyers also demanded a degree of accountability that the Russian state simply was not accustomed to and often unwilling to accept. For the autocracy, the politicization of the justice system never produced the intended results. The problem went beyond the unexpected acquittal; the political trials exposed the state's poor preparation, at times tenuous legal arguments, and willingness to pursue extra-judicial proceedings if the regular courts did not produce satisfactory results. As we will see, however, the fact that the autocracy allowed for a vigorous defense—and did not always emerge victorious—separates the late tsarist political trials from similar proceedings in the Soviet and post-Soviet periods.

More than any other institution in tsarist Russia, the *advokatura* represented modernity, not just in terms of its independent, self-governing corporate structures but also in its liberal, highly developed understanding of law. Both in the courtroom and in chambers, members of the bar waged battle against all three pillars of tsarist justice. The demand by sworn attorneys that the Russian state observe and enforce the law as written struck at the autocratic heart of imperial law. Their advocacy for certain fundamental—and universal—civil rights further undermined the pluralistic nature of Russian law by arguing that one law applied to all Russian subjects. Finally, the legal profession issued the most direct challenge to the underlying duality of Russian law. From the state's perspective, this bifurcated approach allowed for the resolution of mundane disputes in a reasonably orderly fashion without placing any absolute limits on the state's public law powers. But the bar did not accept this highly compartmentalized approach to law. Instead, the *advokatura* distinguished itself as the one institution in tsarist Russia that straddled both sides of the dualistic divide. Sworn attorneys represented big corporations and committed revolutionaries—more broadly property rights and civil rights—but rather than expanding the political middle, the bar and its modern vision of law grew increasingly isolated from the extremes of Russian politics. Russia's leading practitioners, like its great legal theorists, proved unable to bridge the political divide between a revolutionary left and autocratic right, further demonstrating just how elusive a liberal—and legalistic—solution was to Imperial Russia's growing political crisis.[26]

The famous orations of Russia's prerevolutionary lawyers are still published today and represent a home-grown, rule-of-law ideal by which many Russians still measure their country's legal progress.[27] In a speech in 1916, commemorating the fiftieth anniversary of the Russian bar, the sworn attorney O. O. Gruzenberg recounted the brave exploits of his fellow practitioners: "Hundreds of cases involving peasants, workers, pogroms, thousands of purely political cases were pleaded by steadfast and courageous counsels. With the greatest efforts, often forgetting their own interest, our colleagues in all corners of Russia fulfilled their modest but great office—the defense of the individual against the onslaught of the state."[28] But while the orations of Russia's prerevolutionary lawyers upheld an alternative vision of legality, they could not, by themselves, break the strong autocratic foundation of Russian law and state power. That required political change, which arrived in the aftermath of the 1905 Revolution in the form of Russia's first constitution.

The Fundamental Laws of 1906

In 1904, Japan decisively and without warning attacked the Russian naval base at Port Arthur, thereby triggering the Russo-Japanese war. An inadequate military response soon galvanized a political opposition that included striking workers, rebellious peasants, disenchanted liberals, and hardcore revolutionaries. New institutions—worker soviets, alliances of different professional groups—also sprang up in the cities and joined forces with various political movements to challenge the autocracy's monopoly of power. Meanwhile in the countryside, Russian authorities proved incapable of preventing a major breakdown of law and order. This toxic mixture compelled the autocracy to the negotiating table, and in the 1905 October Manifesto, the tsar promised major political concessions. The 1906 Fundamental Laws would transform the manifesto into reality with the introduction of a parliament (the Duma), a defined hierarchy of laws, and basic civil rights.[29] As discussed below, this new founding law was not a picture of legal clarity (Nicholas II never accepted the Fundamental Laws as a full-blown constitution) and left the autocracy with plenty of room for interpretation and self-preservation. Nevertheless, the Fundamental Laws were tsarist Russia's sole attempt at defining in practice what a law-based state looked like and therefore represented a potential turning point in Russian legal history.

One of the most striking aspects of the Fundamental Laws was that it led not with the autocrat but with the state. Article 1 of the preamble proudly proclaimed that the Russian state was "one and indivisible." Yet this provision was immediately followed by a confusing reference to Finland, which stated that while Finland was an inseparable part of the empire, its internal affairs were governed by special decrees based on special legislation.

Why begin a constitution with such an ambiguous set of principles? If the Russian empire was one and indivisible, why was Finland governed by its own distinct set of laws and regulations? Baron Boris Nolde, the early twentieth-century lawyer and legal commentator, later explored this question and concluded that there was, in fact, no contradiction in these first two articles. According to Nolde, Finland, like other distinct regions of the empire, was still subservient to Russian law. Indeed, no matter what grant of autonomy may have been given to Finland, any local institution or regulation could be overturned by the Russian state at any time.[30] Nolde added that this reality had existed for centuries with individual regions enjoying various degrees of autonomy as long as they accepted their ultimate subordination to the autocratic state.

What Nolde described, and what the first two articles of the Fundamental Laws essentially enshrined, was the notion of the unified state. As explained in the previous chapter, this concept had been one of the central ideas of Korkunov's distinctive theory of law. He had argued that the persistence of local law in the Russian empire did not rise to the level of a union or a confederation of independent states. Instead, according to Korkunov, there was only one source of power within the Russian empire—the unified state. Nolde fully supported this notion, and it actually was Nolde's father who had drafted Article 1 with the specific intention of upholding the territorial integrity of the state as the empire's highest legal and national value.[31]

Indeed, Russian leaders to the present day continue to be judged by their ability to uphold this sacred goal.[32]

Thus, the preamble to the Fundamental Laws provided a critical window into the essential principles of imperial law. To begin with, state unity remained the ultimate political objective, and nothing that endangered the integrity of the state could ever be tolerated. Thus, no region was the co-equal of the Imperial Russian state, even if that region retained certain elements of legal autonomy. Instead, the Russian state and state power always outranked local legislation when a conflict of law arose. This did not mean that local law—both national and customary—did not hold sway in vast parts of the empire; the Russian state historically was willing to tolerate a multiplicity of laws and legal traditions as long as a region and the local population recognized their legal subordination to the tsar and the Russian state. Yet the last article of the preamble indicated that this willingness to tolerate such legal diversity was on the decline. Article 3 stated that the Russian language was the general language of the state, and that Russian was compulsory in the army, navy, and state and public institutions. Russification already had been a priority for decades, and it had been accompanied by major efforts to expand the jurisdiction of Russian law throughout the empire. Thus, Article 3 implicitly spoke to the aspirations of the administrative state to use its language policies to spread Russian procedural law at the expense of local practice.

Having started with the state, the Fundamental Laws next devoted considerable attention to the powers of the autocrat. The tsar famously went from the "autocratic and unlimited Monarch" to the mere holder of "Supreme Autocratic Power," a clear demotion, since the tsar no longer possessed the coveted grant of "unlimited" authority. Nevertheless, the residual powers provided to the tsar, especially as they related to his legal standing and prerogatives, remained substantial. To begin with, Article 10 granted the tsar complete control over the administrative state, the institution responsible for the actual governing of the empire. Moreover, the monarch could appoint and dismiss ministers at will without seeking Duma approval. In addition to signing bills into law (or vetoing them), Article 8 assigned the tsar the right of legislative initiative, blurring the distinction between the executive and the newly created legislative branch. The tsar also reserved the right to disband the Duma.[33] Finally, the tsar remained head of the Orthodox Church, and obedience to his power was commanded "by God himself."[34]

The Fundamental Laws further retained certain law-creating powers for the monarch. The tsar reserved the right to issue decrees regarding administrative matters, provided they were countersigned by the appropriate government official, as well as in matters involving his personal estates.[35] Most importantly, Article 87 granted the tsar, at the request of the Council of Ministers, the right to issue decrees in "extraordinary" circumstances if the Duma was in recess. This right was not unbounded. The Fundamental

Laws demanded that within two months of their issuance the government introduce formal legislation in the parliament to replace such extraordinary decrees. Otherwise, they would lose force.

The Fundamental Laws granted the tsar absolute control over other vital areas as well, including the military, foreign affairs, and his personal property. Duma members were allowed to request information via formal questions that probed the legality of the government's actions. According to the historian Marc Szeftel, in practice, such requests did have some impact on public opinion, although they never did result in the dismissal of a government official.[36]

Yet despite the tsar's extensive powers, the Fundamental Laws represented something new and radical, namely the ideal of a law-based state. Most notably, the Fundamental Laws, once and for all, defined what a "law" actually was. For centuries, tsars had issued various rulings—codes, charters, manifestos, decrees—that carried the force of law even if the substance and normative content of such acts differed significantly. Now, Article 86 explicitly stated that no law could be enacted without the approval of the Duma and the State Council, and the signature of the tsar. Moreover, Article 11 stipulated that the tsar issued decrees in accordance to existing laws as well as directives essential for the execution of existing laws. Thus, for the first time in Russian history, a firm hierarchy of laws was established with properly enacted laws standing above executive decrees.[37]

Laws also became truly national in scope; Article 85 stated that Russian laws were equally applicable without exception for all Russian subjects and foreigners living within the Russian state. The Fundamental Laws further recognized certain basic civil rights, such as freedom of the press, religion, and assembly, as well as inviolable property rights. Criminal justice received special attention as well. No Russian subject could be arrested or prosecuted except by procedures established by law.[38]

The Fundamental Laws' grant of civil rights, however, was not absolute. Chapter VIII was portentously entitled "the rights and obligations of Russian subjects." The enumerated duties under this section were not too onerous. They primarily referred to military service and paying taxes. The last provision of this chapter, however, weakened this grant of civil rights. Article 83 stated that "specific laws define exceptions to the rules expounded in [Chapter VIII] regarding localities under martial law or under exceptional circumstances." Pockets of inequality also still persisted under the Fundamental Laws; Article 88 referred to "laws specifically enacted for certain localities or segments of the population," while Article 89 allowed for the retroactive application of justice if the legislation so permitted.

The Fundamental Laws posed one more wrinkle for Russian law. As noted above, the preamble led with a broad notion of the state and its essential unity and then turned to the explicit powers of the autocrat. From the time of Peter the Great, the autocrat and the state represented two separate institutions, although without a clear delineation of powers. Thus, the absolutist state posed no limit on the autocrat's power—indeed, the two terms were naturally combined to describe the political system. According to Nolde, however, while the Fundamental Laws defined the sum total of the tsar's authority, these powers were not coterminous with those of the state.[39] Thus, for the first time in imperial history, autocratic power was separated from the totality of state authority, holding open the theoretical possibility of legally regulating the relationship between tsar and state.

The Fundamental Laws had a short and checkered history. The Duma engaged in substantive and consequential legislative debates and was never formally abolished, which some commentators view as a victory in and of itself. Yet no political movement—socialists, liberals, moderates, right-wing conservatives—seemed satisfied with the new parliamentary system.[40] Moreover, Nicholas II never accepted the loss of his title of unlimited monarch, while the bureaucracy remained largely outside the oversight of the legislature and, according to some commentators, represented a fourth branch of government under the Fundamental Laws.[41]

Prerevolutionary Russia's truncated constitutional experience never overcame the basic autocratic foundations of Russian law. Moreover, numerous violations of the Fundamental Laws subsequently occurred. Notably, on June 3, 1907, Nicholas issued a decree, accompanied by an explanatory manifesto, that disbanded the second Duma, accusing it of legislative obstructionism and outright sedition. He further introduced a new electoral system intended to produce a more compliant and conservative Duma. Nicholas possessed the right under Article 105 of the Fundamental Laws to dismiss the Duma and call for new elections, yet by promulgating a new electoral law without consulting the parliament, Nicholas seemingly violated Russia's newly established hierarchy of laws. The manifesto attempted to provide legal cover for Nicholas by claiming that he was merely asserting his supreme autocratic powers to address a national crisis.[42] Nevertheless, his actions would be remembered as "the coup of 3 June 1907."

Other loopholes around the Fundamental Laws existed as well. Article 87 provided the state with the means to exercise independently the law-creating powers that had served as the backbone of autocratic rule for centuries. In 1906–1907, at the height of the Duma crisis, the government issued sixty decrees under Article 87. Moreover, from 1914 to 1916, the government announced some 365 emergency decrees, not all of which dealt with military matters.[43] Prime Minister Petr Stolypin also implemented two of his most important pieces of legislation—agrarian reform and the Western Zemstvo Bill—via Article 87, in violation of the spirit and, many jurists contended, the actual letter of the Fundamental Laws. Finally, the prevailing state of emergency legislation, which had been ratified every year since 1881, continued to be extended after 1905, casting considerable doubts on the autocracy's commitment to the civil liberties articulated in the new constitution.[44]

Yet in many ways, the first assault against the Fundamental Laws occurred well before the controversial events of June 3, 1907. In the aftermath of the dissolution of the first Duma in July 1906, the liberal Kadet Party along with other disenchanted politicians issued the Vyborg Manifesto in protest of this action. The Vyborg Manifesto was not a neutral document; it called, among other things, for citizens to stop paying taxes and sending recruits to the army. The signatories of this appeal, however, included three of Russia's greatest liberal legal theorists—Muromtsev, Novgorodtsev, and Petrazycki. Muromtsev, in fact, played a pivotal role in the birth of Russia's new constitutional system. He prepared one of the first draft constitutions at the height of the 1905 Revolution that influenced the writing of the Fundamental Laws.[45] He subsequently served as the first elected speaker of the Duma.

While these three men expounded different legal theories, they shared a deep-rooted opposition to the narrow positivist understanding of law that had governed the Russian state for centuries. Collectively, they could have provided critical intellectual and practical expertise in the founding of the law-based state. In the aftermath of the Vyborg Manifesto, however, the Russian state felt compelled to prosecute them for illegal propaganda. It subsequently incarcerated them for three months and then banned all three from elected office. Thus, in one sweeping action, the Russian state managed to criminalize and expel from the political process its leading constitutional law experts. While other liberal lawyers would try to fill this vacuum, the autocracy had already dealt a major blow to the new political system.

1917: The failed transition from autocracy to the rule of law

There would be one last momentous attempt to transform the Russian empire into a law-based state, this time without the tsar. The First World War had been initially greeted with a wave of patriotism by the Russian people, but as Russia stumbled and retreated on the battlefield, public dissatisfaction with the autocracy steadily grew. The Duma reflected this growing discontent but only met intermittently during the war. In September 1915, Nicholas II assumed control of the army himself, thereby taking full responsibility for a faltering war effort. When a series of protests in February 1917 led to the rapid collapse of law and order in Petrograd, the army essentially decided that the only way to continue the war was to abandon Nicholas II. On March 2, 1917, Tsar Nicholas II abdicated both for himself and his son. When his brother Grand Duke Mikhail declined the throne one day later, the political system described in the Fundamental Laws became unworkable. The constitution required an autocrat to oversee the executive branch and state administration, and as of March 3, 1917, no such person existed.

The Duma represented the obvious successor institution, and its leader, Mikhail Rodzianko, clearly envisioned himself as the head of any political transition. Russia's parliament, however, was reluctant to take power in its own name and had, in fact, delegated its negotiating authority at the height of the February crisis to a select committee. The ensuing series of complex and nontransparent negotiations have fueled conspiracy theories for a century, but what emerged was a Provisional Government that had no direct connection to Russia's prevailing system of laws. When Pavel Miliukov, the prominent Kadet leader and foreign minister in the new government, was asked who had elected the Provisional Government, he could only respond, "the Revolution." Indeed, the Provisional Government's primary claim to legitimacy had been quietly inserted into Grand Duke Mikhail's abdication announcement, which stated that the autocrat's "plentitude of powers" had been transferred to the new administration. On this thin reed rested the Provisional Government's assertion of power. The Provisional Government further undermined its capacity to govern by eschewing the right to issue formal laws, delegating the forthcoming Constituent Assembly with the sole authority to pass such final legislation. Still, much was expected of the Provisional Government, including promoting political change, resolving an unpopular war, and restoring stability on the home front. Thus, the Provisional Government could not stand above the fray and wait for the revolution to sort itself out; it had to act.

The Provisional Government began with a joint proclamation on March 3, 1917, with the Petrograd Soviet of Workers' and Soldiers' Deputies, an informal body that nevertheless enjoyed significant legitimacy as the leading representative organ of the capital's working class. This announcement established certain fundamental civil rights: freedom of speech, assembly, religion; the right to unionize; the abolition of all restrictions based on class, religion, and nationality; and universal suffrage.[46] Yet this appeal also included the beginnings of the Provisional Government's demise. It introduced the notion of "dual power" or joint rule among the Provisional Government and the Petrograd Soviet, an anathema to the unified state's long-standing governing principle of a single sovereign. The March 3, 1917, appeal also abolished the police, a fateful decision that soon left the Provisional Government bereft of the necessary force to defend the above new freedoms and its rule-of-law agenda.

The Provisional Government followed up this pronouncement with other progressive legal reforms, notably in administrative law, court procedure, corporate law, and women's rights. However, since the Provisional Government had already denied itself the ability to pass laws—that was reserved for the future Constituent Assembly—its only available option was to rule by decree and executive order. Such practices had been standard procedure for centuries; indeed, the distinction between a law and a decree had only been formally recognized with the introduction of the Fundamental Laws of 1906. Nevertheless, for a new government that espoused the law-based state as the ultimate objective, rule by decree—even in support of progressive agenda—appeared at odds with the stated goals of the revolution.

The Provisional Government also pursued legal reform in specific branches of the law through the establishment of numerous commissions, which ultimately produced little in terms of concrete results. The most innovative part of the Provisional Government's legal program came in the realm of what is today called transitional justice. While the Constituent Assembly looked forward to a new legal regime, the Provisional Government created the Extraordinary Investigatory Commission, which was assigned the responsibility of examining the crimes of the tsarist regime.[47]

The famous defense attorney Nikolai Murav'ev oversaw this investigation and headed what is often referred to as the Murav'ev Commission. Members of the commission included lawyers of all backgrounds, from tsarist investigators and prosecutors to socialist defense attorneys such as Murav'ev. In his June 16, 1917, address to the First All Russian Congress of Workers and Soldiers Deputies in Petrograd, Murav'ev emphasized the truly historic nature of the commission's actions. What made the commission's work unique, Murav'ev argued, was its decision to hold tsarist officials accountable to the laws that existed during the last days of the tsarist regime. As a result, the defendants could never claim that "they had been judged for what was allowed during their time, and had only became forbidden from the moment that [the revolution] entered on the stage of world history."[48]

Murav'ev's speech proceeded to outline what the commission perceived as the major crimes of Russian officialdom prior to 1917. He referred to the illegal delegation of state authority through the use of documents signed by the tsar but purposefully left blank to be filled in by ministers at a later time.[49] Murav'ev further cited the government's abuse of Article 87 of the Fundamental Laws that led to the passage of wartime measures that introduced new taxes and otherwise burdened the working class.[50] Murav'ev's strongest words of opprobrium, however, were directed against the police, whom he described as a thoroughly criminal organization.[51] He specifically referred to the instructions given to the secret police describing how to recruit agents, engage in political provocations, and entrap people in criminal acts.[52] When Murav'ev confronted individual justice officials and asked them on what law they had based their actions, they answered: "There was no law, but that was how my predecessor acted."[53]

The commission's interrogation of witnesses and its vast documentary record provide a final window on how tsarist officials understood—and circumvented—the law. The commission, for example, conducted a comprehensive review of how the government manipulated evidence, spied on jurors, and otherwise violated established legal procedure during the infamous ritual murder trial of Mendel Beilis in 1913.[54] The cross-examination by Murav'ev of I. G. Shcheglovitov, the former Minister of Justice, was particularly revealing in how the highest justice official in the Russian empire interpreted the law. When asked how he understood *zakonnost'* in light of the Judicial Reforms of 1864, Shcheglovitov replied, "It seems to me that the concept of legality incorporates the idea of preserving the existing order."[55] Murav'ev further questioned the witness as to why he had issued pardons of high-ranking government officials in certain cases instead of prosecuting them. "This was done," Shcheglovitov answered, "exclusively for political considerations. Here, legal [considerations], of course, fell by the wayside."[56]

Yet Murav'ev himself clearly straddled the line between politics and law during the course of the investigation. In one instance, when the evidence against one former government official looked particularly flimsy, Murav'ev still refused to release the defendant, claiming that such an action would attract the "indignation of the people (*negodovanie naroda*)."[57] Internal disagreements also existed as to whether the acts committed by the tsarist officials actually rose to the level of a crime. Two prominent members of the commission's presidium wrote to Murav'ev in September 1917 saying that the most serious charge—treason—remained unproven and arguing that other violations were so prevalent through all levels of government that it made no sense to bring individual criminal charges.[58]

The Murav'ev Commission provides no satisfactory point of closure. No grand proceeding ever put the tsarist officials in the dock and forced them to defend their actions in public. Russian historians who have analyzed the Murav'ev Commission's record also have arrived at dramatically different conclusions; it was either the precursor as to how to investigate totalitarian regimes, or alternatively, an overly politicized investigation that by focusing on technically legal activity such as the use of Article 87 and police informants was quickly losing the confidence of the Russian people.[59]

The Provisional Government ultimately was unable to deliver on its vision of the law-based state. In many ways, the lawyers who populated its upper ranks were not revolutionary enough. Indeed, one of the Provisional Government's first steps was to form a special commission to restore the original intent of the Judicial Reforms of 1864, hardly a great act of rebellion. The Provisional Government announced its intention to go after Russian legal pluralism by integrating the peasant courts into the established court structure, but it only made preliminary steps in that direction. The one legal decision that could have brought the Provisional Government strong public support—the expropriation of gentry property for the benefit of the peasantry—was delayed for both legal and military reasons. The Provisional Government hesitated about taking property without compensation but also feared that a peasant army would simply dissolve if the free distribution of land was underway in the village. Therefore, the Provisional Government punted on the question of property to the Constituent Assembly, a legalist solution with disastrous political consequences.

The rise of dual power—or more accurately the multiplicity of powers that blossomed on the local, regional, and national level in 1917—contradicted the historical mission of the Russian state and, along with the Provisional

Government's decision to abolish the police, led to the collapse of law and order. The Provisional Government's pursuit of the law-based state also did not keep pace with the changing mood of the Russian people as a liberal revolution gave way to a broader social revolution whose supporters had little patience for gradual, legal change. Finally, the pursuit of certain universal rights, which pushed Russia away from empire and toward a nation-state, invariably opened up the nationality question. The autocracy during its last decades had changed the notion of the unified state, no longer tolerating the continued influence of local law and pushing for a more national law. But with the collapse of central control in 1917 and the rise of certain universal values, Finland, Poland, the Baltics, and even Ukraine began to assert these universal rights for their own national purposes. The Provisional Government lacked the power to stop the drift of power to the regions and thus found itself presiding over the collapse of an empire, as opposed to the creation of a law-based state.

A long, and largely progressive, legal legacy would soon be washed away by the Bolsheviks. Nevertheless, the Provisional Government showed that the autocracy, despite all its suspicions and counterreforms, had created a common legal language that allowed lawyers from all political backgrounds—conservative, liberal, socialist—to communicate with each other. The same could not be said about the politicians in 1917; they largely had been isolated from one another during the tsarist period and brought their own distinct and rigid views of history to the revolution. The lawyers in the Provisional Government were under the fatal illusion, however, that they had unlimited time to pursue multiple legal reform projects in 1917, when in fact they had only one essential responsibility: the transfer of power to a legitimate government. Their failure to achieve this goal would define the Provisional Government's place in Russian history and open the door to a new, and as yet unarticulated, theory of socialist law.

5

Filling in the Blanks: The Creation of Socialist Law

Two leaders dominate the first half of the USSR's existence. Lenin made revolution and Stalin consolidated the gains of revolution over the course of three-and-a-half decades marked by extraordinary levels of violence. It seems oxymoronic to speak of law—and any notion of restraint on the state—when millions of people were being swept up in the death and destruction of civil war, forced famine, collectivization, and the purges. The Bolsheviks proudly declared their break with the Russian legal tradition, yet as Lenin and Stalin faced the challenge of governing, they were forced to contemplate what role law should play in their newly created socialist society. Marx conspicuously provided no answer to this question, so Soviet legal theorists had to improvise even as the party's core economic program underwent several radical changes, from war communism to the New Economic Policy (NEP) to industrialization/collectivization. The founders of the Soviet legal system also confronted the question of geography and how law might tie the former tsarist empire back together, even as they refused to recognize the Soviet Union as an empire itself.

This chapter traces the Bolsheviks' changing attitude to law during a period of national uncertainty and unprecedented violence. In rapid order, the Bolsheviks would go through three constitutions (1918, 1924, 1936), each of which represents an important benchmark in the party's approach to law and legality. Thus, a review of these early Soviet constitutions sheds considerable light on such fundamental issues as sources of law, civil and social rights, the role of judicial institutions, and Soviet federalism. These constitutions possessed one other distinguishable feature; they all served as a facade for one-party rule. As this chapter demonstrates, the significance of law shrank considerably in comparison to ideology and party. Yet out of all this turmoil, the Soviet Union would forge its own brand of socialist law that, for a brief time, would stand beside common law and civil law as one of the world's three major legal traditions. Hence, both the Bolsheviks' repeated attempts at constitution writing and their instrumental practices merit serious examination even against the backdrop of renewed dictatorship.

Lenin and the Bolsheviks' first constitution

Lenin was no stranger to Russian law. Indeed, he was a product of Russian higher legal education. Having first attended Kazan University law faculty, from which he withdrew (one step ahead of being expelled for taking part in a student demonstration), he graduated with a law degree from St. Petersburg University.[1] Lenin proceeded to practice law in Samara from 1889 to 1893 as an attorney-in-training, the required apprenticeship before joining the bar. Lenin moved to St. Petersburg in 1893 to pursue bigger dreams, but after his revolutionary activities landed him in exile in the Siberian village of Shushensk, he relied on his legal background to advise his fellow prisoners and local residents as an "underground" advocate.[2]

Lenin's creative analysis of Marxism that allowed him to believe a workers' revolution could be achieved in a largely agrarian society remains beyond the scope of this book. Marx said little about law; in theory, there would be no need for it once a worker's state had been established. Lenin similarly paid little attention to the law in his theoretical writings, other than to highlight its distinctive capitalist and bureaucratic features. He also had few kind words for members of his profession, especially those who acted as political defenders: "You have to rule lawyers with an iron rod and put them in a state of siege, for this intelligentsia scum plays dirty," he advised Bolsheviks awaiting trial in the aftermath of the 1905 Revolution.[3]

It was not law but the idea of dictatorship that dominated Lenin's thoughts on any future political transition. During the 1905 Revolution, Lenin wrote about the potential victory of a democratic dictatorship over autocracy. Such a triumph, Lenin asserted, must "inevitably be based on military force, on arming the masses, on an insurrection, and not on any institutions created in a 'legal' or peaceful way."[4] The notion of dictatorship—unbounded by law—always remained central to Lenin's political thinking: "Unlimited power, power beyond the law, power based on force in the most direct sense of the way—this is dictatorship."[5]

Lenin's understanding of power would be further explicated in *State and Revolution*, which he wrote while in hiding in 1917. Only published in 1918, *State and Revolution* never served as a public manifesto of Lenin's intentions prior to coming to power. Nevertheless, it proved highly prophetic in terms of what policies he later pursued. Most notably, Lenin intended to break the tsarist state and replace it with a Russian version of the 1871 Paris Commune.[6] The commune had allowed for freedom of opinion and representative institutions responsible to the electorate but, as Lenin noted approvingly, the commune also had removed the division between executive and legislative branches. The need for experts, added Lenin, would be unnecessary under socialism; literate people could carry out the everyday business of the state, which would be reduced to "registration, recording and checking."[7] The postal system, with its technicians, managers, and bookkeepers—all subject to equal pay—turned out to be Lenin's model for communism.[8]

What was necessary to achieve this level of efficiency was the dictatorship of the proletariat (although in his writings, Lenin scrupulously avoided placing the Bolshevik Party at the head of this dictatorship). And while Lenin generally avoided the subject of terror, he argued in *State and Revolution* that the replacement of the bourgeoisie by the proletariat could only be achieved by violent revolution. Lenin was no shrinking violet in his personal interactions, and he often spoke fondly of how the Jacobins used terror during the French Revolution to pursue the "enemies of the people."[9]

Therefore, Lenin's initial instincts were to overthrow and destroy, and one of his first targets was the tsarist legal system. On November 22, 1917, Lenin abolished all courts except the justice of the peace courts, which were transformed into the people's courts. He further eliminated the institutions that had arisen from the Judicial Reforms of 1864, including the judiciary, juries, and the defense bar. In one fell swoop, Lenin removed the most progressive elements of Russian law that, while not breaking the autocratic state, nevertheless had re-defined the meaning of law over the previous half century. Yet while Lenin was revolutionary in his goals, he relied on a traditional tsarist mechanism to realize his objectives: the decree. Indeed, the connection between all three overlapping legal regimes in 1917—the autocracy, the Provisional Government, and the Bolsheviks—was rule by decree, which in turn linked them all to Russia's statist tradition.

Lenin and the Bolsheviks soon discovered, however, that a war-torn and divided Russia was not the postal service and that its citizens were not natural accountants who could run a country simply by knowing the "first four rules of arithmetic."[10] Thus, Lenin's nihilistic understanding of law and rejection of even the need for basic legal norms were quickly replaced by an instrumentalist approach to law that specifically sought to serve the party's political objectives and to begin transforming peasants and laborers into new socialist men and women. Discipline and education became the buzzwords, and newly appointed judges in the people's courts were instructed to rely on their own sense of revolutionary justice when deciding cases. Indeed, since these judges often lacked a legal or even a secondary education, the established tsarist sources of law—while not disappearing entirely—were necessarily subordinated to revolutionary consciousness.[11]

Lenin did allow the elections for the Constituent Assembly—the only institution broadly recognized among the competing political forces with the right to promulgate formal laws—to proceed as scheduled on November 12, 1917. The Bolsheviks came a distant second in the election with 24 percent of the vote, with the Socialist Revolutionary (SR) party receiving the largest number of delegates. But the Constituent Assembly was destined to meet for only one session (January 5-6, 1918). When its members began considering legislation opposed by the Bolsheviks, Lenin had the assembly shut down.

No Constituent Assembly meant there was no overarching set of principles—or law—that defined Russia's postrevolutionary political reality. The Bolsheviks addressed this vacuum on July 10, 1918, by unilaterally imposing the constitution of the Russian Soviet Federative Socialist Republic (RSFSR). The 1918 constitution articulated an idealistic vision of the future, seeking to abolish the exploitation of man by man and to establish a dictatorship of the urban and rural proletariat and poorest peasantry. The constitution also broke dramatically with the past and the "bourgeois" understanding of law. Most notably, Article 3(b) overturned Catherine the Great's generous grant of property rights, transforming Russia's forests, minerals, and internal waters into state property.[12] With one sentence, the state and the Bolshevik Party became the guardian of Russia's greatest sources of national wealth.

Article 9 proclaimed that the new constitution was presiding over a transition period, thereby indicating its temporary status. Nevertheless, the constitution contained certain fundamental features that would serve as a foundation for socialist law throughout the Soviet period. To begin with, the 1918 constitution endowed multiple institutions with basic law-creating powers. The highest authority under the constitution was the All-Russian Congress of Soviets. Since the Congress did not meet in permanent session, however, it elected an All-Russian Central Executive Committee to serve as the supreme legislative, executive, and controlling organ of the RSFSR.[13] The Central Executive Committee possessed the power to issue its own decrees and regulations, as well the right to coordinate all organs of Soviet authority.[14] The Central Executive Committee further appointed the Council of People's Commissars, which oversaw general administrative matters and issued its own orders and resolutions, subject to the approval of the Central Executive Committee.[15]

Thus, after the autocracy's eleven-year experiment with a recognized yet highly imperfect legislative branch, the Bolshevik Party once again endowed multiple bureaucratic institutions with law-creating powers, thereby undermining any notion of a hierarchy of laws. The 1918 constitution further blurred the distinction between the executive and legislative branches while containing no reference to the judiciary. Finally, the Bolsheviks took the recently enacted universal rights propagated by the Provisional Government and began restricting them. The 1918 constitution did recognize the equal rights of all citizens and further granted everyone the right to pursue religious and anti-religious propaganda.[16] Nevertheless, Article 65 limited the political rights of certain categories of people, including those persons who employed hired labor, private merchants, trade and commercial brokers, monks and clergy of all denominations, and former members of the police.

From the very beginning, therefore, Soviet law was bureaucratic in its origins and unequal in its application. Conspicuous by its absence in the constitution was any reference to the party, the real power behind these political institutions. Finally, the 1918 constitution felt compelled to deal with the nature of the state's national composition at a time of absolute uncertainty. The constitution's drafting coincided with the Brest-Litovsk peace treaty negotiations, which would result in the Bolsheviks' surrender of significant parts of the tsarist empire to Germany. Thus, the constitution was a Russian (and not a Soviet) document and aspired to the title of federation even though significant parts of its presumed territory remained outside its direct control. The constitution further recognized newly independent Finland and the right of Armenia to self-determination.[17]

Nevertheless, while disavowing in Article 5 the pursuit of colonies, Article 11 contemplated the further expansion of the RSFSR. In particular, soviets who differentiated themselves by "a special form of existence and national character might unite [with the RSFSR] in autonomous regional unions, ruled by the local congress of the soviets and their executive organs." The provision added that these autonomous regions "participate in the RSFSR upon a federal basis." The 1918 constitution was outward looking in other ways as well; it called for the victory of socialism in all lands while granting political rights to working-class foreigners who happened to find themselves living within the RSFSR.[18]

Therefore, while the 1918 constitution was an admittedly transitory document, it nevertheless included elements—multiple law-producing bodies, qualified rights, a federation consisting of national subunits—that would become standard parts of the Soviet legal lexicon. It also was an aspirational statement by a political party that found itself in an almost impossible position. Few people, in reality, actually observed the party's decrees and orders, and in 1918, law was secondary to political survival. Lenin's seizure of power invariably invited civil war, and he seemingly welcomed the conflict and violence that accompanied it. During the wide-ranging civil war that lasted from 1918 to 1921, the Bolsheviks specifically pursued war communism, which focused on grain requisitions and the nationalization of industry, but also introduced legal procedures by which to assert the state's coercive powers. Revolutionary tribunals initially were established to respond to the political and economic threats to the new order, but when these bodies ironically proved too lenient, the Bolsheviks turned to the Cheka, the precursor to the Soviet secret police, and outright terror to ensure victory.

The White movement and other anti-Bolshevik forces were no great civil libertarians themselves, and they pursued their own policies of excessive violence and extra-judicial coercion. The progressive lawyers of the Provisional Government were not about to be returned to power, no matter who won the civil war. Nevertheless, Nikolai Murav'ev, the famous political defender and former head of the Provisional Government's investigation of tsarist officials, managed to make one last appearance on the national legal stage. In 1922, the Bolsheviks organized their first large public show trial in which they accused the leaders of the SR party of pursuing an armed struggle against the Soviet regime and outright treason. Lenin wanted a series of "model" trials for educative and propaganda purposes, while largely ignoring the basic rules of criminal procedure. Murav'ev agreed to serve as legal counsel for the SRs, but when demonstrators were invited into the courtroom to denounce the defendants—in total breach of standard criminal procedure—Murav'ev, strongly objected: "Woe to the country, woe to the people, who show contempt for the law and who mock those who defend the law."[19]

The conviction of the SRs was a foregone conclusion, although the death sentences handed out to the twelve defendants were eventually suspended, thanks to pressure from the international socialist movement. But while the proceeding against the SRs served its immediate purpose, namely exposing enemies and rallying people around the new revolutionary power, the public show trial was about to undergo a short-term hiatus. The introduction of NEP in 1921 reopened the debate over what was socialist law, and the ensuing decade would witness the passage of major pieces of Soviet legislation as well as a spirited discussion as to what role law should play in Soviet society. While NEP produced certain legal innovations, however, it primarily would be remembered as the calm before the storm.

NEP and the creation of the Soviet Union

The year 1922 saw the enactment of three landmark pieces of Russian legislation—the Civil Code, the Criminal Code, and the Union Treaty that formally created the Soviet Union—along with the reinstatement of the procuracy, bar, and basic court structures. Collectively, these changes represented a strategic retreat from war communism and its revolutionary attempt to break the tsarist legal tradition. Indeed, the draft civil code previously prepared by the autocracy, along with the partially adopted 1903 Criminal Code, served as models for the NEP legislation. Yet even in retreat, the Bolsheviks made sure that law retained a revolutionary, and highly flexible, character.

The 1922 RSFSR Civil Code represented just such a mixture. From the beginning, Lenin did not want the return of bourgeois law but instead sought to expand the rights of the state. Thus, the 1922 RSFSR Civil Code recognized three forms of property: state, cooperative, and private, with the first two clearly being the preferred categories. Indeed, the Civil Code assigned certain types of property—land, raw materials, forests, water, railroads—exclusively to state control. The state further was given a broad presumption of ownership, unless proven otherwise by the opposing party.[20] Meanwhile the property rights associated with certain types of trade and commercial activities were allowed only under specific conditions; for example, enterprises retained a right to private property but only if they employed no more than twenty workers.[21] Moreover, severe consequences existed for transactions that violated the state's interests or were otherwise shown to be to the state's detriment.

Yet despite its revolutionary gloss, the 1922 RSFSR Civil Code contained enough traditional (i.e., capitalist) legal principles to revive a devastated economy. The headings of the code would have been familiar to civil lawyers: an introductory general part, followed by chapters on property rights, obligations (contracts), and inheritance. The historian M. A. Isaev refers to the 1922 RSFSR Civil Code as an "actual legal document" that was clearly superior, in terms of its clarity and discussion of legal relationships, to later Soviet legislation.[22] The 1922 RSFSR Civil Code further promoted equality among citizens and between men and women. Nevertheless, the legislation made sure that the state retained ultimate discretion over property and commercial activities. As the Civil Code's first article stated, civil rights "are protected by the law unless they are exercised in contradiction to their social and economic purposes."[23]

The 1922 RSFSR Criminal Code also combined old and new principles. It contained the standard infractions against the public order (i.e., theft, robbery, assault, murder). Moreover, like its tsarist predecessor, the RSFSR Criminal Code allowed for a high degree of flexibility and interpretation when defining crimes against the state. Yet according to the historian Peter Solomon, the code made its own unique contributions to criminal law by articulating new categories of state crimes. It introduced three distinctive types of wrongdoing—counterrevolutionary crimes, economic crimes, and crimes by officials—that were so elastic that the "authorities could politicize almost any crime."[24] As a result, market speculation, contract violations (especially with state agencies), and opposition to the revolution all became subject to criminal prosecution.

The year 1922 further witnessed the return of the main institutions of justice. Lenin reinstated the procuracy based on the principles of independence, uniformity, and centralization.[25] In practice, independence required that the procuracy be separate from the judiciary and the state administration. Therefore, it was only responsible to the central government and the Communist Party. The procuracy further was given one overriding mandate—to supervise the full and exact execution of all laws in the Soviet Union. Hence, the party largely restored the original mission of the procuracy established by Peter the Great in the early eighteenth century.[26]

The bar also was brought back in 1922 to promote confidence in the newly revived legal system, although the legal profession did not enjoy the same level of autonomy as its prerevolutionary predecessor. Instead of being controlled by its membership, the bar was placed under the collective supervision of the courts, the soviet executive committee, and the procuracy.[27] The advocate's role in the legal process also changed under

NEP; the bar began to be referred to as a public, as opposed to a private, institution, accompanied by demands that the advocate defend state and social interests, as opposed to the interests of his or her client.[28]

Finally, NEP saw major reforms in the court system. The people's court remained the court of first instance for most cases, but a second regional (*guberniia*) court was established to handle more complex civil litigation and the most serious crimes. Throughout the court system, lay assessors—individual citizens elected to serve alongside judges—began to participate in the rendering of court decisions. The Bolsheviks' underlying suspicion of formal law, however, meant that judges were granted significant discretion in deciding cases. This power was further enhanced by the right to convict based on analogy to another proscribed act in those instances when a given crime was not covered by the existing code. While some Soviet jurists opposed the use of analogy, it ultimately was included in the 1922 RSFSR Criminal Code to provide judges with sufficient flexibility to address unanticipated violations against the state.[29] Lastly, in 1922, the RSFSR Supreme Court was established primarily to hear appeals from the lower courts but also to exercise control more broadly over all judicial organs.[30]

Therefore, the stage was set for a return to a legality based on a combination of old tsarist practices and new Soviet ideals. The Civil Code served its purpose to the extent that regular commercial activity—not only individual traders but also a limited number of private joint-stock companies—was revived under NEP and marked the return of the private sector.[31] In theory, such commercial investment and business activity was only possible if people possessed a minimum confidence in the legal system. Peasants continued to rely on local custom and self-justice (*samosud*) to satisfy the persistent demand for law in the countryside, but they also began to interact with a more official court system that punished speculators, confiscated property, and sentenced peasants to exile.[32] Yet the criminal justice system remained unpredictably lenient during NEP. A high percentage of criminal cases never resulted in indictments, and among those cases that did go to trial, a quarter resulted in acquittals. Moreover, most convictions resulted in compulsory work or other noncustodial sanctions.[33]

The 1922 revival of court institutions and accompanying legislation coincided with the birth of a nation as well. As previously noted, the 1918 constitution left the future construction of the RSFSR unresolved. The civil war itself produced a parade of sovereignties, both within and outside the RSFSR's borders. The RSFSR slowly gathered up these territories through a combination of military conquest, central decrees, and bilateral agreements.[34] Finally, in order to complete this process, Russia, Ukraine, Belarus, and the newly created Transcaucasian Federative Republic (consisting of Armenia, Azerbaijan, and Georgia) signed the 1922 Union Treaty that brought the Soviet Union into existence.

This agreement would quickly be overtaken by events, but one must pause at this historic moment to emphasize that the Soviet Union technically was founded on an agreement between four seemingly independent states. Moreover, this independence was not a complete fiction in 1922. Ukraine had participated in the Brest-Litovsk negotiations as an independent nation, Belarus had negotiated with Poland and Germany, while the Transcaucasian republics had signed treaties with Turkey.[35] Much to the consternation of Stalin, the Ukrainian Communist Party would fight for greater national autonomy up until the signing of the 1924 constitution.[36] But while the 1922 Union Treaty formally marked the birth of the Soviet Union, it quickly would be relegated to second tier importance as other founding legislation provided more clarity regarding the USSR's governing institutions.

One of the most important unanswered questions in 1922 concerned whether the Soviet Union would be a federation, confederation, or a unified state. As Richard Pipes argues, the supranational organization of the Soviet Union was, in fact, quite useful; it theoretically subordinated the role of Russia and the Russian Communist Party in matters of governance while leaving open the possibility of adding new regions as the global socialist revolution continued.[37] Thus, the 1924 Soviet constitution was assigned the specific task of addressing the ambiguous relationship between the center and its constituent members.

Not surprisingly, the need for unity emerged as one of the dominant themes within the 1924 constitution. The preamble referred to a federal state, but Article 1 granted extensive authorities to the supreme organs of power, including not just the standard supervision over foreign affairs but also the right to establish the basic principles (and a general plan) for the national economy.[38] In total, twenty-four items fell under exclusive central control, a detailed list that left few residual powers to the regions. Two provisions did provide the republics with the attributes of statehood—the right of secession and the requirement that a republic's borders could not be re-drawn without its consent—but no legal means to exercise them.[39] Finally, the 1924 constitution designated some powers to regional executive bodies, although all such institutions remained under strict party, and therefore centralized, control.

The powers of the center were reinforced by Chapter 9 of the 1924 constitution, which was entitled "The Unified Political Administration of State." Article 61 assigned the Joint State Public Administration (OGPU)—the successor to the Cheka—with responsibility for "unifying the revolutionary efforts of the member republics in their struggle against political and economic counter-revolution." Yet the OGPU could not be allowed to act solely on its own initiative, so Article 63 granted the procuracy supervisory oversight over the OGPU.

This search for unity, and the unified state, represented one of the essential links between the tsarist and Soviet systems. From the time of Peter the Great, the unified state had meant that no national group reserved the right legally to challenge the supreme power of the ruling authorities. This attribute was true, no matter what sort of bilateral treaty had precipitated the incorporation of a specific territory into the Russian empire or (after 1917) the Soviet Union. Moreover, the 1924 constitution continued Russia's long-term push toward greater centralization. While the new constitution may have presented the country as a union of national republics, it nevertheless emphasized federal, not regional, laws and institutions. Socialism may have replaced Russification as the stated objective, but the end result was essentially the same, namely the expansion of a centralized, highly bureaucratic state.

In addition to addressing the nationality question, the 1924 constitution rejiggered the previous institutions of central authority. It still assigned ultimate legislative power to the USSR Congress of Soviets, but this body remained a part-time legislature. Thus, basic law-creating power again devolved to the Central Executive Committee, which under the 1924 constitution was divided into two branches—the Council of the Union and the Council of Nationalities. The new Soviet constitution, however, felt compelled to even further delegate the Central Executive Committee's authority. It created a twenty-one-member presidium of the Central Executive Committee that met when the full committee and the Congress of Soviets were not in session.[40] During such moments, the presidium served pursuant to Article 29 as the supreme organ of executive, legislative, and administrative power in the USSR, thereby discarding any notion of separation of powers. Article 33 also granted the presidium significant law-creating powers through its right to issue decrees and other legal acts.

Thus, rule by decree—as opposed to the passage of formal laws (*zakony*)—remained *de facto* the most significant law-creating power within the newly created Soviet Union. Article 43 did establish a Supreme Court of the USSR, whose primary responsibility was to maintain "revolutionary legality" by ensuring that regional legislation and court decisions were in full compliance with federal legislation. The Supreme Court, however, remained closely linked to the presidium of the Central Executive Committee. The presidium appointed seven of the eleven judges. Moreover, the procurator attached to the Supreme Court reserved the right to appeal a Supreme Court decision to the presidium for a final decision.[41]

Yet while the 1924 constitution addressed genuine pressing issues and attempted to provide some institutional scaffolding—especially in regard to the nationality issue—it remained, at its essence, a facade. Most notably, like its 1918 forerunner, the 1924 constitution made no reference to the party, the real source of power within all these governing bodies. Tellingly, the 1924 constitution did not include a section on the rights of citizens. Furthermore, it never referred to NEP and the existing economic system. Such gaps were not accidental; the 1924 constitution and NEP were stop-gap measures until a more concrete vision of socialist law—and the Soviet Union's place in a still-promised global revolution—could be articulated.

During the 1920s, several legal theorists took up the challenge of defining the essential features of Soviet law. E. B. Pashukanis advanced his anti-bourgeois legal theory whereby he reduced most Western law to basic contract law principles and the reciprocal consent among the parties. In the process, Pashukanis attacked both the idealism and the substance of Western law. Although his "commodity exchange theory" recognized that bourgeois law would be necessary during the transitional "dictatorship" phase of building communism, according to Pashukanis, capitalist legal principles eventually would be phased out by the promulgation of the national economic "plan."[42] The first five-year plan introduced in 1928 theoretically represented the start of a process whereby law would gradually wither away, as Marx predicted.

Thus, within just a few years of their introduction, the 1922 Civil and Criminal Codes had fallen into disrepute and abeyance. Instead, politics trumped law. As Pashukanis admitted, "[r]evolutionary legality is for us a problem which is 99 percent political."[43] While little of Pashukanis's vision was ever distilled into legislation, his ideas were taught in law schools, where the need for legal simplicity and flexibility soon pushed traditional disciplines (labor law, family law, land law) to the sidelines.[44] In the process of forging a new socialist legal theory, however, Pashukanis undermined the (admittedly) limited procedural guarantees that had been restored under NEP. He paved the way for the introduction of terror that in 1937 would claim Pashukanis himself as one of its many silent victims.

Stalin's assault on law

In the aftermath of Lenin's death in 1924, Stalin began his maneuverings that would ultimately lead to his position of absolute dominance within the party. Stalin started by going after Lenin's economic policies. The dismantling of NEP began as early as 1926 with increased taxes on private traders.[45] In 1927, the notorious Article 58 of the RSFSR Criminal Code appeared, theoretically outlawing counterrevolutionary activity by criminalizing all types of behavior, such as interacting with foreign states or their representatives, rendering assistance to the international bourgeoisie, undermining Soviet industry, or failing to report reliable knowledge about potential counterrevolutionary crimes. According to Robert Sharlet, Article 58 provided "a formal legal rationale for potentially proscribing virtually any type of real or alleged thoughts or behavior."[46] The historian Golfo Alexopoulos further highlights the legal disenfranchisement of certain outcast social groups, including traders, former landowners and tsarist officials, rich peasants, and priests, that began in 1927. This outcast designation soon spread to family members and led not only to the loss of voting rights but also, in the aftermath of the first five-year plan, to the deprivation of other social rights as well.[47]

Stalin formally ended NEP with his decision in 1928 to introduce his twin programs of collectivization and industrialization. Stalin's "revolution from above" emphasized speed; industrialization had to proceed at an accelerated pace both to build the economic foundation of socialism and to allow the Soviet Union eventually to surpass the West. Meanwhile, in order to feed this new industrial state, Soviet agriculture had to be radically transformed as well, even if that meant creating a new category of peasant (the *kulak*) only to have these rich peasants stripped of their possessions and then deported to either a labor camp or a remote village. A few courageous officials resisted, but as the historian Peter Solomon concludes, collectivization "led to the decline in the observance of procedures in searches, arrests, trials, and sentencing, culminating in the breakdown of legality in the countryside during winter 1933."[48]

The radical nature of Stalin's program was not simply that it violently broke with the existing NEP legislation and centuries of peasant customary law. It represented the first time in more than 150 years that economic modernization was not pursued under the cover of law. Catherine the Great modernized in the aftermath of her *Nakaz* and the creation of class-based courts for the gentry and town dwellers. Nicholas I (with an obvious assist from Speranskii) gathered Russia's prevailing legislation and created a separate digest of civil laws to promote economic development. Finally, the demand for the greater protection of property rights ultimately convinced Alexander II to introduce the Judicial Reforms of 1864. So law—in a highly imperfect fashion—had been an integral part of economic modernization for much of the tsarist period. Stalin eventually would invent his own legal theory to solidify his economic modernization program, but after the fact, and after the arrest, detention, and deaths of millions of people.

For Stalin's onslaught against law was not finished after collectivization and industrialization. In the aftermath of the 1934 assassination of Sergei Kirov, the Leningrad party boss, Stalin, began a national purge that affected all classes—the highest party members and the lowest workers fell victim to unjust accusations of disloyalty, sabotage, and espionage. Tsarist criminal law was no model of procedural regularity or fairness, but the fifteen-year Soviet assault on the criminal justice process—war communism, Pashukanis's attack on bourgeois criminal jurisprudence, collectivization—meant that there were no legal brakes on Stalin's pursuit of political enemies, both real and imagined.

Sheila Fitzpatrick defines the terror as "extralegal state violence against groups and randomly chosen citizens [that] was so frequently used that it must be regarded as a systematic characteristic of Stalinism in the 1930s."[49] All pretense to the restraining power of law was lost. Indeed, the Ministry of Internal Affairs created special extra-judicial boards that operated outside the established court system and could imprison and exile all "socially dangerous" individuals for up to five years (later increased to twenty-five years). Stalin further granted the secret police the right to summarily execute prisoners believed to have engaged in acts of sabotage against the new economic order. In 1937, Stalin turned on the secret police (the People's

Commissariat for Internal Affairs or "NKVD") and had thousands of NKVD officers executed as well.[50]

Multiple estimates exist regarding the total number of Stalin's victims, largely depending on the timespan one chooses to investigate. For the 1937–1938 purges, the floor is no less than 1.33 million people arrested, subject to mock trial, and either imprisoned or executed.[51] For the entire Stalin period, the estimates range in the tens of millions of people. The public process culminated between 1936 and 1938 with "show trials" of the old Bolshevik leaders. As previously noted, the first Soviet show trial occurred under Lenin in 1922 and led to the conviction of leading members of the SR party. Under NEP, however, the Bolsheviks moved away from public show trials and instead staged theatrical agitation trials for workers that addressed such topical issues as army discipline, paying taxes, public hygiene, anti-smoking, and sexual misconduct.[52] But in 1928, fiction once again merged with fact with the staging of the Shakhty trial, where fifty-three engineers were charged with wrecking and sabotage under Article 58 of the Criminal Code. Most of the Shakhty defendants admitted their guilt (under duress), turning a legal proceeding, in the words of historian Julie Cassiday, into "a modern morality play with Evil personified on the stage."[53] The next major show trial—the Trial of the Industrial Party in 1930—was actually made into a full-length documentary that not only included mandatory confessions but also utilized various camera techniques to communicate "the vast gulf separating the enemies on trial from their judges and audience."[54]

The stage was literally set, therefore, for the great show trials of 1936–1938. One by one, the former leaders of the Bolshevik Party and Lenin's closest comrades—Zinoviev, Kamenev, Bukharin—confessed to the most heinous acts of treachery and crimes against the Soviet state. The confession was critical to these proceedings, since it essentially amounted to the only available evidence supporting the charges. Bukharin found ways to discredit the government's evidence in his closing argument, but his words had no influence on the trial's outcome. Unlike the great tsarist political trials, no credible defense was mounted to argue either the facts, the law, or the extenuating circumstances surrounding the case. Nor was there an independent jury that had, on occasion, rejected the arguments of the tsarist state. Instead, the proceedings were marked by zealous prosecutors and a fully compliant judiciary. Indeed, the most distinctive commentary was provided by Andrei Vyshinskii, the main prosecutor, who described the defendants as "mad dogs" and demanded that the court "crush the accused reptiles!"[55]

The motivations behind the major defendants' admissions to various fantastic and imaginary crimes have long been a subject of speculation. Torture, isolation, and threats to surviving family members no doubt facilitated the confession process. The historian Robert Conquest argues that the defendants could not live outside the party and that they submitted on the slim hope that they still might be spared and find their place within the party.[56] The reliance on admissions of guilt as the best form of evidence had its historical antecedents; Peter the Great (like other European rulers) viewed a voluntary confession as the best form of proof and was willing to resort to torture in order to extract it. Yet while the show trials only had the appearance of a genuine court proceeding, the act of confession gave substance to the charges and made Bukharin's subtle refutation of the indictment secondary to his overall admission of guilt.[57]

The Great Terror and accompanying show trials represent the height of illegality under Soviet rule, yet it was paradoxically at this exact time that Stalin returned to the question of what was socialist law. The Procurator-General Andrei Vyshinskii had been writing since 1930 about the importance of law as a means of defending the socialist state.[58] He now renounced Pashukanis's theory of Marxist law and argued that rather than withering away, law would serve as the bedrock of socialism. The development of capitalist society, claimed Vyshinskii, contributed to the decay of law and of legality. In contrast, under socialism, "law is raised to the highest level of development."[59] A new course on the Theory of State and Law was introduced, while other traditional areas of law—criminal, civil, family, labor, administrative—returned to the curriculum as well.[60]

The 1936 constitution serves as the major legislative landmark signifying the renewed stature of socialist law.[61] The preamble celebrated the "achievement" of the dictatorship of the proletariat, thereby indicating that the transitional nature of the 1924 constitution had been replaced by full-fledged socialist state. The highest organ of power was renamed the Supreme Soviet of the USSR, but it continued to be divided into two houses and remained the only body endowed with the formal right to pass laws. It also remained a part-time legislature, and when not in session, a full-time presidium with decree powers operated in its absence.[62] The executive/administrative functions under the constitution were carried out by the USSR Council of People's Commissars (renamed the Council of Ministers in 1946), which also retained the right to issue orders and decisions to implement existing legislation.

The 1936 constitution, therefore, continued the tradition of scattering significant decree and other rule-making powers throughout the political system, with a diminished legislature that simply rubber-stamped decisions made elsewhere within the bureaucracy. The constitution further followed the established pattern of providing a detailed list of centralized powers in support of the unified state, leaving little room for genuine regional autonomy, although on paper, the regions continued to possess certain substantive powers. Most notably, union republics were allowed to write their own constitutions and retained the theoretical right to secede from the Soviet Union.[63]

Yet while 1936 constitution relied on its immediate predecessors, it included several important innovations that would provide it with a progressive and democratic gloss. To begin with, the 1936 constitution included a formal list of the rights and duties of Soviet citizens. Several of these provisions focused on social rights—leisure, education, pensions—but the constitution also included the right to privacy and stressed equality among all national groups and the sexes.[64] Article 125 also referred to basic civil rights (freedom of speech, assembly, the press), with the qualification that these civil rights must conform with the interests of working people and strengthen the socialist system. Finally, Article 10 included the notion of "personal" property rights that included earnings, savings, dwellings, and furniture, as well as the right to inheritance. Such personal property rights, however, were clearly subordinate to state, cooperative, and collective farm property, and the socialist system specifically forbade private ownership of the means and instruments of production.

Stalin's constitution undoubtedly represented something new in both Russian and Soviet law. It broke with the tsarist legal practices, which always had relied on custom and a differentiated system of rights, and with the 1918 RSFSR constitution, which had eliminated the political rights of certain categories of people. In contrast, the new constitution emphasized a single all-union citizenship. The 1936 constitution further placed the Soviet Union at the forefront of the debate over human rights, since it elevated social rights to the same level as more established political and civil rights. Yet these rights remained highly qualified and focused on the administrative relationship between state and citizen, as opposed to recognizing a private space that allowed for civil society, private business, and genuine individual rights. Under such circumstances, law lost its dynamic features and invariably moved in a distinctly bureaucratic and punitive direction. Clearly, any attempts to undermine the constitution's central tenets were met with the severest of punishments; as Article 131 stated, "persons committing offenses against public, socialist property are enemies of the people." And for those who fell outside the system, there were no protections. Article 12 proclaimed, "He who does not work, neither shall he eat."

The 1936 constitution further witnessed the triumph of the procuracy over all other judicial institutions. Article 113 assigned the procuracy "supreme supervisory authority over the strict execution of the laws by all People's Commissariats and institutions subordinated to them, as well as by public servants and citizens of the U.S.S.R." This constitutional authority—plus the power of legislative initiative granted in the 1933 status (*polozhenie*) of the *prokuratura*—allowed Procurator-General Vyshinskii to preside over the drafting of the major pieces of Soviet legislation.[65] Thus, the combination of legislative initiative, supervision, and criminal prosecution transformed the procuracy into the most powerful judicial institution in the Soviet Union. In contrast, although the 1936 constitution described the Supreme Court as the "highest judicial organ," it did not possess a monopoly over the interpretation of law. Instead, Article 49(b) assigned the right to interpret the laws of the Soviet Union to the presidium of the Supreme Soviet.

The 1936 constitution made no reference to the bar, but in the aftermath of the collectivization and the purges, its ability to defend Article 127's grant of personal inviolability was essentially reduced to zero. By 1939, according to Eugene Huskey, the subordination of the bar to the party, with a few notable individual exceptions, was complete. Professional qualifications were relaxed in order to create a more politically reliable membership.[66] In terms of daily practice, the rise of administrative entitlements, as opposed to legal rights, shifted civil disputes from the courtroom to the bureaucracy, rendering advocates "actors of secondary importance" within the Soviet legal system.[67]

As had been the case for centuries, it was the state that reigned supreme in the 1936 constitution. Indeed, the constitution referred to the main institutions of governance (national, republic, local) as "organs of state power." Such terminology, however, raised the obvious question: what constituted state power under Soviet law? In 1929, Stalin linked state power with the dictatorship of the proletariat, an unbridled expression of force as well as the essential prerequisite for the withering away of the state.[68] Stalin recognized the philosophical contradiction of maximizing state power in order to eliminate it. Nevertheless, while the 1936 constitution theoretically marked the end of the dictatorship of the proletariat, it retained the notion of state power as an essential organizing principle of governance. Furthermore, the constitution formally acknowledged that the locus of state power was not in its enumerated institutions but in the Communist Party. In contrast to the 1918 and 1924 constitutions, which had been conspicuously silent about the role of the party, Article 126 of the 1936 constitution noted that the "most active and politically most conscious citizens in the ranks of the working class and other sections of the working people unite in the Communist Party of the Soviet Union (Bolsheviks), which is the vanguard of the working people in their struggle to strengthen and develop the socialist system."

Conclusion

After almost twenty years of turmoil and destruction, the Soviet Union re-emerged in 1936 as a unified state with a single source of sovereignty. Despite the establishment of legislative, executive, and judicial institutions, state power rested solely in the hands of Stalin and the Communist Party, which controlled all three branches of government. Moreover, as collectivization and the purges demonstrated, no real legal constraints existed on state power as an expression of force. Instead, the state continued to be ruled by an assortment of decrees and bureaucratic orders, with the legislature—the primary law-creating body—relegated to part-time status. Finally, even though the 1936 constitution granted each republic its own respective constitution, as well as regional linguistic and cultural rights, Article 14 contained a detailed list of centralized powers that effectively nullified any notion of federalism. In retrospect, the Soviet Union would be recognized as an incubator of nations, yet Soviet constitutional law and the Communist Party never acknowledged the republics as somehow limiting the sovereignty of the state until, of course, it was too late.[69]

Some historians argue that the 1936 constitution—and its articulation of legal institutions, rights, and obligations—created a dual state with competing prerogative (force) and normative (law-based) values. The dual state model largely rests on the analysis of Nazi Germany. Germany, however, had a long history of balancing the prerogative and normative state—public law versus private law—that predated the rise of Nazism. Russia's legal evolution had taken a very different course. As noted in Chapter 3, while private law made significant inroads after the Judicial Reforms of 1864, it never served as a realistic counterbalance to the public law powers of the autocracy. Moreover, two decades of socialism had clearly subordinated private law—and property rights—to the Soviet state. Thus, while Stalin may have desired the stability that law affords, he had no intention of subjecting state power to legal regulation, promoting private law, or introducing genuine adversarial procedures to provide for the defense of individual rights. Stalin's attack on the legal system and accompanying ruthless assault on private spaces remains one of the essential features of the Soviet Union's totalitarian model and distinguishes it from the authoritarian practices of its tsarist predecessor.

The 1936 constitution recognized Stalin's major contributions to building socialism—the economic plan, socialist ownership of the means of production, collective and cooperative farm property—and converted them into founding legal principles, thereby putting a gloss over the terror (which still had two years to run). The constitution also provided a veneer of stability to a traumatized population. Other commentators argue, however, that the intended audience for the constitution lay not inside but outside the country and that Stalin wanted to present the Soviet Union to the world as a democratic state.[70] But no matter who was Stalin's ultimate target group, the pursuit of legal stability roughly coincided with the end of the Soviet Union's search for utopia. The historian Yuri Slezkine describes the religious, messianic fervor that the early Bolsheviks brought to the building of communism, arguing that they were true believers who genuinely thought they were building a new socialist paradise.[71] But while the 1924 constitution still spoke of "revolutionary legality," the 1936 constitution retreated to the more conventional task of the administration of "justice (*pravosudie*)." The 1936 constitution further abandoned the notion of the withering away of the state, one of the essential theoretical foundations of Marxism. Instead, the 1936 constitution confirmed that state and law would be permanent features of Soviet life, and Vyshinskii provided no justification for this philosophical deviation other than the assertion that socialist law was inherently better than capitalist law. The constitution represented not just stability but usurpation of the revolutionary dream for power politics.

Obviously, Stalin's dual objectives of stability and terror contradicted each other and represent an enduring paradox that historians—searching for the roots of socialist legality—still find difficult to reconcile.[72] From Stalin's perspective, however, there was no reason why he could not have both law and terror, and in Vyshinskii, Stalin found someone who willingly pursued both tasks.[73] Soviet law after the Second World War would become increasingly professionalized and bureaucratized. More law graduates entered the field, but success in the procuracy and judiciary depended on avoiding acquittals and ensuring low rates of reversals, eventually resulting in a strong accusatorial bias within the Soviet criminal justice system.[74] Stalin, however, never abandoned his reliance on terror—he used it, for example, when exporting socialist law to the newly occupied eastern bloc countries after 1945. The gulags remained full, and Stalin continued the policy of forced relocation of suspect ethnic groups into the Soviet hinterland.[75] At the time of his death in 1953, he was preparing yet a new round of show trials revolving around the anti-Semitic so-called Doctors' Plot. Stalin had reinvented "state and law" in its most violent and extreme form. His successors would struggle with curbing its most excessive features while maintaining a monopoly over state power.

6

Socialist Legality and Illegality

Soviet law gained traction under Nikita Khrushchev (1953–1964) and Leonid Brezhnev (1964–1982). Khrushchev sought to reinvigorate socialist legality by addressing Stalin's crimes and by promoting law as a source of public regulation and social mediation. Brezhnev pursued a less innovative and more restrictive "law and order" policy but still oversaw the adoption of a new constitution. Thus, socialist law reached its fullest expression under Khrushchev and Brezhnev, as reflected in the emerging legal professionalization and stability of the late Soviet period. But while Soviet law provided a forum for addressing everyday disputes (albeit on its own terms), it responded with overwhelming force to any individual or group that challenged the ideological underpinnings of the state. Such excessive responses, along with corruption and the rise of informal practices, exposed the underlying weaknesses within the Soviet legal system. This chapter explores the competing trends within late Soviet law as it unwarily approached its greatest and final test.

Khrushchev's revival of Soviet law

The post-Stalin era began with the decision soon after his death on March 5, 1953, not only to end the investigation of the Doctors' Plot, and its eerily familiar pursuit of enemies, but also to release and rehabilitate the defendants in the name of upholding "socialist legality."[1] The subsequent arrest and execution in 1953 of Lavrenty Beria, Stalin's henchman and head of the security services, sparked confusion and uncertainty among citizens regarding the arbitrariness and lawlessness that were now tacitly recognized as having flourished under Stalin. The removal of Beria opened up the path to power for Nikita Khrushchev, who would soon push his other rivals aside and assume the leadership of the Communist Party. Khrushchev would continue to address the excesses of the Stalinist criminal justice system as general secretary while introducing numerous pieces of legislation—on a national and republic level—that attempted to provide substance to his understanding of socialist legality.

Khrushchev began where no other Soviet leader had started: procedure. He abolished the Ministry of Interior's special troikas that had received the right in 1934 to send people to labor camps in secret administrative proceedings. He also granted the procuracy supervisory powers over the investigations by the secret police, deprived military courts of their jurisdiction over civilians, refocused the burden of proof on the prosecution, and repudiated the evidentiary force of confession in counterrevolutionary cases.[2] Dismantling Stalin's repressive machinery, however, required more than introducing new procedural guarantees. The gulags still contained millions of innocent victims, and the prevailing legal system was incapable of handling these appeals without itself being called into question. Therefore, since extra-judicial proceedings had created the problem, Khrushchev relied on extra-judicial procedures to resolve it. The process began with the amnesty issued on March 27, 1953, which announced that prisoners who displayed a conscientious attitude toward work and were not a significant danger to society would be released.[3]

But how was this amnesty to be administered and what sorts of rights were to be restored? No single agency or piece of legislation ultimately governed the massive release of inmates from the gulag.[4] Prisoners had to work their way through the bureaucracy and prepare elaborate appeals to get their jobs back, receive pensions, return to their home cities, and otherwise obtain access to basic public services. The historian Miriam Dobson described the dilemma confronting petitioners as they tried to navigate their way through the system. "On the one hand, they knew the camps should be seen as a site of correction and redemption. On the other, they wanted to present themselves as deserving, loyal, Soviet people, not as dark degenerates whose pre-arrest lives were futile and unwholesome."[5]

The poet Anna Akhmatova later would famously describe the collision of two worlds in the aftermath of the release of gulag prisoners. "Now those who were arrested will return, and two Russia's will look each other in the eye; the one that sent people to the camps, and the one that was sent away."[6] Khrushchev further articulated the crimes of Stalinism in more detail during his Secret Speech in February 1956, although he limited their scope and placed the blame squarely on Stalin and his cult of personality. But while party historians were given the unenviable task of trying to reconcile Stalin's crimes with post-Stalinist Soviet governance, they produced no satisfactory explanations as to why the party had tolerated such massive illegalities for so long.[7]

Thus, the crimes of the gulag largely went unanswered and hung over the Soviet legal system in a way that the excesses of the tsarist Siberian exile system did not. The legal parallels between these two penal regimes were self-evident; both displayed similar arbitrary, extra-judicial, and repressive characteristics. Like the gulag, the prerevolutionary system of administrative exile also undermined any notion of due process while leaving significant numbers of tsarist subjects with no legal recourse to challenge their sentences. The main difference between these two periods was one of scale: the number of political detainees was significantly lower under the tsars than during the Soviet period. In 1901, political exiles in Siberia totaled 1,800.[8] In the aftermath of the 1905 Revolution, the number of exiles jumped to 30,000 in 1910, still just a fraction of what occurred during Stalin's purges.[9] Moreover, one of the recurring problems of the tsarist exile system was the inability to provide proper surveillance over the detainees. If one had the right social standing—such as Lenin—exile would have turned into a challenging yet still productive sabbatical to catch up on one's scholarly pursuits. In the words of the historian Daniel Beer, exile communities became "academies of sedition in which new recruits could study doctrine and established figures could churn out a stream of revolutionary theory and journalism."[10] No such options existed under Stalin's gulags, where despite flowery statements about reeducation and the "purification of society," the goal of prison labor was to work the inmates to near-death. In Stalin's camps, the best one could hope for was survival.

To break with the Stalinist past, Khrushchev concentrated on the need to return to the "Leninist norms of socialist legality," although such terminology provided little clarity as to the path forward. The one available legal alternative associated with Lenin—NEP—was no longer viable, since it relied on customary law as well as prerevolutionary civil and commercial law principles, none of which survived Stalin's campaign of industrialization and collectivization. Moreover, the phrase "socialist legality" was not a new term but traced its origins back to the Stalin era. A journal bearing that name had been published since 1946 by the procuracy, Ministry of Justice, and Supreme Court; it highlighted, among various issues, the growing problem of bribe-taking and corruption among Soviet officials.[11] Khrushchev clearly linked legality with the new restraints on the security services and a more engaged citizenry.[12] Yet socialist legality fell far short of notions of rule of law or the law-based state, as Khrushchev had no intention of placing absolute legal restraints on either himself or the party.

Thus, Khrushchev's pursuit of socialist legality focused not on rewriting broad constitutional principles but on providing a clearer statutory basis for everyday law. Most importantly, he presided over the codification of Soviet law—the culmination, albeit under radically different circumstances, of what Speranskii envisioned when he had collected Imperial Russia's laws and decrees more than a century before. Yet the codification of Soviet law promoted both national unity and a theoretical decentralization of power. Thus, Khrushchev began the process of adopting supranational principles in a specific branch of law (civil law and procedure, criminal law and procedure, family, labor, land, etc.), which then served as templates that were translated into national codes by each republic. Historians have not paid much attention to the regional distinctions among these law codes;

certain national civil law guidelines, for example, were mandatory, while in other matters, such as criminal law, some regional deviations and references to local custom were tolerated.[13] While obviously not independent, each republic nevertheless now possessed the legal trappings of statehood, most notably its own constitution and regional law codes, further highlighting the Soviet Union's unique (and unintended) role as the incubator of nations.

Khrushchev was not satisfied, however, simply with re-invigorating the legal process. He also revived a preexisting Soviet legal institution—the comrade courts—as a means to pursue a more populist, informal vision of legality.[14] The jurisdiction of the comrade courts included not only petty cases transferred from the regular courts but also disputes referred by the local soviets as well as private matters (i.e., family disputes, drunkenness, truancy, intra-apartment conflicts). The name of this tribunal was deceptive; comrade courts were classified as an elective social agency, not a judicial institution, meaning that they did not follow the formal rules of procedure.[15] Instead, they relied on the volunteer participation of fellow workers and neighbors and a general understanding of what constituted proper socialist behavior. When the American law student George Feifer visited a comrade court in 1964, he found little sign of rigging or excessive party supervision but also few signs of actual preparation.[16]

Thus, the comrade courts relied both on the application of social pressure and the prospect of reeducation—and not a formal legal verdict—to address both real and perceived antisocial behaviors. A healthy degree of utopianism also ran through these proceedings. The comrade courts represented society's attempt to correct deviant conduct without overtly relying on the state's coercive powers, thereby partially returning to the Bolsheviks' original romantic vision of the future where formal law was no longer necessary to regulate everyday life. This idealism, however, was tempered with a level of pragmatism; an overburdened Soviet court system was only too happy to remove these petty cases from its jurisdiction.[17]

The reliance on informal rules in low-level legal proceedings was not without historical precedent. The peasant courts of tsarist Russia also had depended on unwritten procedures and local standards, although with a very different orientation. The imperial peasant courts reflected the habits and customs of the local population, which allowed for bottom-up legal decision-making and a significant amount of legal diversity across the empire. In contrast, the comrade courts pursued a more ideological agenda; they sought to promote a communist morality that, while open to interpretation, nevertheless flowed from the top-down understanding of acceptable socialist behavior and values.[18] That the comrade courts regularly resorted to public humiliation and embarrassment as part of their overall education strategy only further detracted from their usefulness as a source of grassroots legality.[19]

Khrushchev's emphasis on socialist legality marked the end of terror and a return to everyday law in the Soviet Union, albeit with a distinct socialist flavor. Feifer's discussion of civil cases in the people's courts in the 1960s is particularly notable for its absence of basic contract disputes. In a planned economy, where profits were outlawed and "speculation" criminalized, citizens appear to have had little incentive to reduce everyday transactions to a formal agreement. Contract disputes regularly occurred among state enterprises, large and small, but they were adjudicated separately in the state *arbitrazh* (commercial) courts. Therefore, the regular courts were left with a high number of property disputes that focused on a uniquely Soviet problem, namely how to divide an already small communal apartment.[20] Such property issues often accompanied divorce proceedings, which were further complicated by questions of whether a separated spouse still retained the legal right to live in a city as per the Soviet Union's restrictive residency requirements. Feifer specifically highlighted the sharp, emotional exchanges that occurred among the parties in civil cases, as well as the lack of procedural regularity in the courtroom.

Criminal proceedings were much more structured with the judge being joined by two lay assessors to provide an appearance of public participation. These citizen jurors, however, lacked legal expertise and were sarcastically referred to as "nodders," since they seldom challenged the judge's decisions. Moreover, since prosecutors rarely participated in criminal trials (it was not required under 1960 Criminal Procedure Code), the judge assumed responsibility for reviewing the evidence and *de facto* representing the state. While such involvement may offend the sensibilities of a common law jurisdiction and its image of an impartial judge, civil law countries accept a more engaged judiciary, although Soviet judges regularly crossed legal boundaries and provided ideological commentary and advice. Criminal trials often involved theft of state property, and Feifer noted that these types of cases were dealt with particularly harsh sentences. A Soviet judge, concluded Feifer, was not concerned with a single crime or criminal act but possessed a larger pedagogical purpose: "[A] greater task faces the court—no less than the remaking of a society."[21]

Yet it was the procuracy, with its broad supervisory powers, and not the judiciary that emerged as the most powerful legal institution in the post-Stalin era. From Peter the Great onward, the pursuit of legality had always been balanced by the need for supervision and central control. Vyshinskii secured these public oversight responsibilities for the procuracy during the 1930s, and it would retain them until the end of the Soviet Union.

Supervision was divided into two categories: specific and general. Specific supervision covered oversight over criminal investigations and the prosecution of cases, prisons, the organs of public order (the Ministry of Internal Affairs, the Committee for State Security), and the affairs of minors. The procuracy further was granted specific supervisory powers over civil cases, enabling prosecutors to review all judicial decisions involving such personal disputes.[22] The procuracy's general grant of supervision included the right to oversee the execution of laws in all ministries, enterprises, and social organizations, and the exact observance of laws by all officials and citizens.[23] These powers were so broadly interpreted that they essentially allowed prosecutors to micromanage enterprises, factories, and collective farms to ensure compliance with the state's economic plans.[24]

Khrushchev's pursuit of legality—never absolute to begin with—waned during his later years. He decided that too many lawyers were being produced in the Soviet Union and subsequently limited the growth of the *advokatura*.[25] The new procedural protections under Soviet criminal law also impeded Khrushchev's fight against parasites, speculators, hooligans, and other perceived violators of socialist norms. Khrushchev aggressively pursued such anti-Soviet behavior without letting the technicalities of socialist legality get in the way. Most notoriously, in 1963, the poet Joseph Brodsky was convicted for social parasitism in part because he held no apparent job and, more importantly, because the state objected to his writings. In another egregious case, a currency speculator, Ian Rokotov, was sentenced to eight years in prison. His ill-begotten gains became part of a public exhibit organized by the Committee for State Security (KGB). When Khrushchev visited, he supposedly remarked that these speculators needed to be shot. Suddenly, the presidium of the Supreme Soviet issued a decree that called for the death penalty for bribes and theft in particularly large amounts, including currency speculation. Moreover, this edict was applied retroactively. A separate edict—this one unpublished—applied this provision specifically to Rokotov and his accomplice, and they were subsequently executed.[26] The legal journalist Yuri Feofanov covered the original trial and still remembered the case more than two decades later when he revisited the controversy. The Rokotov execution, he concluded, showed "that the 'restoration of Leninist norms of legality' was pure fiction, a legal cover for arbitrariness; it did not inhibit the party in any way in dealing with the undesirable people and in asserting force over law."[27] Thus, despite Khrushchev's pursuit of a revived socialist legality, the Stalinist foundations of Soviet law remained firmly in place.

The dissident challenge to Soviet law

Khrushchev's peaceful removal from office in 1964 and subsequent quiet retirement signified that there would be no return to terror as state policy. In fact, Leonid Brezhnev's assumption of power posed little threat to the legal status quo. The state continued to meet the demand for law and provide a venue for everyday justice, as long as citizens' complaints remained within the scope of conventional Soviet practices. Brezhnev did back away from the comrade courts in favor of increased professionalization and more regular rules of procedure. Yet Brezhnev soon asked the Soviet courts to assume a new responsibility: to adjudicate the limits of acceptable political behavior via the criminal process. Thus, a new round of political trials began. These proceedings differed from the show trials of the 1930s; they were not staged for mass audiences but instead remained largely hidden from public view, although unofficial transcripts circulated among the dissident community. The trials further did not rely on confession—forced or otherwise—but had to deal with pleas of innocence and arguments provided by defense counsel. Although the outcomes were preordained, the trials themselves provided moments of unpredictability while exposing the ideological limits of Soviet law. The proceedings also allowed defendants to question Soviet practices and expose the hypocrisy of official government pronouncements, starting with the 1936 constitution itself.

The first major political trial of the Brezhnev era was that of two writers—Andrei Siniavskii and Iulii Daniel'—who had published abroad under pseudonyms novels that were, to put it mildly, critical of the Soviet Union. The Soviet state indicted them under Article 70 of the RSFSR Criminal Code for conducting activities that weakened and defamed the Soviet political and economic system. Thus, the state put literature itself on trial, and the cross-examination of Daniel' and Siniavskii exposed the surreal nature of Soviet law as prosecutors held the authors criminally accountable for the words of fictional characters. "The most rudimentary thing about literature," argued Siniavskii in his closing statement, "is that words are not deeds, and that words and literary images are conventions: authors are not identical with the characters they create. This is an elementary truth, and we tried to talk about it. But the prosecution stubbornly rejected the idea as an invention, a means of evasion and deceit."[28]

Siniavskii and Daniel' were sentenced to seven and five years of hard labor, respectively. While many viewed the trial as a return to Stalinist practices, a few dissidents saw an opportunity to turn the tables on Soviet officialdom and hold the authorities accountable to their own laws. In particular, they seized upon the Soviet concept of legality—the demand that citizens fulfill the law as written—and expanded it as a means to impose a higher rule-of-law standard on the Soviet state.[29] In 1967, a small group of demonstrators gathered in Moscow's Pushkin Square with various placards denouncing certain provisions of the RSFSR criminal code and demanding the release of political prisoners. The unsanctioned meeting was quickly broken up by the authorities and charges filed against the demonstrators for violating the public order. The prime defendant was Vladimir Bukovskii, a university dropout and a self-taught expert on Russian criminal procedure.

Bukovskii's case was handled by Dina Kaminskaia, a member of the Moscow bar and one of the few lawyers willing to take on political cases. The active presence of defense counsel by itself represented a radical departure from the show trials of the 1930s. The *advokatura* had managed to retain a modicum of corporate autonomy in comparison to other Soviet institutions, mainly because it remained a fee-for-service profession. And while the Communist Party controlled the bar's leadership, lawyers retained some leeway to make a legal argument, provided that they did not cross the line and make a politically charged speech in court. In such instances, Kaminskaia noted, a lawyer would be expelled from the bar with no chance for reinstatement.[30]

Thus, Kaminskaia and Bukovskii brought different legal strategies to the case. Bukovskii wanted to make a constitutional argument, that the criminal code provisions regarding gross violations of public order violated the 1936 constitution and its promises of freedom of speech and freedom of the press. Operating under different constraints, Kaminskaia understood that it was not possible to make a constitutional argument: "No court in the Soviet Union is empowered to declare a law unconstitutional," she later explained. "The courts have no right to criticize the law; their sole obligation is to administer it."[31] She also knew that advocates in political cases had to separate themselves from the political views of their client. What Soviet law allowed Kaminskaia to make was a purely legal argument, namely that based on the law's exact wording and prohibitions, no crime actually occurred under the statute.[32]

Kaminskaia knew that the verdict was predetermined even as she poked holes in the government's evidence. But whereas in tsarist Russia the lawyer's closing argument was the most memorable speech, in the Soviet Union the "last word" of the defendant often produced the most powerful moment of the trial. Bukovskii did not disappoint. "Freedom of speech and a free press is primarily the freedom to criticize; no one is ever forbidden to praise the government. If you include articles on freedom of speech and freedom of the press in the Constitution, then you must tolerate criticism."[33] Bukovskii concluded by addressing the bench: "There are such concepts as honor and civic courage. You are judges and you are presumed to possess these qualities. If you really are persons of honor and civic courage, you will give the only possible verdict in this case—a verdict of acquittal."[34] Not surprisingly, the judge did not possess such resolution; Bukovskii received the maximum three-year sentence.

Bukovskii and other dissidents lacked the open political space to pose a genuine threat to the Soviet state. Nevertheless, they consistently challenged its legal foundations, not only in calling for basic civil rights but also by demanding greater recognition of various national groups (Ukrainians, Lithuanians, Armenians, Crimean Tatars, etc.) and religious freedom. In the aftermath of the 1975 Helsinki Accords, various Helsinki groups were set up throughout the Soviet Union. These activists managed to establish close communications with Western journalists to draw attention to political trials. They also demanded that the Soviet Union live up to its human rights commitments as set forth under the Helsinki Accords. The Soviet state was able to deflect the latter claim, in part because no legislation had been enacted incorporating the Helsinki Accords into domestic Soviet law.[35] Whether international treaties immediately became a part of Soviet law was subject to debate among Russian scholars, but this question never was resolved to the advantage of the dissidents.

Reliance on legality and the law as written ultimately provided no protection for the dissidents. Yuri Orlov, a cofounder of the Helsinki Watch Group, was charged in 1978 with anti-Soviet agitation and propaganda. He described in his memoirs how his lawyer had been so intimidated by the KGB that he refused to make any political arguments at the trial.[36] Moreover, since Soviet law looked for the discovery of objective truth—as opposed to an adversarial examination of contradictory evidence—the judge possessed full discretion as to which witnesses could take the stand. Not surprisingly, none of Orlov's witnesses testified. The judge even prohibited any citation from the fifty-nine volumes of collected evidence, determining that the activities of the Helsinki Watch Group were somehow not relevant to the case, when in fact they were essential to the indictment.[37] The appearance of adversarialism—without its procedural guarantees—was the hallmark of the dissident trials, but Soviet officials eventually found ways to bypass the legal process entirely, most notably by sending dissidents to psychiatric hospitals.

Not all of the dissidents embraced traditional liberal ideas, nor did they represent a fully united political movement. It would take time before their indictment of the Soviet system would gain traction beyond their own world of self-publication (*samizdat*) and in the West. Yet Bukovskii had exposed a profound defect in Soviet law and one that it would never overcome. Simply stated, the Soviet constitution and its enumerated rights were not a "living" constitution because no court was allowed to interpret it. To cite just one example, the US Bill of Rights do not stand by themselves. They can only be understood by working one's way through hundreds of Supreme Court decisions. How could the broad civil and social rights described under the Soviet constitution be understood if no court was empowered to clarify and enforce them?

The USSR Supreme Court did provide "guidance" on various aspects of Soviet law that was theoretically binding on lower courts, thereby indirectly providing a degree of judicial interpretation.[38] The absence of constitutional review, however, represented one of the fundamental distinctions between Soviet law and its fellow continental civil law systems. They both may have theoretically relied on detailed codes and the law as written—as opposed to Anglo-American use of judicial precedent. In the aftermath of the Second World War, however, national constitutional courts gradually were established throughout much of Western Europe, and although their specific mandates and procedures varied, these courts assumed responsibility for interpreting the civil and social rights articulated in each country's respective constitution. Individual human rights achieved even greater recognition with the signing of the European Convention on Human Rights in 1950 and the subsequent creation of a European Court of Human Rights with the power to enforce these rights even over the objection of national law. Thus, while commentators noted the similarities between Soviet law and the continental civil law tradition, the goal posts moved after 1945. Civil law countries added their own distinct brand of constitutional review to their jurisprudence, thereby raising the status of the courts in any discussion of the division of powers. The Soviet Union never joined this debate and therefore remained a true outlier in the civil law system.[39]

The 1977 Soviet constitution and late Soviet law

The Soviet Union did take one last crack at constitutional reform in 1977, but it was motivated by neither political necessity nor a poplar groundswell for change.[40] Instead, history itself seemingly dictated the need for a revised founding document. In 1961, Khrushchev called for a new constitution to reflect the next stage in the USSR's inevitable march to communism. Despite Khrushchev's ouster, Brezhnev completed this task by introducing a constitution suitable for a country living under "developed socialism." No one, of course, contemplated that the Soviet Union would meet its swift and definitive end just fourteen years later and that the "Soviet people"—if they had ever existed—would be no more. Nevertheless, the 1977 constitution commands attention. It represents the final expression of the goals and ideals of Soviet law. Moreover, within its text, one can identify the seeds of the Soviet Union's impending demise, as well as the problematic legacy that the 1977 constitution would bestow on the newly independent Russian Federation in 1991.

The 1977 constitution began with a long, rambling preamble that summarized the sweeping trajectory of Soviet history. It recognized the Communist Party's great triumph in 1917, then paid homage to the Soviet Union's victory in the Second World War, and concluded with praise for the Soviet Union as a society of "mature socialist social relations" that had created a new community of people: the Soviet people. Yet unlike previous constitutions, the Communist Party was placed front and center, moving up from Article 126 in Stalin's 1936 constitution to Article 6. This provision proclaimed that "the leading and guiding force of the Soviet society and the nucleus of its political system, of all state organizations and public organizations, is the Communist Party of the Soviet Union."[41]

The state also featured prominently in 1977 constitution. Pursuant to Article 70, the Soviet Union was an integrated, federal, multinational state that embodied the state unity of the Soviet people and drew all its nations and nationalities together for the purpose of jointly building communism. The 1977 constitution also preserved the most innovative features of the 1936 constitution, namely its recognition of equality among all citizens and its detailed grant of social and civil rights. These social rights were expanded to include rest and leisure, health care, retirement, education, housing, and cultural benefits, while other provisions guaranteed freedom of speech, the press, assembly, and religion, as well as privacy.

Yet like its predecessor, none of the above rights were absolute under the 1977 constitution. According to Article 39, enjoyment by citizens of their rights and freedoms must not be to the detriment of the interests of society or the state nor infringe on the rights of other citizens. The assignment of rights was further qualified pursuant to Article 59 and its requirement that citizens perform certain duties and obligations. Finally, as the historian Benjamin Nathans argues, all of the above rights were predicated on one activity: the provision of labor.[42] As long as Soviet citizens were employed, they had access to the above rights and the accompanying benefits. But if one fell outside this category—if one was a poet, refusenik, dissident, or entrepreneur (i.e., speculator)—he or she no longer performed acceptable labor and, in fact, posed an existential threat to the system. Thus, Soviet law became highly compartmentalized; if a citizen stayed within its political and social boundaries, then a person enjoyed a plethora of rights. However, Soviet law could not handle exceptions to the rule, inevitably provoking a legal overreaction that only highlighted the arbitrariness and inadequacies of its system of rights.

The 1977 constitution's attempt to promote stability failed on other fronts as well. Like its Soviet predecessors, the 1977 constitution granted the USSR Supreme Soviet with the exclusive power to draft formal laws, but it remained a part-time legislature that met twice per year. In its absence, the constitution assigned various law-creating powers to the presidium of the Supreme Soviet, although any amendments issued by the presidium to existing laws required subsequent Supreme Soviet approval. The Soviet Union's primary sources of law included the detailed fundamental principles for civil, criminal, and other branches of law that were subsequently reduced to republic-level law codes, decrees issued by multiple government bodies, and court judgments and guiding explanations.[43] Other actions, while not necessarily rising to the level of law, nevertheless still found their way into Russian legislation and were sometimes viewed as indirect sources of law, including enactments of the Communist Party and other social organizations.[44]

These multiple and often inchoate sources of law had profound consequences for the very idea of law in the Soviet Union. From a statistical standpoint, the number of "laws" (*zakony*) represented a tiny fraction of all Soviet legislation; from 1945 to 1965, only 200 formal laws were adopted. During the same twenty-year period, the presidium of the Supreme Soviet issued 10,000 decrees, while all union-level bodies issued an additional 57,400 resolutions.[45] Laws may have held a higher status than decrees in the Soviet Union's legal hierarchy, yet they played a diminished role in the actual governance of the nation. And this problem was only compounded by the fact that a large number of bureaucratic decrees and resolutions were never published, making it impossible in many instances to determine what the law actually was.[46]

Thus, despite the codification of certain branches of law, Soviet law remained as messy and impenetrable as its tsarist precursor. Custom was also included among the prevailing list of sources of law, and it appears to have been occasionally applied in some regional courts.[47] Nevertheless, the primacy of socialist law as set forth in Article 4 of the 1977 constitution pushed customary practices into the informal, as opposed to formal, sector of society. Such traditional practices, however, persisted and had a profound impact on Soviet law. As the historian Ronald Suny notes, "So powerful [were] the obligations of one's relatives and friends that the shame incurred by nonfulfillment was, for many in the southern tier of Soviet republics, much more serious than the penalties imposed by law."[48]

Pursuant to the 1977 constitution, justice continued to be organized along regional, not federal, lines with proceedings to be conducted in the union republic's national language.[49] Each union republic further was granted its own constitution, as well as the seemingly anachronistic right of secession. Appeals worked their way through a union republic's supreme court and ultimately to the USSR Supreme Court, which possessed broad legal and supervisory powers. Yet under the 1977 constitution, the Supreme Court was not the sole branch of government assigned the right to interpret the law; according to Article 121(5), the presidium of the Supreme Soviet also was granted the right to interpret the laws of the USSR.

It was the procuracy, and not the judiciary, however, that emerged as the most powerful legal institution under the 1977 Soviet constitution. Article 164 granted the procuracy the supreme power of supervision over the strict and uniform observance of all laws. Virtually every institution in the Soviet Union—ministries, state committees and departments, local executive-administrative bodies, enterprises, cooperatives, and collective farms—was constitutionally subject to the procuracy's supervision. The procurator-general further oversaw the appointment of most procurators throughout the country, thereby making the procuracy one of the most centralized—and pro-statist—institutions in the USSR. Finally, Article 113 granted the procuracy (among other state and judicial actors) the right to initiate legislation before the Supreme Soviet.

The 1977 constitution referred to the bar and its need to provide legal assistance to the population but left the profession's future organization to subsequent legislation. According to the political scientist Pamela Jordan, the late Soviet *advokatura* gained a semblance of control over its corporate affairs, including over admissions, disbarment, professional conduct, and fee schedule. Advocates further staffed legal aid consultation bureaus to ensure that citizens obtained access to professional legal advice. Yet ultimate control over the *advokatura* still resided in the state and party. The state kept the number of advocates artificially low, openly discriminated against Jewish applicants, and forbid certain lawyers from participating in high-profile political trials.[50]

No unified legal profession existed in the Soviet Union in the sense that while lawyers shared certain experiences (i.e., law school, a common body of legal literature, courtroom interactions), there was no single professional body that represented the joint interests of the procuracy, judiciary, and bar. The Communist Party objected to such an organization on the grounds that it potentially could undermine loyalty to the party itself.[51] Nevertheless, under late socialism, the Soviet Union possessed the standard legal actors that provided the appearance, and to some extent, the reality of everyday law. As Robert Rand described in his book *Comrade Lawyer*, an analysis of the daily activities of a Moscow legal consultation bureau, Russians regularly sought legal advice and went to court to litigate matters of divorce, small personal property disputes, housing disagreements, illegal firings, as well as to defend themselves against criminal charges. Yet noticeably absent from Rand's discussion of common disputes were contracts and torts, although Soviet legislation allowed for such cases as well. In reality, a highly circumscribed system of private law emerged in the late Soviet period, one that shared many of the statutory trappings of continental civil law but not the same core values and incentives. The Soviet Union lacked privately owned goods used for trade and production, criminalized transactions that produced profits and other sources of "unearned" income, and possessed no "deep" pockets (other than the state) to compensate plaintiffs in tort actions.[52] Rand further communicated a certain weariness around late Soviet law; the courtroom "was old and tired," while the reception room at the consultation bureau resembled an "inner city welfare office in the United States."[53]

Socialist legality distinguished itself from other civil law and common law jurisdictions in other ways as well. To begin with, as part of its supervisory functions, the procuracy took on the role of pseudo-ombudsman, reviewing thousands of citizen complaints each year and demanding that administrative bodies address these grievances.[54] Such appeals were cheaper and faster than court review. Yet, unlike a true ombudsman, the procuracy was neither independent nor overly concerned with the protection of individual rights. Thus, by filing a complaint with the prosecutor, Soviet citizens passively surrendered their rights to an institution that was unlikely to assert their interests vis-à-vis the state.[55] The option to bypass the court system altogether and to pursue an administrative remedy to one's legal claim only reinforced the underlying bureaucratic nature of Soviet law.

The procuracy possessed another unique privilege, namely the right to petition for supervisory review. This power essentially meant that even after a criminal or civil case had been decided, the procuracy—at the behest of a party or on its own initiative—could file a protest requesting that the case be reopened.[56] Such a request could be filed years after a legal action had been decided. Thus, no finality of judgments (*res judicata*) existed under Soviet law, creating a major source of instability within the legal system.

The Soviet Union further lacked independent legal institutions. The Communist Party controlled all three pillars of justice, and state interference in individual cases was so rampant that it acquired its own distinctive moniker: telephone law.[57] Moreover, it was not only political dissidents who faced certain conviction. Various mechanisms existed that enabled prosecutors and investigators to dismiss charges during the pretrial phase, that is, a *de facto* acquittal that was not accurately reflected in court statistics.[58] Nevertheless, the professional stigma against acquittals was so great that once indicted, Soviet courts convicted defendants at a 99 percent rate, throwing serious doubt on the legitimacy of the Soviet adversarial system.[59] Russian commercial law also failed to provide for certain essential legal remedies, such as specific performance, that could realistically compel the parties to abide by a contract. Instead, enterprises received money damages, which were essentially meaningless because the real problem was not compensation but bottlenecks in the supply chain that delayed production. Companies appealed directly to ministry or party officials to break this jam, thereby confirming, according to Kathryn Hendley, that "people had little reason to turn to the law when their rights had been violated."[60]

The shortcomings of Soviet private law, along with the rise of informal practices—most notably, the notorious exchange of favors (*blat*) that enabled Soviet citizens to gain access to scarce goods and services—created an alternative means of exchange that existed outside the formal constraints of law. According to the sociologist Alena Ledeneva, *blat* focused on reciprocal personal networks that facilitated access to basic consumer goods that were in permanent short supply.[61] Yet despite its pervasiveness, Ledeneva argues that *blat* did not rise to the level of illegal economic activity; it was based on connections, not money, and simply "reorganized the official distribution of material welfare."[62] Because such informal activities eased daily life, the state largely tolerated *blat*. Nevertheless, *blat* operated at the public expense, since the target of such redistributive activities often involved state property.[63]

Ledeneva distinguishes between *blat* and corruption (i.e., the use of public office for private gain), but even after separating these two concepts, corruption proliferated throughout the Soviet Union.[64] Widespread bribery dated back to Stalin's rule, although some of its most egregious instances were kept secret so as not to discredit the government and the Soviet legal system. For example, the 1949 bribery trials of corrupt USSR and RSFSR Supreme Court judges and staff were held behind closed doors to prevent negative publicity from reaching the general public.[65] Such closed proceedings, however, invariably reduced the state's ability to deter future acts of corruption, and by the Brezhnev period, the payment of bribes regularly accompanied ordinary social interactions, whether they be with the police, enterprise managers, auditors, doctors, judges, university professors, or service workers.

But corruption began at the top, within the upper echelons of the party and government. Indeed, since so much of the Soviet economy was not properly monetized, corruption often took the form of access to privilege (a better apartment or a fully stocked grocery store) as opposed to actual financial reward. Corruption was top-down, unchecked by law, and impossible to eradicate. According to the émigré Russian lawyer Konstantin

Simis, the ruling party-government apparatus would have to destroy itself in order to end corruption, but this would never happen, since "the nature of any unrestricted power is such that it inevitably corrupts those who wield it and constantly generates the phenomenon of corruption."[66]

Professor Kathryn Hendley took one last scholarly look at Soviet law at the end of the Soviet period and found little to recommend. The specific subject of Hendley's research—Soviet labor law—failed on multiple grounds. Despite their symbolic enshrinement in Communist Party ideology, the rights and interests of workers were an illusion. The courts did the bare minimum, rubber-stamping management decisions and "going through the motions with respect to their legal duties."[67] On a broader level, Hendley described Soviet law as simply the "one-way projection of state authority."[68] It did not engage in an interactive dialogue that reflected the "shared values of society" and proved unable to protect citizens from encroachments by the state.[69] To the extent that law mattered, it only did so by invoking fear and not as "a means for achieving justice or even solving problems."[70] Hendley further emphasized the duality of Soviet law, where the mundane cases generally proceeded without state interference but where the political cases allowed party elites "to manipulate law and legal process to further their own agendas."[71]

Yet even to refer to the duality of Soviet law is to overestimate the vitality of the Soviet legal system. All civil law systems possess an underlying dualism; it is in the nature of the division between private law—the rights of the individual—and the public law powers of the state. These two realms may be separate, but they are also interdependent and build upon each other.[72] Yet Soviet private law played no effective role in limiting or influencing the public law powers of the Soviet state. The enumerated rights offered under successive Soviet constitutions were always qualified by certain duties and often unrealizable in practice. Moreover, Soviet property rights never allowed for the accumulation of capital whereby a commercial sector, exercising its economic rights under private law, could challenge the powers of the state. What was left was a pale imitation of private law, focusing on family and housing disputes instead of contracts and torts. And even the family was not sacrosanct; Article 66 of the 1977 constitution called on Russian parents to train their children "for socially useful work, and to raise them as worthy members of socialist society." In retrospect, tsarist private law provided more protections and made far more inroads on autocratic power than its Soviet successor.

Conclusion

A present-day nostalgia persists around the late Soviet period that extends to Soviet law. Aleksandr Makovskii, at the Ninth Senate Readings before the Russian Constitutional Court in 2013, spoke of the contradictions within Soviet law but also about its own internal logic. In the forty years before the collapse of the Soviet Union, he noted, a huge amount of work had been done to systematize Soviet law. This effort had resulted in a "brilliant success" that first resulted in a chronological collection of laws, then a multivolume systematization of laws, and finally the drafting of Soviet (i.e., federal) codes of laws as well as the beginnings of the creation of law codes for all union republics.[73]

Soviet law changed Russian society in other ways as well; it put forward notions of equality and social rights that previously did not exist in the Russian empire. Soviet law further sought to educate citizens on what it meant to be a Soviet citizen and his/her role in creating a socialist society. Yet the ability of law, by itself, to create a new man has always been elusive. The prerevolutionary legal philosopher Bogdan Kistiakovskii recognized this fact in 1909, when he stated that "every social organization needs legal norms, that is, rules regulating not the inner conduct of people, which is the task of ethics, but their external conduct."[74] Given the Bolsheviks' ideological drive, education often crossed over into outright propaganda, undermining any notion of impartiality under the law.

Other current Russian commentators do not share the same attachment to Soviet law. The Russian legal historian M. A. Isaev summarily dismisses the presumed legal advancements of the Soviet period. The reforms of Vyshinskii, he writes, established a "banal form of legality, without which any society would find itself in a state of ungovernable, anarchic self-disintegration."[75] The people's courts, Isaev further noted, were nothing less than courts of inquisition from the middle ages transferred to the twentieth century.[76] The Soviet legal system was not about the realization of justice, Isaev concludes, but the preservation of the state system.[77]

State preservation had been the first priority of every Russian ruler since Peter the Great, so the subordination of Soviet law to the needs of the state fit an established pattern that had existed for centuries. It was Stalin, however, who originally set the terms of Soviet law, and neither Khrushchev nor Brezhnev ultimately was able to erase Stalin's considerable imprint. Khrushchev did succeed in ending the terror—a momentous break from the Stalinist past—while attempting to re-instill a degree of idealism into Soviet law. Yet Khrushchev's vision of "socialist legality" included his own willingness to bypass the law when convenient and never addressed the anti-legalist and instrumentalist roots of socialist law forged by Lenin and Stalin. Similarly, while Brezhnev rewrote the Stalin constitution, he retained much of its original spirit and content, including the Communist Party's monopoly on power, a part-time legislature, qualified rights, an opaque system of sources of law, an ascendant procuracy, and a subservient judiciary that was not empowered to provide substance to the rights set forth in the constitution. Thus, the ability of Soviet law to evolve and change with the times was limited. Nevertheless, when an agent of change—Mikhail Gorbachev—finally appeared in 1985, legal reform quickly moved to the top of the political agenda.

7

Russia's Long Constitutional Crisis: 1985–1993

Many factors played into the collapse of the Soviet Union. Attempts to revive socialist ideology quickly exposed the country's underlying rigidity and inability to embrace reform. The Communist Party itself was sharply divided, and a deteriorating economic situation only highlighted the extreme lack of consensus regarding the best strategy going forward. The nationality question also played a critical role in the breakup of the Soviet Union as the republics increasingly asserted their independence from Moscow. Finally, the twists and turns in the political relationship between Mikhail Gorbachev and Boris Yeltsin make the demise of the Soviet Union a personal story.

This chapter adds another dimension to the analysis of the Soviet Union's collapse by examining the country's constitutional crisis that unfolded from 1988 onward, when the national question came to the forefront. At its essence, this emergency asked the question of what overarching understanding of law held the country together. As a single system of law gradually disappeared, dual power—or more accurately, multiple sources of sovereignty—appeared and slowly rendered the Soviet Union ungovernable. Yet for the newly created Russian Federation, the constitutional crisis did not end in 1991 with the collapse of the Soviet Union. It continued all the way to the close of 1993 when a new constitution was hastily adopted after Yeltsin's violent confrontation with the Supreme Soviet. Therefore, this chapter focuses on the long constitutional crisis and its two main protagonists as they both turned to traditional Russian legal principles in a desperate attempt to preserve national unity.

The collapse of socialist law

Much consideration has been given to the fact that Mikhail Gorbachev received a legal education in the Soviet Union. This training distinguished

Gorbachev from most of his peers in the Politburo who possessed technical, and not legal, backgrounds, as well as exposed him to comparative and international issues that other university faculties simply did not address. Moreover, Gorbachev's tenure at Moscow State University straddled a critical historical period—he began in 1950 toward the end of Stalin's reign and finished in 1955, on the eve of Khrushchev's consolidation of power. He initially was going to be part of the legal reform process. Upon graduating, he was offered a position with the USSR procuracy to supervise the state security organs. Gorbachev pictured his future work "as a struggle for the victory of justice, in accordance with my political and moral beliefs."[1] Yet Gorbachev's expectations were summarily dashed when the procuracy suddenly revoked the job offer, evidently because it did not want to hire inexperienced lawyers to investigate these controversial cases. Gorbachev ended up in the procuracy back in his home region of Stavropol, a position he quickly sought to escape. He soon found employment in the local Komsomol in its agitation and propaganda department. Thus began his remarkable climb that culminated in his appointment in 1985 as general secretary of the Communist Party.

Gorbachev began with economic reforms and an attempt at accelerating (*uskorenie*) the Soviet economy, but when confronted with the deep rot within the socialist economic system, Gorbachev turned to political reform as his best chance to achieve some early successes. Gorbachev's twin campaigns of *glasnost* (openness) and *perestroika* (restructuring) unlocked a previously closed public space that brought numerous troubling issues—past and present—to the forefront, ranging from Stalin's crimes to the inadequate response to the 1986 Chernobyl nuclear disaster. The meaning of perestroika also evolved over time, from an early focus on economic reform to a more broad-based call to change both party and government structures.

Both glasnost and perestroika naturally raised questions about the prevailing legal order, yet Gorbachev initially brought a highly compartmentalized approach to law. He introduced commercial law reforms without proposing more substantial legal changes that would address the planned economy or the prevailing political system. Thus, in June 1987, Gorbachev introduced a new law on state enterprises that gave Soviet companies control over their own finances as well as the opportunity to enter into joint ventures with foreign partners, provided that the foreign partner remained a minority shareholder.[2] Approximately one year later, the law on cooperatives gave newly formed small private businesses the right to own property, maintain bank accounts, employ workers, conduct commercial transactions, and otherwise engage in regular business transactions.

Gorbachev's attempt to update the Soviet Union's commercial legislation with infusions of Western practices would continue until the end of his time in power. Yet such legal reforms were not only highly technical and narrowly focused, they also were placed in a uniquely hostile environment. The Soviet Union lacked the institutions, infrastructure, and people to put private business on an equal footing with state enterprises. Gorbachev himself never abandoned the planned economy or state-owned enterprises, which sucked up virtually all of the Soviet Union's financial resources and left little in reserve to spur private investment. Moreover, the prices of goods produced in Russia's fledgling private sector were significantly higher than state-produced goods. Public opinion soon turned on private business, viewing these new cooperatives as speculators. Gorbachev also grew disillusioned and referred to intermediaries in the cooperative sector as "pure rogues."[3] If the Soviet economy had experienced some immediate returns from these market reforms, as had occurred previously under NEP in the 1920s, Gorbachev may have been more patient and seen if the Soviet Communist Party, like its counterpart in China, could maintain political control over a more mixed economy. The lack of results, however, soon forced Gorbachev to think beyond economic restructuring and limited commercial law reforms and consider a more radical political transformation of the Soviet Union.

Gorbachev named this second round of change "democratization," a word with multiple meanings that, while broadly calling for greater public participation in everyday decision-making, did not necessarily translate into one man, one vote. But democratization did not exist in a legal vacuum. Gorbachev also called in 1988 for a "law-based state (*pravovoe gosudarstvo*)" a prerevolutionary term that, as discussed in Chapter 4, emphasized a state subordinated to, and not outside, the law. The legal scholar Harold Berman further distinguished the European law-based state from the Anglo-American concept of the rule of law; the latter included implicit references to natural law that provided a moral basis when considering the legitimacy of a specific law.[4]

The law-based state had been a popular rallying cry among opposition Russian liberals during tsarist times, but Gorbachev now expropriated this term in the name of the Soviet ruling elite. Gorbachev did provide an important qualification by referring to a "socialist" law-based state, thereby implying a distinction between Soviet and Western understandings of the concept. He left unanswered, however, what the law-based state meant for the Communist Party's constitutionally mandated monopoly of power.[5] Sufficient ambiguity surrounded Gorbachev's vision of the law-based state, yet as events would later bear out, with one turn of a phrase, Gorbachev went from committed reformer to unwitting revolutionary.

Gorbachev's flirtation with the law-based state began with constitutional reforms. The Brezhnev constitution had been revised just once during its first decade. By the end of 1988, however, approximately one-third of the 1977 constitution had been amended with additional changes to come.[6] In particular, Gorbachev substantially changed the legislative branch. He introduced a new Congress of People's Deputies, two-thirds of whom were selected in competitive elections, while the remaining delegates came from the Communist Party, Komsomol, the Academy of Sciences, trade unions, and other officially recognized social organizations. The Congress of People's

Deputies in turn elected a newly revamped Supreme Soviet that henceforth would meet eight months a year, a dramatic increase in comparison to the previous Supreme Soviet, which had met fewer than eight days per year.[7]

While the Congress clearly outranked the Supreme Soviet as the country's highest legislative organ, both institutions possessed the right to pass laws with an expectation that an indirectly elected but more permanent Supreme Soviet would possess greater public legitimacy than its Brezhnev predecessor when adopting legislation. At the same time, the list of institutions with the right of legislative initiative before Russia's legislature expanded significantly to include people's deputies, the presidium of the Supreme Soviet, the USSR Council of Ministers, the union republics, the USSR Supreme Court, the procuracy, the USSR Academy of Sciences, and other social institutions.[8] Finally, Gorbachev created a new executive sinecure for himself as chairman of the USSR Supreme Soviet, thereby granting himself a governmental title to go along with his position as head of the Communist Party.

The 1988 constitutional reforms temporarily resolved most of Gorbachev's legal problems. He had injected more democracy into the system by allowing for multicandidate (but not multiparty) elections, all the while making sure that the Communist Party remained in control of the legislative bodies. He further raised the stature of laws within Russia's legal hierarchy. No longer would a decree issued by a government body become a law via the rubber-stamped approval of a part-time legislature; instead laws would emerge from a more permanent, albeit indirectly elected, Supreme Soviet, thereby putting Russia on the road to the law-based state. Finally, Gorbachev accomplished all of these legal changes without abandoning the Communist Party, the real power behind these governmental structures and the institution responsible for maintaining state unity.

Gorbachev would introduce other progressive legal reforms over the course of the next two years that included increasing the independence of the judiciary, expanding the right of defense counsel in preliminary investigations, and creating a Constitutional Supervision Committee theoretically responsible for ensuring that all laws complied with the constitution.[9] He also allowed, to an unprecedented degree, a discussion of Stalin's terror as nongovernmental organizations gathered evidence and published prison memoirs in an effort to document Stalin's crimes.[10] While the focus was on the past, however, these investigations inevitably implicated the present-day Communist Party, since its monopoly of power and system of laws could still be traced back to Stalin and the 1930s.

Yet despite such openness and democratization, events were already beginning to spin out of control for Gorbachev by the end of 1988. By allowing for elections to both Soviet and regional institutions, he opened up the question of national sovereignty and the underlying relationship between Moscow and the republics. Pursuant to prevailing law, each republic possessed its own constitution, legislature, legal codes, and court system, as well as the theoretical right of secession. The assumption was that these law-creating functions would be tightly controlled by the Communist Party and would not break with federal legal principles. The rise of nationalist movements and the holding of local elections, however, upset these long-standing assumptions and suddenly initiated a war of laws. The Estonian Supreme Soviet issued the first declaration of sovereignty on November 16, 1988, with Latvia, Lithuania, Azerbaijan, Moldova, Uzbekistan, and Georgia soon following suit. Moreover, the continued fighting between Armenia and Azerbaijan over Nagorno-Karabakh suggested that certain ethnic disputes were beyond any legal regulation or political compromise.[11] Finally, the decision to send troops against peaceful demonstrators in Tblisi in April 1989 backfired, revealing the potential human cost of keeping the Soviet Union together by force.

The mobilization of the Soviet Union's national groups led to a constitutional emergency that quickly overwhelmed all other reform efforts. The roots of this crisis dated back to the very founding of the Soviet Union. The 1922 Union Treaty theoretically had resolved the nationality question; the four signatory republics surrendered their national sovereignty to create a unified socialist state that in practice recognized only one source of state power. Such a "unified" state, in fact, had been at the center of Russian governance for centuries. The tsar exercised exclusive state authority for all but the last eleven years of imperial history, and while the 1936 and 1977 constitutions created various state institutions, the Communist Party still monopolized state power during the Soviet period.

The 1922 Union Treaty proved so successful that Soviet leaders came to believe that they ruled over a fully integrated nation-state. This illusion was quickly stripped away in 1989 and 1990, when the weak federal underpinnings of state power suddenly became obvious to everyone. Soviet law would play a critical role in first exposing and then exacerbating this problem. Individual republics passed laws on citizenship and regional language requirements. Other legislation changed street names, allowed local residents to avoid the national draft, promoted a free press, created alternative legal institutions, and otherwise ignored federal law. The Baltic States posed the most immediate threat to the Soviet Union's integrity. Annexed after the Second World War, they were not parties to the 1922 Union Treaty. Therefore, they simply demanded the return of their national independence that had been illegally taken away from them.

Instead of focusing on his liberal agenda, Gorbachev was forced to pass laws on such difficult subjects as secession and how to declare a state of emergency. The April 1990 law on secession exposed Gorbachev's deteriorating position. Both the 1936 and the 1977 constitutions upheld this right for union republics, thereby making it awkward to ignore. Yet Gorbachev had no desire to sanction procedures that made it possible for a republic to leave the Soviet Union. Thus, his law on secession imposed numerous conditions—including a five-year waiting period, the resolution of all border disputes, and the endorsement of the Soviet legislature—that left none of the key players satisfied. From Gorbachev's perspective, he had been required to legalize a process that, if implemented, would end his rule. Meanwhile, the individual republics believed that Gorbachev had not acted in good faith and later simply ignored the law on secession when formulating their demands for independence.[12]

The socialist law-based state seemed increasingly out of reach despite multiple constitutional amendments and the passage of progressive legislation. Gorbachev ultimately came to the conclusion that the primary obstacle to change was the Communist Party itself. On March 6, 1990, at his behest, the Congress of People's Deputies repealed Article 6 of the 1977 constitution, thereby ending the Communist Party's monopoly of power. In so doing, Gorbachev gambled that he could rule through existing government institutions (i.e., state power) and not through party structures. The Congress of People's Deputies elected Gorbachev to the new position of president of the Soviet Union, an elevation that was simultaneously a political triumph and grave miscalculation. Gorbachev biographer Archie Brown argues that at this stage, Gorbachev most likely would have won a national election and gained political legitimacy as the popularly elected leader of a country.[13] Instead, Gorbachev won with a rather lackluster level of support within the Congress (1,329 for, 495 against, 313 abstaining or submitting invalid votes), reflecting his declining political standing.[14]

Gorbachev soon found himself embattled on multiple fronts. The party was fracturing, the economy continued to decline, and the nationalist opposition had moved from the smaller, peripheral republics to Russia and Ukraine, the Slavic heartland of the Soviet Union. Increasingly isolated, Gorbachev began to rely less on law and more on the traditional form of Russian legislation, namely the decree. The Supreme Soviet granted Gorbachev the right to rule by executive decree in September 1990, leading to constitutional changes that expanded the president's decree-making power.[15] Yet this increased authority neither advanced Gorbachev's self-professed goal of the law-based state nor won him more popularity. As the political scientist Robert Sharlet notes, "Gorbachev's decrees became increasingly arbitrary and controversial, resembling more the proclamations of a monarch than the considered executive decisions of a constitutional leader mindful of the division of power within a constitutional system."[16]

As Gorbachev tacked to the right and the left in 1990–1991 in search of popular support, he confronted what all Russian leaders feared most: dual power. For more than 300 years, the unified state, with its notion of subordination to a single sovereign by all national groups, had governed the Russian empire and the Soviet Union. The one fatal breakdown in this system—the 1917 revolution—had been precipitated by the rise of a multiplicity of powers that culminated in national collapse. Gorbachev now faced the same dilemma; various national groups were asserting their sovereignty at the expense of the union as a whole. One last attempt at coercion occurred in January 1991, when Soviet troops were sent into Vilnius, Lithuania, to take over the local television station. Gorbachev's role in these events remains disputed; he heated up the rhetoric prior to the violence, but he later blamed the military for pursuing a provocation against him and his reforms. Nevertheless, the resulting death of fourteen civilians only diminished Gorbachev's democratic credentials without actually solving the Lithuanian situation.[17]

With force seemingly off the table—and rule by decree undermining the goal of the law-based state—Gorbachev turned to the treaty-making process as the only other established means of holding the country together. Bilateral peace treaties and other agreements had brought different territories into the Russian empire, always with the understanding (on the Russian side at least) that these regions recognized the tsar as the sole sovereign. The 1922 Union Treaty similarly brought the main national groups into the Soviet Union under the umbrella of socialism and the supremacy of the Communist Party. However, the Union Treaty, as incorporated into the 1977 constitution, was no longer viable, and Gorbachev in March 1990 proposed drafting a new founding law. Prospects for a definitive solution were dashed almost immediately when the Baltic States, Armenia, Georgia, and Moldova opted not to participate in the discussions.[18] The union was already disintegrating, and in many regions, theoretical discussions on such topics as the supremacy of Soviet federal law, the language rights of citizens, economic relations among republics, and the division of powers between the center and the regions were being overtaken by daily events. Moreover, it was Russia, with Boris Yeltsin as its newly chosen head of the Supreme Soviet, that most directly challenged Soviet power.[19] Yeltsin clearly used his authority to undercut Gorbachev, both by asserting the RSFSR's economic sovereignty and by negotiating bilateral treaties between Russia and other union republics.

Gorbachev's efforts did receive a modest boost on March 17, 1991, when a large majority of Soviet citizens voted in support of maintaining the Soviet Union in a national referendum, although six republics boycotted the voting.[20] Gorbachev further managed on April 23, 1991, to bring together the heads of nine republics (including Yeltsin) in the "9+1" talks to begin preparing a new draft of a union treaty, in the process exiling the Communist Party to the political sidelines. A new country—the Union of Sovereign Soviet Republics—was contemplated that, while retaining the same USSR acronym, nevertheless would espouse such basic principles as the national sovereignty of the republics, human rights, civil society, and the national development of an all-union market.[21] Many details regarding how a highly centralized state would give way to a *de facto* confederation remained to be worked out. Meanwhile, Gorbachev's political position continued to diminish, especially in the aftermath of the June 12, 1991, national election of Boris Yeltsin as president of the RSFSR. Yeltsin now possessed a direct electoral mandate; Gorbachev did not.

In early August 1991, Gorbachev left Moscow to vacation at a government dacha in Crimea. He planned to return to the capital on 19 August, the day before the signing of the new union treaty. Yet events intervened one last time as eight high-ranking Soviet officials formed the State Committee for the State of Emergency and attempted a *coup d'etat* to save both the party and the Soviet Union. Resistance in Moscow, led by Boris Yeltsin, and also in other major cities throughout the Soviet Union, quickly revealed a fatal lack of preparedness by the plotters. Gorbachev found himself held captive in Crimea, unable to act, but his pursuit of the law-based state manifested itself in one final and ironic way: both parties appealed to prevailing law to justify their actions.[22] The coup plotters referred to the legal transfer of power from president to vice president under Article 127 of the constitution to highlight the legitimacy of their actions. They further highlighted the people's loss of rights that had occurred "in gross violation of the Fundamental Law of [the Constitution of] the USSR."[23] In response, Yeltsin issued a series of appeals, demanding the return to regular constitutional order and the convocation of the Congress of People's Deputies. He further asserted the constitutional supremacy of the RSFSR, stating that the "organs of local power will unswervingly adhere to constitutional laws and decrees of the President of Russia."[24]

The above exchange of legal opinions represented a pyrrhic victory for Gorbachev. He may have transformed the constitutional discourse in the Soviet Union, but Gorbachev no longer possessed sufficient political authority to keep the country together. A fifth draft of the Union Treaty would be published on November 25, 1991, but there were no takers.[25] Indeed, in what turned out to be the final nail in the coffin, over 90 percent of Ukrainians voted for independence in a national referendum on 1 December.[26] One week later, the heads of the Russian, Belarusian, and Ukrainian republics met at a hunting lodge in Belavezha Forest. Yeltsin made one last attempt to save the union, but the president of Ukraine, Leonid Kravchuk, citing the results of the referendum, refused to participate in any revival of the centralized state. With no way to preserve the union, the leaders now required a means to end it. They did so by formally renouncing the 1922 Union Treaty, a seemingly long-forgotten agreement that nevertheless provided a legal pretext for the heads of three of the four original signatories to dissolve the Soviet Union.

The collapse of the Soviet Union involves the confluence of crises—economic, political, national—that all occurred simultaneously and with cumulative effect. At each turning point, Soviet law was put to the test and, on its own terms, ultimately found deficient. Gorbachev initially thought that he could graft commercial law and limited private enterprise onto the Soviet legal system, yet the prevailing state sector proved so dominant and all-encompassing that this transplant failed to take root. Gorbachev next tried to separate party and state institutions while advancing an independent political foundation for state power, infused with Western notions of the rule of law and the law-based state. The Soviet constitution, however, had always served as a facade for the Communist Party, and once it was removed from the equation, the Soviet state began to fall apart. Gorbachev was left with ruling by decree, a traditional yet increasingly impractical method of governance because he could no longer rely on state bodies to implement his orders.

Finally, Gorbachev confronted a collapse of the unified state as the republics asserted their national autonomy at the expense of central authority. Ironically, the Soviet state had endowed the republics with the theoretical trappings of law and judicial independence on the assumption that these powers would never be exercised. When these constraints suddenly disappeared, the Soviet Union fell into a war of laws where regional legislation trumped federal law, a fatal condition that, if unaddressed, invariably leads to national collapse. In order to prevent this catastrophe, Gorbachev turned to procedures that had been utilized since Muscovy to bind disparate parts of the empire together: the treaty-making process. From the outset, however, six republics refused to participate in the negotiations, meaning that the composition of the Soviet Union was going to change no matter what the final agreement. And after the failed August 1991 coup and Ukrainian referendum, the prospects for Gorbachev's union treaty were reduced to zero.

The Soviet flag came down from the Kremlin for the last time on December 25, 1991. The end of the Soviet Union, however, did not mean the end of Soviet law. In particular, Russia continued to be governed by the 1978 RSFSR constitution, a document largely derivative of the 1977 Brezhnev constitution. The 1978 RSFSR constitution had been significantly amended from 1989 to 1991 to reflect Russia's desire for greater independence, but it possessed no track record as the highest source of governing law. The same problems that plagued Gorbachev would now bedevil Yeltsin. These included major ethnic divisions, a deteriorating economy, and an ill-defined system of division of powers. One constitutional crisis was ending, and a second one was just beginning.

The troubled birth of the Russian Federation

Boris Yeltsin stands out as the only opposition politician in Russian history to both overthrow and then consolidate state power. That achievement, in and of itself, makes him one of the most compelling figures in Russian history. The fact that he transformed Russian law in the process, albeit in an uneven and imperfect manner, makes him a pivotal person in Russian legal history as well. A discussed below, Yeltsin's political odyssey coincided with his growing awareness of the deficiencies within the Soviet legal system. Legal reform became an integral part of his platform, but as political tensions mounted in the aftermath of the Soviet Union's collapse, Yeltsin hastily resurrected the state as the only institution capable of maintaining the integrity of the Russian Federation.

An engineer by training, Yeltsin started his career in construction but later joined the party and eventually rose to become First Party Secretary for the Urals region of Sverdlovsk in 1975. Yeltsin distinguished himself as a party apparatchik with a populist touch who got things done. In 1985, he moved to Moscow to become head of the Central Committee's Department of Construction, but within eight months, Gorbachev tapped him to become First Secretary of the Moscow Party Committee.[27] To a certain extent, Yeltsin was a team player who supported the broad objectives of glasnost and perestroika while using his position to expose the debilitating corruption in everyday Moscow life. Yet at the same time, Yeltsin was a master self-promoter, and reports of the crusading public servant who eschewed the privileges of the ruling party elite only enhanced his image both in the Soviet Union and among the foreign press.

In 1986, Yeltsin further moved up the party hierarchy to become a candidate (nonvoting) member of the Politburo. Yet as Yeltsin's public profile grew, he became more disillusioned both with the pace of reform and the Communist Party's overall commitment to it. On October 21, 1987, he announced his intention to resign from the Politburo.[28] His speech by itself was political suicide, but rather than let Yeltsin quietly fade away, Gorbachev and other party officials piled on and issued several humiliating public rebukes. Yeltsin's downfall was complete, yet it was at this moment that Gorbachev made a critical and still unexplained decision; rather than banishing the disgraced Yeltsin back to Sverdlovsk and political oblivion, Gorbachev chose to keep him in Moscow. Some commentators suggest that Yeltsin had become a leading symbol of perestroika who could not be easily discarded. Others speculate that Yeltsin was still useful to Gorbachev, in that Yeltsin could still be called upon if Gorbachev needed to confront the party hardliners at some later date.[29] Whatever the reason, Yeltsin remained in Moscow and thus began the most improbable political comeback of all time.

Gorbachev provided one more key ingredient that contributed to Yeltsin's unlikely success: free elections. Yeltsin reappeared on the political stage in June 1988, when he managed to get invited by the Karelian delegation to participate at the Nineteenth Communist Party Conference. There he gave a memorable speech in which he not only highlighted the corruption within the party but demanded his own political rehabilitation "while I am alive," a not-so-subtle reference to the many victims of Stalin's repressions who only managed to be rehabilitated long after their deaths.[30] Over the next three years, Yeltsin would win four elections: USSR Congress of People's Deputies (March 1989), RSFSR Congress of People's Deputies (March 1990); chairman (speaker) of the RSFSR Supreme Soviet (May 1990), and finally president of Russia (June 1991). Such a string of victories highlighted Yeltsin's underlying support as well as his unique appeal as a politician in a country dominated by dull party apparatchiks.

During these election campaigns, Yeltsin gathered new constituencies and raised issues that struck at the legal foundation of the Soviet Union. Decentralization emerged as one of his central causes, and Yeltsin encouraged both union republics and the regions within the RSFSR to assert their independence. Yeltsin backed up this demand with action. Most notably, he presided over the RSFSR's declaration of national sovereignty in June 1990, when Russia announced its theoretical independence from the Soviet Union.

Yeltsin further experienced a dramatic philosophical conversion during his years in the political wilderness. He went from party apparatchik to ardent supporter of basic civil rights, including freedom of speech, press, assembly, and religion, as well as an advocate for private property rights.[31] Many commentators questioned the depth of Yeltsin's transformation. Yet, although he did not initially abandon the Communist Party, he did call for the end to its absolute political monopoly. In June 1990, moreover, he resigned from the party, declaring himself to be a social democrat.

Yeltsin's political transformation, and his championing of such issues as civil rights and anti-corruption, required fundamental legal reform. But whereas Yeltsin excelled in playing the renegade to the ruler Gorbachev, his position changed after the collapse of the Soviet Union, when he became the primary target of the opposition. Moreover, Yeltsin faced the same toxic mixture of economic, political, and national problems that had undone Gorbachev, only instead of trying to keep the Soviet Union together, Yeltsin now confronted a splintering Russia. The most pressing problem concerned the nationality question. The Russian Federation consisted of diverse component parts: autonomous republics, districts, territories, and autonomous regions. The autonomous republics presented the most immediate challenge to the unity of the Russian Federation. They were named after the titular national group and long aspired to the same sovereign rights as the recently departed union republics. Soviet law had not given them the right of secession and other trappings of independent statehood, however, because they did not border other countries.[32] Nevertheless, the Soviet Union was no more, and Tatarstan, Chechnya, and other regions were demanding greater autonomy.

Yeltsin, of course, had staked his political reputation on decentralization, and he could not easily reverse course. Therefore, like Gorbachev, he now turned to the treaty-making process as the only available means to preserve the Russian Federation. On March 31, 1992, the Federation Treaty was signed, consisting of a series of three agreements with: 1. republics; 2. districts, territories, and the cities of Moscow and St. Petersburg; and 3. autonomous districts and regions. The Federation Treaty sought to clarify the relations between the center and the regions, but it was at best a temporary solution and it was added as an appendix to the 1978 RSFSR constitution.[33] Several regions used the negotiations to extract economic concessions from Moscow, making an already asymmetric federalism even more disparate.

More ominously, two republics—Tatarstan and Chechnya—did not even sign the Federation Treaty, casting serious doubts on the viability of the Russian state.

The nationality crisis hovered over an equally divisive debate, namely the nature of state power itself. This struggle ultimately was played out both in the political and the legal arenas, in the process putting the deficiencies of Soviet and post-Soviet law on full display. Yeltsin probably possessed sufficient political capital in the aftermath of his victory in August 1991 to disband the Congress and demand a new constitution. Yeltsin declined to act, however, in part because a sufficient number of legislators, elected under the revised 1978 constitution, rallied around him during the August coup. More importantly, in November 1991, the Congress approved broad emergency powers for Yeltsin, including the right to issue binding decrees. These emergency powers were only good for one year, but they nevertheless allowed Yeltsin's economic pronouncements to go into effect unless the Supreme Soviet objected within seven days.[34] With such authorization in hand, Yeltsin decided to keep the 1978 constitution—and sitting legislature—so that he could concentrate on economic reform.

Yeltsin used this decree authority to commence a major transformation of the Russian economy and commercial law, cutting subsidies to industries, freeing prices, and authorizing the privatization of major state enterprises.[35] From the very beginning of Yeltsin's reforms in 1991, however, the reliance on commercial law represented a true leap of faith. In Imperial Russia, the establishment of corporations was highly regulated and required a specific act of law before they could operate, while during the Soviet period all business consisted of state enterprises until Gorbachev's last-minute effort to create independent cooperatives. Yet despite this long-standing suspicion of the corporate structure, commercial law was the only instrument in the economic reformers' toolbox that could meet their immediate objectives; by privatizing factories, creating shareholders, and installing new management, the reformers could begin determining what enterprises still retained value and what businesses were no longer viable.[36] The alternative was to pursue a gradualist approach—to let a new system of Russian private law evolve and take root in society, an admittedly more appealing strategy, except that it meant spending money that the state did not possess and hoping that Russia did not revert back to Soviet law principles.

The relative merits of Yeltsin's economic reforms remain a subject of heated historical debate and criticism.[37] The transition to a market economy undoubtedly required certain bold steps, but this strategy was not without real economic hardship, and as the economy spiraled downward, the Congress began to clash with Yeltsin. His adversaries now included several prominent former allies. His vice president Aleksandr Rutskoi switched sides, increasingly presenting himself as the logical alternative to Yeltsin. Moreover, Ruslan Khasbulatov, the speaker of the Supreme Soviet (the permanent legislative body that met when the Congress was not in session) also moved to the opposition, even though he owed his position largely to Yeltsin's efforts.

Thus began a battle that is often characterized as a conflict between the executive and legislative branches. This observation, however, implies that there was some tradition of division of powers in Russian history, when in fact none existed. Indeed, the Russian executive branch had only been appended to the 1978 constitution in May 1991 with relatively weak powers.[38] Yeltsin did possess a national electoral mandate as well as the broad right to issue decrees, but only as so authorized by the Congress. He also held a political wildcard, namely his credibility as the person most directly associated with the 1991 revolution and the defeat of the Communist Party. Nevertheless, despite Yeltsin's lofty status, the law as written clearly favored the Congress of People's Deputies. Like Yeltsin, its members possessed their own mandates, having been elected in March 1990. More importantly, the intended beneficiary of the 1978 constitution—the Communist Party—had lost its monopoly status. Thus, the phrase "all power to the Soviets" once again came to life as the Supreme Soviet and the Congress assumed the sole authority under the 1978 constitution to pass laws.

As previously discussed, the difference between laws and decrees had not been strictly observed under the Soviet Union's inchoate sources of law. In the ensuing political battle between Yeltsin and the legislature, however, the distinction became critical. The Congress used its law-creating powers to derail Yeltsin on numerous fronts, both by asserting greater parliamentary control over the executive branch as well as by opposing major pieces of Yeltsin's economic agenda. The Supreme Soviet, for example, extracted several concessions from the government regarding its privatization plans, thereby ensuring that insider management and work collectives, and not outside shareholders, would retain majority control over privatized industry.[39] Thus, the anticipated rewards of privatization—determining the actual value of an enterprise, greater efficiency, increased capitalization—failed to materialize rapidly. Moreover, the Congress retained an additional advantage in its ability to change the rules of the game in midstream. As Yeltsin and Khasbulatov negotiated the terms of a possible referendum on a new constitution, the Supreme Soviet changed the law, eliminating the right of Russian citizens to call a referendum on their own initiative. Instead, this power became the exclusive prerogative of the Congress of People's Deputies, significantly limiting Yeltsin's ability to go directly to the people.[40]

An unlikely intermediary emerged during this struggle that hinted at a possible settlement to this crisis. On December 12, 1992, Valerii Zorkin, the head of the Russian Constitutional Court, managed to lower the tensions between the executive and legislative branches by brokering an agreement for a national referendum on Russia's future constitutional system. The Constitutional Court had only been in existence since October 1991, but during its short lifespan, the court had already issued several major decisions. It not only overturned Yeltsin's decree on merging the KGB and the Ministry of Internal Affairs, it also managed to convince Yeltsin to abide by the decision, thereby providing the first example in Russian history of a court declaring a government action unconstitutional.[41] Other decisions proved more difficult to enforce; the court could not prevent Tatarstan's referendum on independence, even though it held that the vote was illegal,[42] nor was it able to fully implement its (admittedly) convoluted decision on the legal status of the Communist Party.[43]

Zorkin's popularity soared in the aftermath of the December 1992 compromise, but by March 1993, the referendum was off the table, and the two branches of government were back at each other's throats. The Supreme Soviet further began to strip Yeltsin of his emergency powers, including his right to issue decrees.[44] In order to break this deadlock, Yeltsin announced on March 20, 1993, that he was imposing direct presidential rule, yet even before Yeltsin published his order, Zorkin and the Constitutional Court ruled that the president had violated nine clauses of the 1978 constitution. When Yeltsin actually published his decree four days later, he removed all of the controversial references, thereby rendering the court's decision moot. More importantly, from Yeltsin's perspective, Zorkin ceased to be an honest broker, sharply reducing the chances of political compromise.[45]

The feuding parties eventually agreed to hold a referendum, essentially asking the Russian people to choose between Yeltsin and the Congress of People's Deputies. On April 25, 1993, four questions were put forward, concerning the Russian people's confidence in President Yeltsin, their opinion of his socioeconomic program, and on whether elections were necessary for the president and parliament. For the referendum to be binding, however, a majority of all eligible Russian voters, and not a majority of those who actually voted, had to be achieved. Yeltsin fell short of this requirement. Nevertheless, the results from the referendum provided a major boost for Yeltsin, as he received clear majority support among the participating electorate both for his presidency and his policies.

Yet for a second time, Yeltsin failed to follow up a major political victory with decisive action. Instead, he convened a constitutional assembly in June 1993 that sought to bridge the gap between the Supreme Soviet's draft constitution and the constitution prepared by the presidential administration. The Supreme Soviet assigned major powers to the parliament, including the right to approve all government ministers, while precluding any right to dissolve the parliament and call early elections.[46] Ironically, Yeltsin initially had presided over the Supreme Soviet's constitutional commission when he served as the highest elected official of the RSFSR, but as president of the newly independent Russian Federation, Yeltsin's thinking clearly had shifted.[47] Therefore, Yeltsin proposed a pro-presidential system of government while insisting that the days of the soviets were over. According to Yeltsin, the current soviets were the direct descendants of those institutions that had usurped the lawful power of the Constituent Assembly in 1917 and could not be reformed. Soviets and democracy, Yeltsin concluded, were simply "incompatible."[48]

No consensus emerged as to the contents of the new constitution or whether it should be approved by the Congress or in a national referendum. By September 1993, the Supreme Soviet not only challenged Yeltsin's economic policies but was moving into foreign affairs and defense policy, matters that until then had been under exclusive presidential control.[49] Russian law degenerated into a slugfest of competing decrees issued by Yeltsin and Khasbulatov.[50] Such conflicting orders undermined any notion of the supremacy of law while simultaneously pushing the Russian Federation ever closer to collapse.

On September 21, 1993, Yeltsin issued decree number 1400, disbanding the Congress of People's Deputies and calling for new parliamentary elections. From a political standpoint, Yeltsin had reached a dead-end. He realized that the Congress would never adopt his constitution and that any attempt to bypass the Congress by holding a national plebiscite still required approval from the Congress, an impossibility in the current political environment.[51] In his speech to the nation, Yeltsin referred to his 1991 election as president in a nationwide election—as well as the results of the April referendum—as granting him the authority to issue such a decree. He further justified his actions by stating that the decree provided the only means to save Russia's infant democracy and economic reforms. His final card, however, was the need to defend the one institution that had governed Russia for centuries: the state. According to Yeltsin, the only way to overcome "the paralysis of state power in the Russia Federation" was through constitutional reform.[52] Therefore, as the "guarantor of the security of our state, I am obliged to break this ruinous vicious circle."[53] Failure to act, he added, could have catastrophic consequences; it could lead to the "disintegration of the Russian state," a country that still possessed "an enormous arsenal of nuclear weapons."[54]

Thus, Yeltsin acted both in the name of democracy and the preservation of the Russian state, two principles that historically occupied opposite ends of the Russian political spectrum. Yeltsin's justifications, however, could not overcome the fact that he had also acted in clear violation of prevailing law. The Congress responded by stripping Yeltsin of his authority, while the Constitutional Court concluded that Yeltsin's decree served as grounds for impeachment. The ensuing two-week standoff ultimately was resolved by force. The defenders of the Supreme Soviet broke through the police cordon surrounding the White House on the night of October 3, 1993, and they nearly succeeded in capturing the main television station. Yeltsin responded the next day by ordering tanks to fire on the Russian White House—the symbol of his 1991 triumph—ending the crisis and leaving 187 people (according to official statistics) dead in the process.[55]

In the aftermath of this violence, Yeltsin announced new parliamentary elections as well as a national plebiscite on the new constitution to be approved by a simple majority of participating voters. In choosing this path, Yeltsin sought to limit the involvement of the regions, which were making increased demands for greater sovereignty.[56] He also skirted the constraints of the law on referendum, which required a majority of eligible, as opposed to participating, voters. Finally, in light of the Constitutional Court's support of the Supreme Soviet during the October events, Yeltsin suspended the court indefinitely, although no individual justice was removed.

Not surprisingly, Yeltsin selected his pro-presidential draft constitution for consideration, and on December 12, 1993, the new constitution was ratified by 58.4 percent of the participating electorate. The vote was not an overwhelming mandate for Russia's new founding law; only 54.8 percent of all eligible voters even participated in the plebiscite.[57] Moreover, it took a month to publish the official results, inevitably leading to charges of fraud in calculating the final tally.

Conclusion

Historians will long debate whether the rule of law was saved—or betrayed—by the events of October 1993. The letter of the law may have been violated, but according to Russian legal expert Leonid Batkin, by 1993, "constitutionalism" had become "a refuge for reactionaries, communists, as well as nationalists, who wished to restore the status quo."[58] Had Yeltsin defeated the Soviet Union only to see the reestablishment of Soviet law, with its long-standing biases against private law, civil liberties, and the division of powers? In the end, despite all the clouds that hung over the plebiscite, the new constitution was broadly accepted as the law of the land. Oleg Rumiantsev, the head of the Supreme Soviet's constitutional commission, suggests that part of the reason was political fatigue: "The vast majority of political forces in the country were exhausted, just tired to death of the enervating political battles and confrontations."[59] The constitution was also accepted, according to Rumiantsev, because the political classes had no choice. "All the problems with its adoption and its birth trauma were accepted as a lesser evil than having no fundamental law at all."[60] The last bulwark of Soviet power—the 1978 constitution—was dismantled, and Russia finally moved into the post-Soviet era.

8

The 1993 Constitution: A Framework for Reform

The 1993 constitution set the agenda for the future development of Russian law. Much still needed to be done. The constitution's legal hierarchy, which placed laws over decrees, still had to be enforced. The nature of center-regional relations demanded further clarification, property rights required more concrete protections, and basic corporate law structures still had to be put into place. Finally, the existing legal institutions, and in particular the judiciary, needed to be transformed to meet the advanced rule-of-law standards set forth in the country's new founding law. Yeltsin pursued reform in all of the above areas, yet none would go according to plan or live up to their original expectations.

This chapter provides a detailed analysis of the 1993 constitution and its subsequent implementation during the Yeltsin presidency. It pays particular attention to the three main philosophical pillars—federalist, democratic, and statist—that were articulated within the constitution. Yeltsin relied on all three principles, paradoxically turning himself into both a pro-Western legal reformer and a staunch defender of Russian state power. Yeltsin's legacy further would be affected by the politicians and businessmen who took advantage of his reforms to gain wealth and power and who subsequently used the law to protect their interests. As this chapter demonstrates, the 1990s included several important legal milestones. Yeltsin undoubtedly took steps that reconnected Russia with the general norms and practices of the continental civil law tradition. Yet overcoming the Soviet legacy, forging a common political and economic space, and transforming existing legal institutions proved much more difficult than originally expected. The chaos and corruption that accompanied the process of legal reform have left a lasting stain on Yeltsin's overall reputation as a politician and a transformational leader.

The 1993 constitution

Starting in the late 1980s, Russian politicians and legal scholars made multiple visits abroad to learn from experts about the major Western constitutions. The American constitution initially attracted much interest, in light of its democratic traditions, institutional restraints, unique status, and ability to shape both government and politics.[1] Over time, however, Russians turned to continental examples of parliamentary and mixed systems, such as the French semi-presidential model. One can identify various American, French, German, Belgian, and Spanish ideas in the 1993 Russian constitution.[2] However, the most immediate influence remained the bitter political standoff that directly preceded its adoption, as well as the broader historical context that shaped these events. Thus, as discussed in detail below, the 1993 constitution stands out as a product of Russian history with numerous links to its statist past, rather than a wholesale foreign borrowing.[3]

One of the most distinctive features of the 1993 constitution concerned the prominent role given to the Russian state. No one chapter articulated the power of the state, yet it was omnipresent from the start. The constitution's preamble spoke of the need to preserve Russia's historic "state unity" and of renewing its "sovereign statehood."[4] Article 5(3) declared that the federative makeup of the Russian Federation would be based upon its "state integrity" and a "uniform system of state power." The "unity" of the Russian state was also described under Article 77(2), where the executive bodies of federal and regional government formed "a single system of executive power in the Russian Federation."

The 1993 constitution divided "state power" along federal and regional lines; but, while this term was nowhere defined in the constitution, it carried ominous historical overtones. State power was associated with the unconstrained use of force by the autocracy and Stalin's dictatorship of the proletariat as well. Some post-Soviet scholars describe modern-day state power in relatively benign terms, linking the idea to general notions of sovereignty and standard governing institutions.[5] Other commentators, however, associate state power with rudimentary force. According to one definition, state power is:

> a system of relations of supremacy and subordination, a concentrated expression of will and force of the dominating social, national stratum (class, nation) or of the people, embodied in the state-legal institutions. [State power] guarantees stability and order in society, defends its citizens from external and internal encroachments by utilizing various methods and means, including state coercion and military force.[6]

Prior to 1993, state power had never been equated with democracy in Russia, yet the Yeltsin constitution attempted to make just such a connection. Under

Article 3, the multinational people of the Russian Federation represent the highest source of power, but they exercise their sovereignty both directly as well as through bodies of state power and local self-government. State power also stands at the center of an ambiguous and fundamental provision of the Russian constitution. Article 10 declared that "state power shall be exercised on the basis of a division (*razdelenie*) into legislative, executive, and judicial branches." These bodies, the clause continued, "shall be autonomous." Western analysts naturally turned to the second half of the clause and highlighted a notion of separation of powers as the essence of the provision. Russian commentators, however, noted that Article 10 began with a notion of state power, which under Russian legal theory at all times remains single and unified, and then introduced a division of functions that operated as part of a united state system.[7] Therefore, rather than marking a radical transformation, Article 10 can be seen as establishing a fundamental contradiction at the heart of the Russian constitution. The provision incorporated the idea of a division of powers but subordinated it to the principle of a single system of state power. Thus, a reasonable interpretation under Article 10, as noted by a prominent Russian jurist, would be to refer to the judiciary as an "organ of state power" (i.e., a part of the state apparatus) as opposed to an equal and independent branch of government.[8]

Who, then, exercises state power under the 1993 constitution? The answer is not one of the three designated branches of government, nor an overarching system of checks and balances, but the president of the Russian Federation. Technically, the president was not included in Article 10, since under the 1993 constitution, the executive branch refers to the government headed by the prime minister. Article 11, however, listed the president first among the other main branches of government (the legislature, the government, and the courts) entitled to exercise state power. The presidency also appeared first in the constitution's enumeration of the four main governing institutions. According to Article 80, the president served as head of state and guarantor of the constitution. The president further was responsible for protecting the sovereignty, independence, security, and state integrity of the Russian Federation while ensuring the coordination and integration of the organs of state power.

Other presidential powers under the 1993 constitution included the right to appoint the head of the government (the prime minister), dissolve the Duma, mediate intergovernmental disputes, sign international treaties, and serve as commander in chief. Article 85 further granted the president quasi-judicial powers by allowing the president to suspend acts of regional executive authorities prior to a judicial determination. The president can be impeached by a two-thirds vote in both houses of the legislature. However, if the State Duma (the lower house) twice votes no confidence in the government over three months, or three times rejects the president's nominee for prime minister, the president can dissolve the Duma and call for new elections.[9]

In light of recent history, Yeltsin made sure that in any future confrontation between the Duma and the president, it would be the Duma that faced the prospect of imminent dismissal. The legislature's primary counterweight against presidential power was its right to approve all federal laws, including laws related to the federal budget, taxes, international treaties, and peace and war.[10] The constitution further called for the passage of federal constitutional laws by a supermajority vote in order to implement certain requirements specified within the constitution itself. The president retained the right to veto legislation, but this veto could be overridden by a two-thirds vote in both the Duma and the upper house (the Federation Council).

But while the legislature remained the only body that could pass a formal "law" (*zakon*), it was not the only institution that could propose legislation. The 1993 constitution preserved the long-running tradition (dating back to at least the early nineteenth century) of providing the right of legislative initiative to multiple institutions, including the president, the government, the three high courts, and the legislative bodies of the subjects of the Russian Federation. More importantly, the president under Article 90 preserved the right to issue decrees and orders that are obligatory on the entire territory of the Russian Federation. The only limitation on the president's decree authority pursuant to the 1993 constitution was that these directives cannot violate the constitution or federal laws. The Russian government also received the right to issue its own decisions and orders under Article 115 so as to implement federal law and the normative decrees of the Russian president. The president can cancel such orders, but they do carry some legislative weight: the normative acts of the government (and the president) can be appealed to the Constitutional Court to review their compliance with the constitution.[11]

Therefore, as throughout Russian history, the sources of Russian law included a combination of laws, decrees, and various administrative orders. The 1993 constitution, however, imposed a specific legal hierarchy on this legislation. The constitution served as the highest source of law, followed by federal constitutional laws, federal laws, presidential decrees, and administrative orders. The constitution also contained a legal wildcard: international law. Article 15(4) stated that the universally recognized principles and norms of international law and international treaties and agreements of the Russian Federation shall be a part of its legal system. Treaties regularly are incorporated into domestic law, so the clause appeared fairly standard and provoked little discussion. What made this provision exceptional was its openness to the "principles and norms" of international law. As will be discussed in Chapter 9, after Russia joined the Council of Europe in 1998, decisions by the European Court of Human Rights began to be cited in Constitutional Court and other domestic court determinations. By so doing, the court acknowledged a non-Russian source of law that nevertheless had direct ramifications for Russian justice.

In addition to the horizontal division of powers between the three branches of government, the constitution introduced a vertical division of powers between the center and the regions. Article 5(1) recognized all territorial subdivisions within Russia (republics, districts, regions, etc.) as equal, thereby upholding the essential unity of the Russian Federation. Article 71 provided a long list of topics (organization of the federation, foreign policy, the federal budget, customs, human rights, etc.) under exclusive federal jurisdiction, while Article 72 contained an equally detailed list of topics under the "joint" jurisdiction of federal and regional authorities. The matters under "joint jurisdiction" included taxation, public health, family issues, human rights, and the demarcation of federal property. Finally, Article 73 assigned all residual authority to the regions.

Previous Soviet constitutions had attempted to itemize various federal and regional powers. For most of the Soviet Union's existence, however, these designations possessed little practical significance, since the Communist Party controlled all levels of government and its centralized decision-making left little room for local experimentation. The 1993 constitution opened up the possibility of a genuine federal state, but the above provisions were, in many ways, as unrealizable as their Soviet predecessors. For example, the constitution was far from clear as to how federal and regional law would be harmonized to regulate matters under joint jurisdiction. Moreover, what did it mean, in terms of actual legislation, that human rights were subject to both federal and joint jurisdiction?

This ambiguity was only compounded by the fact that Articles 71 and 72 did not exhaust the 1993 constitution's discussion of center-regional relations. Russian federalism was also governed by the most traditional means of delimiting authority between the center and the regions, namely the treaty process. Article 11(3) specifically upheld the right of federal state organs to transfer unspecified authorities and powers via treaty to the regions. Other constitutional provisions further contributed to regional inequalities and the development of asymmetrical federalism. National republics retained the right to enact their own constitutions as well as the right to establish their own state languages.[12] The other regions were not without their own founding charters but the republics seemingly possessed a higher status; well into the first decade of the 2000s, the leaders of republics carried the more prestigious title of "president," while the heads of regions were simply known as "governor." The constitutional distinction among the constituent parts of the Russian Federation as well as the incorporation of the treaty-making process directly into the 1993 constitution—would have major consequences for Russia's internal stability during the Yeltsin's presidency as the country teetered between federation and confederation.

The most progressive section of the 1993 constitution concerned the civil rights and liberties set forth in Chapter 2. For the first time in Russian constitutional history, the chapter heading defining the rights and freedoms of Russian citizens was not immediately qualified by certain state obligations and duties. Indeed, from a theoretical standpoint, the Soviet dissidents—by commandeering Soviet legality as a means to assert basic rule-of-law principles—had won the day. Article 2 proudly declared that "man, his rights and freedoms, are the supreme value" and that it was the state's obligation to recognize, observe, and protect these freedoms. The constitution proceeded to list the universally recognized civil liberties and human rights: equality before the law and the court, the right to privacy, freedom of movement, freedom of speech, freedom of religion, the right to association, the right to own property, and the right to engage in entrepreneurial and economic activities as otherwise not prohibited by law. No state ideology could be imposed, and all public associations were considered equal before the law.[13] The above rights only could be limited by federal law, and even in that case, only to the extent necessary to protect the fundamental principles of the constitutional system, morality, health, the rights of other people, and national security.[14] The primary duties imposed on Russian citizens by the constitution were paying taxes, preserving the environment, and defending the country—a dramatic departure from the 1977 Soviet constitution that included demands on citizens to train their children for socially useful work and more generally directed them to comply with the standards of socialist conduct.

The 1993 constitution followed up these basic civil liberties with fundamental due process principles.[15] Moreover, in an implicit reference to the Judicial Reforms of 1864, the 1993 constitution restored the right to be tried before a jury in those cases defined in federal law.[16] The listing of these civil rights and criminal protections was largely aspirational.[17] The commentator Leonid Batkin noted that "there is much here that is new and substantive for citizens of Russia, although it is like a suit of clothes they must grow into."[18] The above rights, however, were not exhaustive; Article 7 proudly proclaimed that Russia also was a social state, and the constitution listed numerous social rights, including, the right to free medical care and education, social security, and various types of creative activity. The Soviet advancement of social rights, therefore, was directly incorporated into the 1993 constitution, providing yet another historical link in Russia's constitutional evolution.

The final major section of the 1993 constitution dealt with the question of judicial power. Article 120 recognized the independence of the judiciary, and subsequent provisions provided judges with grants of irremovability and immunity. Three distinct high courts were originally established under the constitution—the Constitutional Court, the Supreme Court, and the Higher Commercial (*Arbitrazh*) Court—each containing specific grants of jurisdiction, although in practice, some overlap invariably existed. Only the Constitutional Court's jurisdiction was spelled out in detail, a reaction to the court's political engagement during the previous year.[19] Various government bodies received the right to appeal different types of legislation (i.e., laws, decrees, treaties) to the Constitutional Court, while individual citizens could only petition in cases involving violations of federal law.[20]

Chapter 7 on judicial power contained one last, and rather incongruous, provision dealing with the procuracy. This influential and longest-running legal institution barely survived the constitutional crisis of 1991–1993. Many reformers had called for the abolition of the procuracy's supervisory powers and oversight over criminal investigations, and it was only thanks to the last-minute intervention by the Procurator-General Aleksei Kazannik that a proposed constitutional provision limiting the procuracy to prosecuting criminals was removed.[21] Instead, the 1993 constitution included a general provision (Article 129) that defined the procuracy's structure and appointment procedures but left its actual powers to be defined by later legislation. Therefore, the 1993 constitution, unlike its Soviet predecessor, contained no explicit recognition of the procuracy's right to supervise the implementation of laws. The procuracy lost the right of legislative initiative; nor was it one of the recognized state institutions empowered to appeal directly to the Constitutional Court.[22] Even the chapter heading assigned to the procuracy under the 1993 constitution—judicial power—appeared ill chosen, since the procuracy was not a part of the judiciary and, by process of elimination—since it possessed no legislative power—belonged to the executive branch.[23] A diminished procuracy emerged from the new constitution; however, it retained significant political connections—and leverage—to fight another day.

On the surface, the 1993 constitution contained the standard institutions and liberties necessary to transform Russia into what it proclaimed to be in Article 1—a democratic, federal, law-based state with a republican form of government. Commentators recognized the lop-sided powers granted to the president, but one nevertheless could still identify such fundamental building blocks as a division of powers, a law-creating legislature, an independent judiciary, and a detailed and largely unqualified articulation of civil rights and freedoms. Russia still needed to implement these institutions and principles—a daunting task—yet the general scaffolding appeared to be in place.

But while many commentators aptly referred to the 1993 constitution as super-presidential, it could have just as well been described as traditionally statist, for within the 1993 constitution were all the tools and legal principles that had governed an empire for centuries.[24] This inheritance included the centrality of state power, a flexible treaty-making process to forge a unified state, the right to issue decrees, and the broad assignment of legislative initiative to multiple branches of government. Moreover, even though the 1993 constitution punted on the question of the procuracy's general supervisory authority, the procuracy retained its long-standing pro-statist orientation and a place in Russia's founding legislation. Throw in the preservation of social rights from the Soviet Union, and an alternative constitution emerges, one that emphasizes a more conservative and traditional understanding of Russian and Soviet law.

Defining Russian federalism

The most immediate practical problem confronting Yeltsin in 1993 concerned the national question. The new constitution supplanted the 1992 Federation Treaty that Yeltsin had signed to keep the country together during the constitutional crisis. Nevertheless, doubts remained whether Tatarstan, Chechnya, and other republics would accept the new distribution of authority under Articles 71–73. To clarify this relationship and make a stronger federation, Yeltsin entered into a bilateral treaty with Tatarstan on February 15, 1994. Additional treaties followed so that eventually forty-seven out of eighty-nine regions would have such bilateral agreements in place.[25]

Yet far from clarifying the situation, the treaties only exacerbated the country's asymmetrical relations and generated greater legal confusion. On a theoretical level, the treaties were neither federal constitutional laws nor federal laws, since they had not been approved by the legislature, nor had they been published according to the official legal requirements.[26] Therefore, their legal standing remained tenuous at best. Moreover, on the practical side, the treaties contained numerous tax breaks and other economic concessions, thereby creating unequal relationships between Moscow and the individual regions. The treaties further obscured the issue of sovereignty. The Tatarstan treaty, for example, did not even refer to the republic's status as a subject of the Russian Federation; instead, the treaty appeared to be an agreement between two sovereign states as reinforced when Tatarstan began to establish its own overseas representation offices.[27] Numerous other legal irregularities appeared in these treaties, including assertions of a right of secession when the 1993 constitution (unlike its Soviet predecessors) did not recognize such claims.

In reality, Yeltsin stretched the historic idea of the unified state to its absolute extreme in order to keep the country together. The roots of Yeltsin's strategy could be found in tsarist Russia's treaty-making process, with the crucial distinction being that these long-ago agreements had been a sign of military victory and imperial expansion, not political retrenchment. Nevertheless, tsars had signed treaties with different national groups on numerous occasions, incorporating them into an empire based on the fundamental concession that the region recognize the ultimate sovereignty of the supreme ruler. For much of the imperial period, the tsar was willing to tolerate significant legal diversity as long as that critical promise was extracted from the region. It was only at the end of the tsarist period—and during the Soviet Union—that the treaty-making process was accompanied by attempts to forge a more uniform and national system of laws. Yeltsin's central institutions were too weak to pursue such a strategy in 1993, so the president essentially retreated to early imperial notions of Russian statehood and legal pluralism. But despite Yeltsin's sacrifice of legal uniformity for the sake of national unity, the regions' recognition of Moscow's sovereignty remained shaky at best.

Most radically, Chechnya refused to commit itself to the unified state. Chechnya had declared its independence in September 1991 and essentially escaped Moscow's oversight for the next two years. The prospect of transporting oil through the south Caucasus brought the republic under renewed scrutiny, and when it continued to defy Moscow, Russian troops attacked on December 11, 1994. Despite promises of an easy victory, the Russian army proved incapable of retaking the republic, and when a ceasefire was finally declared in 1996, Chechnya *de facto* achieved independence. Chechnya represented more than a military defeat for Yeltsin; human rights violations perpetrated by the military on a massive scale severely undermined the promises of civil rights expounded upon in the 1993 constitution. The human rights community decisively broke with Yeltsin in the aftermath of the Chechen war, and though Yeltsin may be credited for allowing independent—and highly critical—media coverage of the conflict, his reputation as a "democrat" never recovered.

The Chechen war subsequently would have an even broader impact on the evolution of Russian law. In 1995, the invasion of Chechnya became the one of the first high-profile cases argued before the re-instated Constitutional Court. Representatives from the Duma and the Federation Council challenged Yeltsin's legal right to attack Chechnya without first consulting the legislature and without following the procedures set forth in the law on the state of emergency and other existing legislation. A convoluted discussion of the legal issues accompanied the oral arguments as Yeltsin's lawyers disputed whether legislation that predated the 1993 constitution still applied to the unique circumstances in Chechnya. In the end, the Constitutional Court ruled that the preservation of national integrity and the broad powers granted to the president under the 1993 constitution trumped Russia's nascent system of checks and balances, especially in times of national crisis.[28] In other words, the Court—whether knowingly or not—confirmed the essential legal principle that had governed Russia for centuries, namely that the preservation of state unity prevails over any body of legal regulation.

The Constitutional Court was strongly criticized for not holding the government accountable for its human rights violations in Chechnya. In many ways, however, the Constitutional Court had no good options; it had already been suspended once, and a second confrontation most likely would have resulted in the court's dissolution and the transfer of constitutional disputes to the Supreme Court.[29] Here the Court took into account political realities in its decision, but it avoided the direct engagement in politics that had characterized its predecessor during the 1992–1993 crisis. Thus, by pursuing a more discreet, less confrontational strategy, the Court reestablished its ability to engage in constitutional review.[30] Over the next few years, the Court issued numerous decisions clarifying the rights and due process requirements set forth in the constitution. The Court published both its final rulings and all dissenting special opinions, as well as referenced its past decisions within the body of its determinations, thereby creating an informal system of precedent. The Constitutional Court, however, still faced serious difficulties in implementing its decisions, particularly in cases involving federalism; on three separate occasions during the 1990s, for example, the court declared that the internal passport and registration system (*propiska*) violated the constitutionally protected right of freedom of movement, yet this practice persists to the present day.[31]

The inability to enforce court decisions confirmed that despite the enhanced status of the judiciary under the 1993 constitution, any final resolution of center-regional relations required a political answer. Ironically, Yeltsin straddled both sides of the issue. He welcomed the Constitutional Court's push for a more symmetrical federalism and increased central powers. At the same time, he was the primary driver of the treaty-making process that, while devolving significant power to the regions, established fundamental inequalities among the subjects of the Russian Federation as well. Yeltsin tried to address the problem in 1997 by appointing presidential representatives in the regions, but by then most governors had been popularly elected and felt little need to heed the word from Moscow. The end result was a more democratic but highly fragmented state where top-down legality, which for centuries had been considered a critical element of Russian governance, essentially stopped working.

Legal modernization and economic reform

The 1993 constitution sparked a second fundamental legal transformation in the areas of property rights, commercial law, and private law. The new constitution included such fundamental rights as the right to possess, use, and dispose of property; freedom of contract; and the protection of intellectual property, to name just the most prominent. While such rights are standard features in any Western legal system, one must recognize the historic nature of their inclusion in the Russian constitution. The 1993 constitution did not simply overturn seventy-plus years of socialism, which clearly discriminated against most types of private ownership. It further crossed a philosophical threshold that Imperial Russia failed to cross in the decades leading up to 1917, namely the broad recognition of property rights as a fundamental civil right. In a nod to the immediate Soviet past, the drafters balanced property rights with social rights. Nevertheless, the 1993 constitution should be recognized for peacefully resolving an issue that had divided Russian society for centuries.

Critical legislation soon gave these economic rights more substance. Parts 1 and 2 of the Civil Code were introduced in 1995 and 1996, respectively, containing all the legal mechanisms—including contract rights, an interstate commerce clause, and commercial (corporate) law—to transform Russia into a market economy.[32] As Soviet law lacked these basic procedures, Russia borrowed from Dutch, Italian, and Swiss law to flesh out the internal workings of its new civil law system.[33] The Russian Civil Code, however, provided more than just the ground rules for a capitalist economy. It also served as the "economic constitution" of the Russian Federation that simultaneously reinforced the hierarchy of laws set forth in the 1993 constitution. For example, Article 3(3) specifically allowed the president to regulate civil legislation, but not if his executive decrees contradicted the Civil Code or other laws. In such instances, the law always trumped a decree. Furthermore, the Civil Code preempted any regional legislation that conflicted with it, thereby making Russian private law truly national in scope.[34]

Only once before in Russian history, under the 1906 Fundamental Laws, had law definitively superseded decrees and then only with major loopholes. Yeltsin's acrimonious relationship with the Duma from 1994 onward is well-documented—the parliament's first act upon reconvening in 1994 was to approve an amnesty for the instigators of the October 1993 events, and in 1999 the Duma nearly impeached Yeltsin for (among other things) the collapse of the Soviet Union.[35] Nevertheless, Yeltsin largely accepted this new legal hierarchy, and he coaxed significant civil and commercial legislation out of a reluctant Duma. In addition to the Civil Code, Yeltsin signed laws on joint stock companies, limited liability companies, anti-monopoly regulations, Part 1 of the new tax code, and bankruptcy. Moreover, the failure to pass legislation and instead rely on decrees often did not produce the desired results. For example, the Duma never approved a law on the privatization of land, and although Yeltsin began the process via decree, significant legal uncertainty persisted concerning ownership rights until such a time that the Duma approved a law. Yeltsin tried to jumpstart reform via decree in other areas as well, such as the reorganization of state welfare benefits, but he could never get the Duma to go along with these changes, and without a law, his welfare reform agenda soon stalled.[36]

Yeltsin could still deliver targeted economic benefits via decree—a genuine source of power and corruption—but such executive orders were not sufficient for many major initiatives.[37] Yeltsin therefore presided over a subtle yet fundamental shift in Russian law. He still exercised state power and reserved almost exclusive discretion over how to maintain the unity of the country. Nevertheless, his ability to rule directly by decree was limited by the need to seek legislative approval of his policies, thereby leading to an uneasy separation of powers during his presidency. He also raised the level of legal transparency as all major laws were published and often accompanied by legal commentaries that addressed how the statute was being interpreted. Practicing attorneys with sufficient resources could also access legal databases that grouped relevant laws, decrees, and court decisions together and could be easily updated as new legislation was approved. Thus, the inchoate organization of Soviet sources of law gave way to a much more systematic presentation of the law of the Russian Federation.

Russia's newly established legal hierarchy and growing commercial legislative base provided renewed optimism for Yeltsin's pursuit of economic modernization. As previously mentioned, the first round of post-Soviet privatization did not live up to expectations. In 1992, the Supreme Soviet changed the direction of the program by allowing existing Soviet management—as opposed to outside investors—to remain in control of former state enterprises. Long-standing Soviet managers were not concerned with the niceties of corporate law, such as observing the independence of the board of directors, obtaining shareholder approval for major transactions, or even going to court to sue deadbeat partners.[38] While so-called red directors largely remained on top, the average Russian worker was left out in the cold. Individuals were granted vouchers to bid on companies, but they were often sold to speculators like "worthless candy wrappers."[39] Needless to say, this early round of privatization did not create a nation of shareholders; instead, people became increasingly disillusioned with the supposed efficiency of private law and the market as they watched Soviet assets being purchased for pennies on the dollar.

The privatization process did allow individuals with foresight and resources to purchase state companies and to accumulate major property holdings, thereby producing in the mid-1990s a new class of Russians: the oligarchs. These ambitious businessmen purchased vouchers in bulk to acquire state assets, often over the strong resistance of the previous enterprise directors. The optimism surrounding private law could not mask, or compensate for, the lawlessness that accompanied the rise of the oligarchs. As the journalist David Hoffman notes, money and property "brought competition and conflict. And conflict needed a place to settle its disputes, but since the rules were still not drawn—the laws not enforced, the courts not effective—the new money and property interests created their own rules outside the law, using bribery and corruption, using violence and coercion, all of which could easily be purchased."[40]

The oligarchs, however, at least theoretically bought into the concept of private and commercial law and any accompanying respectability that might come with it. The other new prominent economic player—organized crime—showed no such inclination. These "violent entrepreneurs," as the Russian sociologist Vadim Volkov dubbed them, engaged in various protection rackets and acts of extortion for financial gain, with no apparent qualms about using force when required.[41] Supply quickly met demand as legitimate business could not rely on the courts to enforce contracts or collect debts, thereby forcing them to seek alternative means of enforcement and/or protection. By the mid-1990s, former members of the security services also entered the protection business. They relied on their connections with their former state agencies to provide a "roof" for their clients, and while such arrangements obviously raised corruption issues, the private protection companies paradoxically helped limit the expansion of organized crime. With time, a desire to protect dubiously acquired property even began to shift incentives toward the use of the law.[42]

It was the oligarchs, however, who remained the public face of privatization and Russian capitalism, and they only became more rapacious over time. As the 1996 presidential election approached, they used the cover of commercial law to gain control of some of the most valuable assets in the country. The deal known as loans-for-shares essentially boiled down to low-interest loans from oligarchs to a cash-strapped government in exchange for shares in state companies as collateral. Two additional considerations sweetened the deal: 1. the oligarchs could actually manage the companies while they were theoretically only temporary owners and 2. the auctions for these shares would be organized by the oligarchs themselves. Thus, in the most egregious example, Mikhail Khodorkovskii's bank (Menatep) organized the auction of a state oil company that (surprise, surprise) was won by Khodorkovskii. Vladimir Potanin walked away with 38 percent of Norilsk Nickel, a metals-producing giant, while Boris Berezovskii gained control of the oil company Sibneft. All of them barely bid above the starting price, and all three soon joined the ranks of billionaires.[43] The loans-for-shares deal demonstrated just how far privatization had strayed from its original goals, in the process discrediting the commercial and private law principles that were supposed to provide the legal foundation for a modernizing, capitalist Russia.

The cynicism surrounding private law only made its primary alternative—state capitalism—that much more attractive. The leading proponent of this approach was the mayor of Moscow Yurii Luzhkov, who had kept Yeltsin's national privatization program out of the city and instead pursued his own brand of economic reform. Luzhkov possessed a key advantage, namely that Moscow served as Russia's financial hub and therefore he had access to resources that simply were not available to other cities. Luzhkov's model centered on the link between government and business, where Luzhkov himself, and not the market, picked the winners and losers. The results were outwardly impressive—new buildings, monuments, restaurants, roads—but they came with extreme corruption that enriched the bureaucrat and a few select businessmen.[44] Yet even as Luzhkov and his wife (the owner of a major construction company) acquired great wealth, he still retained a popular touch with voters and found creative ways to extract money from business to pay for basic social services and his glossy image of a renewed Moscow.[45]

Practitioners of state capitalism emerged in other cities as well. Most notably, an enterprising deputy mayor in St. Petersburg named Vladimir Putin used his administrative powers to issue licenses and contracts that returned significant financial rewards to him and his coterie of friends.[46] Both privatization and state capitalism contributed to breaking the foundation of the planned economy and socialist law. Yet in order to regulate this process, Yeltsin pushed through a new system of private law that, while necessary for modernization, had no established roots in post-Soviet Russian society. Oligarchs, organized crime, and corrupt bureaucrats equally relied on private law to conduct business but without buying into the underlying pro-market reform agenda. Indeed, they all believed in property rights and corporate protections to the extent that they were happy to send their profits abroad to shell companies located in various offshore tax havens. As a result, Yeltsin never received the economic and political payback for his commercial law reforms.

Yeltsin's economic legislation was not totally in vain. Despite unprecedented levels of corruption, private law practices began to filter down into everyday life. In 1998, in the aftermath of yet another financial crash, Russian entrepreneurs filled the gap left behind by departing Western businesses, relying on the legal protections within Russian commercial and property laws to pursue their investments.[47] At the same time, the many irregularities that accompanied the privatization process only served to discredit Russia's nascent commercial and private law, thereby undermining Yeltsin's economic reforms and opening the way to the return of state capitalism.

Re-balancing Russia's legal institutions and the pursuit of judicial independence

A final area of legal reform that consumed significant attention under Yeltsin's presidency concerned the relationship between the three main pillars of justice: the judiciary, procuracy, and *advokatura*. The *Conception of Judicial Reform* published in October 1991 by leading scholars and criminal law specialists served as the main blueprint for judicial reform until the mid-1990s. Judicial independence represented the *Conception*'s ultimate goal, and the reformers introduced several measures to raise the status of the judiciary, including life tenure for judges (albeit with an initial probationary period), the establishment of independent corporate bodies with control over admissions and disciplinary actions, significant judicial oversight over pretrial investigations, and judicial review of complaints against government officials.[48] The authors of the *Conception* further demanded increased state support for the legal system—and for the salaries and social benefits of individual judges—to ensure that the judiciary achieved true independence.

Other institutional reforms occurred as well, including a push away from the inquisitorial system of justice and toward more adversarial proceedings. The hallmark of this reform was the reintroduction of jury trials. Gorbachev actually called for jury trials as part of his criminal justice reforms, but legislation restoring the jury was only approved in July 1993. Jury trials initially were piloted in nine regions and only covered "serious" felonies, thereby limiting their potential impact.[49] Jury trials faced major logistical and legal challenges. Russian courtrooms were not built to seat a jury, so new facilities had to be prepared. Judges also had to adapt to their new role as impartial arbiters, as opposed to *de facto* representatives of the state. Notably, the Russian jury system possessed its own procedural rules that differed from the Anglo-American system. For example, the aggrieved person was allowed to participate as an equal party at trial with the right to introduce motions, cross-examine witnesses, make a closing argument, and appeal a final judgment. Like other civil law countries, all jury verdicts could be appealed, including not-guilty verdicts.[50] Some commentators questioned whether the reintroduction of jury trials was worth the financial cost, but juries were at least willing to acquit—a statistical rarity in the Soviet system—and trial judges enjoyed the enhanced stature that accompanied presiding over a jury trial.

But while jury trials held both historical and practical value, their small rollout during the 1990s inevitably limited their impact on the Russian criminal justice system. A much broader transformation occurred in commercial law with the conversion of the Soviet state commercial (*arbitrazh*) system into one of the three constitutionally mandated judicial branches, complete with its own supreme court (the Higher Commercial Court) to set its agenda. The commercial courts covered economic disputes between legal entities, and between legal entities and the government. The 1995 passage of the Commercial Procedural Code lowered fees for filing cases while demanding more adversarial proceedings, resulting in a noticeable increase in the use of the commercial courts by the end of the 1990s.[51] But while the commercial courts became more professional and gradually integrated a new cadre of judges, the enforcement of decisions remained a persistent problem.[52]

By the mid-1990s, the *Conception* was replaced by a more moderate agenda that focused on practical concerns, such as the financing of courts and the need to tame the growing caseload assigned to individual judges.[53] The latter problem was addressed in 1998 by creating a new layer of adjudication to handle smaller claims—the justice of the peace court—which borrowed its name from its distant tsarist predecessor. Yet while an independent judiciary served as the *sine qua non* of the legal reformers, this goal proved elusive as other informal means of state control reasserted themselves. The perseverance of old habits and practices was most visible in the courts of general jurisdiction where the bulk of Russia's criminal and civil cases take place. In particular, the chairman of the courts retained significant control over the distribution of cases, as well as the career advancement of individual judges.[54] Regional officials also possessed significant input in the judicial appointment process, which naturally encouraged judges to avoid offending local politicians.[55] Given that no lustration of the judiciary occurred, Soviet judges, along with Soviet mindsets and incentives, continued to populate the courts of general jurisdiction.

The failure to transform the judiciary created an opening for Russia's longest-running legal institution—the procuracy—to regain some of its clout. Most importantly, the 1995 law on the *prokuratura* incorporated most of the procuracy's standard supervisory powers over the implementation of legislation and administrative organs, as well as the right to investigate any violation of the civil liberties and freedoms articulated within the 1993 constitution. The procuracy further received the right to participate in law-creating (*pravotvorchestvo*) activities, thereby at least partially addressing the 1993 constitution's failure to reaffirm the procuracy's right of legislative initiative. Finally, while the procuracy lost the right to supervise the courts, it otherwise kept its power of general supervision and the ability to hear citizen complaints.[56]

Therefore, the procuracy fundamentally remained a pro-statist institution with most of its traditional powers intact. It just never fell in line with the Yeltsin regime. Instead, Yeltsin regularly clashed with the procuracy as various criminal investigations reached into the highest levels of his administration.[57] The conflict culminated with a fight between Yeltsin and Procurator-General Yurii Skuratov, who was investigating corruption in the Central Bank, Boris Berezovskii's corporate empire, and a series of construction contracts that potentially implicated Yeltsin's family. Yeltsin's aides evidently convinced Skuratov to resign in February 1999 by threating to release a videotape of Skuratov carousing with prostitutes. However, when the tape was played in March on national television, it tarred Yeltsin as having engaged in an unseemly form of blackmail. The Federation Council then refused to accept Skuratov's resignation, thereby allowing him to remain procurator-general against Yeltsin's expressed wishes. It was at this point, according to the journalist Steven Lee Myers, that Vladimir Putin, the newly appointed head of the Federal Security Service (FSB), intervened. He convinced Skuratov to resign based on additional compromising materials that would expose Skuratov to criminal prosecution. Yeltsin took notice. "[Putin] had demonstrated his loyalty to the president," argues Myers, "impressing him with his quiet efficiency; others might promise, but Putin achieved results."[58]

Changes to the bar and private legal representation represent a final area of substantive institutional reform during the Yeltsin era. The traditional top-down Communist Party control of the *advokatura* dissolved as new markets and well-paid practice areas opened up, most notably in the area of commercial law.[59] The national and local bar associations, however, proved incapable of preventing new associations of lawyers from emerging, thereby undermining their ability to set professional standards and defend corporate interests. Most importantly, the bar never received a professional monopoly over civil complaints, meaning its members were largely stuck with the more mundane state-appointed criminal cases that were far less lucrative. Civil society organizations also sponsored new legal aid bureaus that advised visitors on public interest matters and everyday disputes, thereby appropriating one of the legal profession's most important public service functions.[60] In the end, the bar remained vulnerable to the whims of the state, such as when the government attempted in February 1997 to raise monthly contributions from advocates to the state pension fund from 5 percent to 28 percent. The Constitutional Court ultimately overturned this decision in 1997, citing the bar's nonprofit status, but in the same year, the Ministry of Justice assumed oversight over all nongovernmental organizations, including the bar.[61]

The uphill struggle to break with the past can best be seen in the evolution of Russian criminal law. The 1993 constitution promised judicial independence and basic due process protections. The Yeltsin administration, however, never got a new criminal procedural code through the Duma, meaning that Russian criminal law continued to be governed by the RSFSR Criminal Procedure Code of 1960, albeit with numerous amendments. Even the amended code, however, was not reflected in the everyday interactions with the criminal justice system, as the legal scholar Stanislaw Pomorski discovered when he studied a lower criminal court in the Siberian city of Krasnoiarsk in 1999. According to Pomorski, the traditional prejudices of Soviet law were all still present, including a desire to avoid acquittals, the failure to hold public hearings, prosecutorial bias, a reliance on confession, and the unwillingness to inform defendants of their newly established right against self-incrimination. Moreover, advocates in state-appointed cases often went unpaid and therefore took a rather casual approach to their assigned criminal defense responsibilities, with no major professional repercussions.[62] Pomorski concludes that "the correspondence between earnestly declared legal principles and the mundane reality of judicial practice is loose, and at some crucial junctions, plainly non-existent."[63] Thus, despite all of the reforms, the Russian criminal process remained largely unchanged—a belated acknowledgment of the resilience of Soviet law and just how ingrained its institutions and practices were at the time of the Soviet Union's demise.

Conclusion

Yeltsin famously asked for forgiveness in his December 31, 1999, farewell address to the Russian people, noting "that what seemed simple to us turned out to be tormentingly difficult. I ask forgiveness for not justifying some hopes of those people who believed that at one stroke, in one spurt, we could leap from the gray, stagnant, totalitarian past into the light, rich, civilized future. I myself believed in this, that we could overcome everything in one spurt."[64] While Yeltsin did not enumerate the list of obstacles, it undoubtedly included legal reform. To Yeltsin's credit, he had presided over the transformation of Russia's legal system and underlying laws to a degree unprecedented in Russian history. He was the first Russian leader to enumerate the fundamental civil liberties of the Russian people without any immediate qualifications. In the process, he forged a political consensus that recognized property rights as a fundamental civil right. He reintroduced jury trials to Russia, thereby creating the possibility of genuine adversarial proceedings. With the exception of several months following October 1993, he also allowed for an independent media and freedom of assembly, even when he was the target of much of the opprobrium.

Yeltsin further observed a hierarchy of laws under the 1993 constitution that placed statutes passed by the legislature over his own personal decrees. Yeltsin admittedly struggled with this principle and did not always appreciate that his pronouncements did not carry the force of law. Nevertheless, he accepted this distinction far more than his Soviet and tsarist predecessors. Yeltsin also transferred significant legal authority to the regions, although his improvised system of asymmetrical federalism carried its own risks for the country's long-term stability. He revived Russian private law, which had been redefined and marginalized by the Bolsheviks, while establishing a system of constitutional jurisprudence that for the first time in Russian history allowed individual citizens to make constitutional arguments before the court. In the process, Yeltsin became the first Russian leader to accept a decision by a high court that declared one of his actions unconstitutional.

But while Yeltsin incorporated the rule-of-law ideal into his reform program, he also was an inveterate statist who understood, and had relied upon, an unlimited notion of state power as he worked his way up the Soviet political system. This experience also influenced how Yeltsin pursued legal reform. Most notably, Yeltsin emphasized the historic notion of state power as expressed in his decrees during his confrontation with the Congress of People's Deputies in 1992–1993. Yeltsin next made sure that various pro-statist elements, including the right to issue decrees with the force of law as well as the ability to dismiss the Duma if it proved to be too intransigent, were incorporated into the 1993 constitution. Yeltsin later used the concept of state power—and the need to preserve national unity—to attack Chechnya, and while a politically cautious Constitutional Court ultimately upheld his actions, Yeltsin's standing as a legal reformer clearly suffered as a result.

Without question, Yeltsin was not afraid to employ state power to his political advantage. However, for both political and personal (mainly health) reasons, he turned out to be a rather poor steward of the Russian state tradition. His bilateral treaties with the regions sacrificed centralized control and top-down legality for the higher goal of maintaining state integrity. What emerged was a weak state that faced major obstacles in transmitting its orders down to the regional level, the historic minimum requirement for preserving Russia's national integrity. Yeltsin also never cultivated the procuracy and its extensive coercive and supervisory powers; indeed, instead of being a natural ally of Yeltsin and the state, as was its historical mission, the procuracy largely worked against Yeltsin. Finally, while considerable state resources went into reviving private law, introducing jury trials, and promoting an independent judiciary, these reforms failed to stop the unprecedented rise in crime and corruption that also is part of Yeltsin's legacy. To be sure, corruption did not begin with Yeltsin; it possessed deep roots in Soviet and imperial history. Yeltsin, however, monetized corruption and gave it a price via privatization, and the Russian legal system was woefully unprepared to deal with the consequences.

The optimism that motivated many Russians during the 1990s to take a chance, start a company, or defend their rights has given way to memories of lawlessness and political dysfunction. Yeltsin undoubtedly left behind an ambiguous record, one that had combined new civil liberties, property rights, and legal values with deep-rooted statist principles. Moreover, none of Yeltsin's legal reforms were firmly grounded in Russian society at the time of his departure. Therefore, Yeltsin's legacy as a legal reformer was highly contingent on the policies of his successor. In his farewell address, Yeltsin announced: "Russia will never return to the past. Now, Russia will always move only forward." In choosing Vladimir Putin as his designated heir, however, Yeltsin selected a man who deeply believed in the Russian state and traditional state power. Russian law would continue to evolve but on a different path than Yeltsin envisioned.

9

Vladimir Putin and the Restoration of State and Law

Vladimir Putin belongs to that select group of Russian leaders whose long tenures in office have defined an era in Russia's history. "Putinism" is now associated with a renewed sense of patriotism, the recentralization of government, economic recovery, shrinking civil liberties, territorial expansion, and Russia's return to the ranks of leading powers. Throughout his reign, Putin has relied on a very traditional understanding of state and law that allows him to maintain control over a continental, multinational state. Putin also has demonstrated patience and restraint in putting his system in place, including a four-year period where he stepped aside and allowed Dmitry Medvedev to serve as president and to propose his own set of legal reforms. Yet Putin quickly abandoned Medvedev's agenda when he took up his third term as president in 2012. By exploring the development of Putin's statist legal stance and the Medvedev interregnum, this chapter traces the parameters of present-day Russian legality and explains why liberal legal reform remains so problematic.

Putin's rise to power

Little is known about Vladimir Putin's days as a law student at Leningrad State University. Admittedly, he never intended to practice law but viewed law school as a necessary stepping stone to a career with the KGB, which he ultimately achieved.[1] He did manage to attend some lectures by the prominent Leningrad law professor and future elected mayor of the city Anatolii Sobchak. Sobchak would later reappear in Putin's life as his most important mentor.[2] But the start of perestroika found Putin stationed in Dresden. Thus, he missed all the excitement, energy, and openness that accompanied the first few years of glasnost and economic reform.[3] Instead, he lived at the periphery of a declining Soviet empire. When East Germany imploded in 1989, Putin bravely defended the last outpost of Soviet rule, the local KGB headquarters. When he called Moscow for orders as to how to handle an excited crowd of rowdy protestors, however, "Moscow was silent." He later bitterly remembered this as a sign of the Soviet Union's "paralysis of power."[4]

Putin returned to Russia in 1990 with a need to reassess his long-term career prospects. He continued to work in the security services as assistant rector for international affairs at Leningrad State University but also joined the staff of Anatolii Sobchak, who by then had been elected chairman of Leningrad's city council. Putin's decision to work for Sobchak paid major professional and financial dividends as Sobchak emerged as one of Russia's most important democratic leaders in the aftermath of the August 1991 failed coup attempt. When Sobchak shortly thereafter became the first popularly elected mayor of the newly renamed St. Petersburg, Putin was his right-hand man. For the next five years, Putin learned the ins-and-outs of local politics and free market economics, all the while looking out for his own personal benefit. When Sobchak lost his bid for reelection in 1996, however, Putin found himself at another professional crossroads, but thanks to personal connections, he landed a new job in Moscow in the Presidential Property Management Directorate.[5] Thus, for a third time, Putin began the climb up the career ladder, becoming in short order director of the Federal Security Service, prime minister, and Boris Yeltsin's designated successor.

On December 29, 1999, just two days before Yeltsin's unexpected resignation, Prime Minister Putin published a manifesto entitled "Russia at the Turn of the Millennium" in which he laid out his strategy for what was about to be his presidency. At the top of his priorities was the restoration of the Russian state. "Our state and its institutes and structures have always played an exceptionally important role in the life of the country and its people," Putin argued.[6] "For Russians a strong state is not an anomaly which should be got rid of. Quite the contrary, they see it as a source and guarantor of order and the initiator and main driving force of any change." Putin, however, did not envision a return to the Soviet totalitarian model; instead, he saw the state as "an efficient coordinator of the country's economic and social forces that balances out their interests, optimizes the aims and parameters of social development and creates conditions and mechanisms of their attainment."[7]

Putin's manifesto foreshadowed the direction of his legal reforms as well. He announced his intention to go after crime and corruption while pursuing an investment strategy that combined "purely market mechanisms with measures of state guidance."[8] While the latter statement broke with the immediate Soviet past, it was quite compatible with previous Russian approaches to economic growth; tsarist bureaucrats played a prominent role in promoting the private sector from the middle of the nineteenth century onward.[9] Putin supported Russia's integration into global economic structures, most notably the World Trade Organization (WTO). And while he called for the restoration of traditional values—most notably patriotism—he praised the individual rights and freedoms enumerated in the Russian constitution.

Putin's millennium message rejected any attempt to reimpose a state ideology. Russia had a "good" constitution, Putin contended, and he accepted Yeltsin's attempt to combine state power and democracy; what was needed, however, was "a streamlined structure of the bodies of state authority and management."[10] And one of the biggest threats to the state was the growth in regional laws that violated constitutional norms. If left unaddressed, Putin warned, these unconstitutional laws would undermine the security of the state, its ability to govern, and the integrity of the country.

Putin the legislator

It was in the area of federalism that Vladimir Putin made his first move as president. On May 13, 2000, just four days after his inauguration, Putin issued a decree that divided the Russian Federation into seven federal districts. These new areas corresponded with Russia's military districts and, more importantly, grouped multiple republics, regions, and territories together, thereby undermining the individual autonomy of the then eighty-nine subjects of the Russian Federation. He subsequently appointed in each district a presidential envoy, who was part of the presidential administration and reported directly to Putin. The envoys' assigned task was to monitor federal agencies in their districts and ensure compliance with federal law, a supervisory function in the spirit of Peter the Great and his reforms.[11] The envoys were soon joined in each district by representatives of other state legal and administrative bodies to pursue this mission, including the procuracy, Ministry of Justice, the Audit Chamber, the FSB, the Ministry of Internal Affairs, and the Federal Tax Police.

Thus, Putin used a decree—a pure exercise of state power—to reestablish top-down legality in the regions. Putin would further deploy his decree powers—without going to court—to overturn regional legislation that he contended violated federal law.[12] Yet rule by decree was not sufficient to reassert central control over the regions; Putin also required substantive legal changes, and he turned to the procuracy as his primary ally to restore the legal unity of the Russian Federation. As previously noted, numerous regional constitutions and normative acts passed during the 1990s openly violated the 1993 constitution. Putin called on the procuracy to review these laws and, if necessary, overturn them. Since the procuracy no longer possessed the right of legislative initiative, it found itself going to court to enforce federal law.[13] The procuracy's success rate was impressive; of the more than 6,000 regional laws identified in 2000 as needing to be harmonized with federal law, some 5,800 were brought into conformity by 2002.[14]

Putin's recentralization plan also required the passage of legislation to change the composition of the parliament's upper house, the Federation Council. Under Yeltsin, the heads of regions doubled as members of Federation Council; however, while they retained significant loyalty to Yeltsin, they turned out to be highly protective of their regional prerogatives. Putin eventually persuaded the regional executives to approve a law that gradually removed them from the Federation Council, although the regional executives were allowed to select their replacements (unless rejected by the regional legislature by a two-thirds vote). Putin also passed legislation granting the president the right to dismiss regional legislatures and executives for long-running and/or gross violations of federal law.[15]

Putin's actions formally brought the post-Soviet internal treaty-making period to a close. Putin did sign one last agreement with Tatarstan in 2007, but this treaty was more perfunctory in nature and broadly followed the division of powers set forth in the 1993 constitution. Most treaties either expired or were formally revoked.[16] Commentators both at the time and in retrospect expressed ambivalent feelings about the demise of the treaty-making era. The agreements had facilitated the transfer of significant economic power to the regions and served as the beginnings of genuine local politics. The regions, however, were not only a laboratory for change but also a source of unbridled corruption. Many local leaders had paid lip service to Moscow but focused on lining their pockets. The treaties also had produced an unequal relationship among the Federation's constituent members, with various economic privileges distributed haphazardly across the regions. With Putin's rise, the pendulum clearly swung away from Yeltsin's asymmetrical federalism, although outposts of legal pluralism and local custom remained, particularly in the North Caucasus. Nevertheless, Putin's emphasis on a single federal law restored centralized control while pushing Russia in the direction of the nation-state.

Putin pursued other legal reforms as well. He filled in the gaps in Yeltsin's economic legislation, including Part 3 (inheritance and conflict of laws) and Part 4 (intellectual property) of the Civil Code, Part 2 of the Tax Code, and the Law on Bankruptcy. Other laws were adopted as part of Russia's attempt to join major international organizations, such as the Financial Action Task Force (FATF), a global anti-money laundering organization.

Two pieces of legislation deserve special attention: the 2001 Land Code and the 2001 Criminal Procedure Code. The Land Code was long overdue; the provisions in the Civil Code relating to the ownership of land could not be activated until the adoption of the Land Code. Admittedly, the Land Code only covered urban land (about 2 percent of all land in the Russian Federation), but it was followed in 2002 by the Law on Agricultural Land Transactions. The Land Code established the right of private land ownership both by Russians and foreigners with the noted exceptions that foreigners could neither purchase agricultural land nor own land in the border areas so designated by the president.[17]

The new Criminal Procedure Code was also long in anticipation and, on balance, a major improvement over the previous RSFSR code. It opened up the preliminary investigation to more adversarial challenges; a lawyer could now be present from the time a person was detained or arrested.[18] Defense counsel also could conduct his/her own preliminary investigation and demand that this information be considered by the criminal investigator. The code reduced the judge's discretionary powers by eliminating the Soviet practice of sending a case back for supplemental investigation in order to avoid career-damaging acquittals. The 2001 Criminal Procedure Code did permit judges as a preliminary measure to return cases back to the prosecutor for up to five days to correct technical violations but not as a means to end a trial.[19] Finally, the 2001 Criminal Procedure Code offered a well-recognized workaround to the newly-revived adversarial process, one that exists around the world: plea bargaining. By 2010, approximately 64 percent of all criminal cases were resolved via such special procedures, reflecting recognition of the miniscule chance of being acquitted and the hope that a plea might facilitate a more lenient sentence.[20]

The passage of the Land Code and Criminal Procedure Code, along with other legislation, solidified Vladimir Putin's early reputation as a lawgiver. Unlike Yeltsin, Putin possessed sufficient political leverage over the Duma to pass these landmark pieces of legislation with little opposition. Putin also presided over one of the most progressive advancements in Russian legal history: the recognition of European law as a part of Russian law. Admittedly, this process began under Yeltsin. Russia joined the Council of Europe in 1996 and subsequently ratified the European Convention on Human Rights in 1998. Russian citizens soon flooded the European Court of Human Rights in Strasbourg with appeals, although it would take several years for them to master the procedural technicalities and to begin to win judgments against the Russian government.[21] Cases from Russia raised fundamental violations of civil liberties, criminal procedure, social rights, and property rights, with a disproportionate number of cases involving human rights abuses in Chechnya. On a practical level, most decisions involved the Russian government paying fines to the aggrieved party. Other European Court determinations calling for more substantive changes to the legal system—such as the need to improve the enforcement of domestic court decisions—produced more tepid responses from the Russian government and often were left unimplemented. Nevertheless, the European Court represented a new and increasingly attractive venue where Russian citizens could pursue their individual claims against the state in a much more favorable legal environment.

European Court decisions also became an essential element of Russia's legal dialogue pursuant Article 15(4) of the Russian constitution, which acknowledged that the "generally recognized principles and norms" of international law—as well as international treaties—constituted an integral part of the Russian legal system. While the scope of this provision remains controversial and subject to debate, its impact was profound. To begin with, the European Convention actually became a part of Russian law and buttressed the human rights provisions in the 1993 constitution. Russian court decisions also began to cite European Court rulings even though Russia did not officially recognize judicial decisions as a source of law. In 2011, the Constitutional Court chairman Valerii Zorkin highlighted the fact that more than fifty court determinations made reference to European Court decisions.[22] Finally, in a few instances, the European Court's demand for legal change actually produced significant results. Most notably, the European Court struck down Russia's use of supervisory review under its civil procedure code, thereby forcing Russia to initiate major reforms of its civil appellate process. While not abolishing *nadzor* outright, these changes resulted in a much more streamlined review of civil cases and greater stability of judgments. In other words, thanks primarily to a decision by the European Court, Russia recognized the principle of *res judicata* (finality of judgments) as a central part of its judicial process.[23]

Petitions to Strasbourg were just one example of Russia's increased litigiousness. Under Putin, Russians also turned with increased frequency to domestic courts.[24] As Kathryn Hendley convincingly has demonstrated, private law returned to Russia with an increasing number of citizens pursuing tort, contract, family, inheritance, and tax disputes via the courts.[25] Hendley further reveals a growing sophistication among Russian litigants about when to pursue legal action and, alternatively, when to try other informal methods of dispute resolution, thereby avoiding the expense of going to court. Hendley finds little evidence of corruption in Russia's justice of the peace courts; instead, she describes hard-working, overburdened judges trying to keep pace with the strict time limits imposed by the state for resolving such low-level disputes.[26]

Increased access to the courts, however, did not mean the end of corruption; on the contrary, Russian business remained a sitting target for various nefarious actions with corrupt judges, prosecutors, and criminal investigators often serving as willing enablers in the process. In the early 2000s, a new word entered the Russian lexicon: *reiderstvo* or corporate raiding. Unlike its Western counterpart, which rewards shareholders with above-market payouts in purchasing companies, corporate raiding in Russia involves various illegal schemes designed to seize some (if not all) of the target's assets. Thomas Firestone, the former US Department of Justice legal advisor in the Moscow Embassy, argues that corporate raiding reflected the underlying deficiencies of Russian commercial law, including uncertainty over property rights and poor corporate governance, as well as a deep-rooted corruption in law enforcement and the judicial system as a whole.[27]

The expansion of Russian private law and its accompanying accomplishments, struggles, and outright distortions provide an appropriately mixed picture of Putin's early attempt at legal reform. Putin was interested in promoting legality—or as he more bluntly described it, "a dictatorship of laws"—but the adjudication of civil disputes remained a secondary objective. The larger goal, as reflected in Putin's millennium message, was the return to the founding principles of "state and law" and the subordination of law to state power.

Consolidating state power

Putin pursued a consistent and multifaceted strategy to reassert state authority. He began with Russia's newly minted media tycoons. He used various strong-armed legal tactics to wrest control of Russia's major television stations from Vladimir Gusinskii and Boris Berezovskii, thereby completing the initial stage of his state-building project.[28] Henceforth, the Russian state would control the message delivered to the people on television.

Yet neither the Gusinskii nor Berezovskii takedowns would have the same ramifications for Russian law as the arrest and trial of the Russian oligarch Mikhail Khodorkovskii. As previously noted, Khodorkovskii was no poster child for corporate governance. He purportedly rigged the original auction of the oil company Yukos in 1996, and he showed little deference to minority shareholders during the 1998 financial crisis.[29] Yet in the early 2000s, as the price of oil skyrocketed, Khodorkovskii changed his corporate behavior. He appointed independent directors to his board, ordered audits by Western accounting firms, and pursued deals with major international oil companies. He also expanded his corporate philanthropy and support for civil society, funding groups dealing with social welfare, public health, and higher education. Yet in the process of raising his public profile, Khodorkovskii took several steps that were bound to upset Putin and his efforts to restore the Russian state. For example, Khodorkovskii entered into pipeline negotiations with China while pursuing a separate deal with ExxonMobil that contemplated a foreign stake of up to 40 percent in Yukos.[30] More ominously, Khodorkovskii pursued an active policy of lobbying domestic lawmakers as well as provided direct financial support for multiple political parties. By 2003, half of the Duma purportedly owed their allegiance to Khodorkovskii.[31]

Putin could not tolerate such challenges, and while he provided Khodorkovskii with several subtle warnings, Khodorkovskii chose to ignore them. The suspense ended on October 25, 2003, with Khodorkovskii's arrest on charges of tax evasion, falsifying documents, and theft. The subsequent investigation and trial of Khodorkovskii would serve as a test of the new 2001 Criminal Procedure Code, and it failed on multiple levels. Bail was denied. The judge granted prosecution motions without even hearing any defense objections and further restricted the cross-examination of witnesses. Defense lawyers were detained and called in for questioning, while their offices were illegally searched and documents removed in violation of attorney-client privilege.[32] Although the proceedings took on all of the trappings of a political trial, the state insisted that the case remained a criminal manner. Khodorkovskii's closing statement reflected how politics had intervened in his case: "I was the wrong sort of oligarch, therefore the authorities not only confiscated Yukos but are now holding me in prison for the second year running."[33]

With the verdict never in doubt, Khodorkovskii received nine years in jail. Yukos soon would be seized, broken up, and auctioned off in a less than transparent manner with the ultimate winner being Rosneft, a state-owned oil company. Thus, Putin and the state received the bounty of Yukos's oil revenues, a boon for economic growth throughout Putin's second term in office. Yet the Khodorkovskii case had profound repercussions for Russia's legal system. It left in tatters the 2001 Criminal Procedure Code, which proved unable to withstand the specific demands of the state. Moreover, with the case, Putin put limits on the role private law would play in Russian society going forward. Putin allowed the remaining oligarchs to keep their money, but these prosperous Russians could no longer use private law to challenge the prerogative powers of the state. Instead, Putin demanded, and the oligarchs supinely agreed, to use their wealth to support various public works and charitable projects that promoted the goals of the state. Peter the Great's service requirements had found their twenty-first-century equivalent, to the detriment of the property rights set forth in the 1993 constitution.

Putin's second major assertion of state power occurred in 2004 in the immediate aftermath of the tragedy in Beslan, North Ossetia. Chechen rebels had seized a school and held hundreds of teachers and students hostage. Russian commandos eventually stormed the building, but 334 hostages, including 186 children, died in the process.[34] Ten days after the events, Putin issued a decree abolishing elections for the heads of regions as well as for mayors. With little explanation, Putin cited the need to fight terrorism as justification for such a dramatic step. Henceforth, Putin would nominate candidates to such offices to be confirmed by regional parliaments. In the same decree, Putin announced that going forward all Duma elections would be conducted by party lists, thereby eliminating the single mandate districts that previously had elected half of the Duma representatives.

Putin's order would be written into law, but he demonstrated that the preemptive strike of the decree still carried significant weight when used decisively and with the element of surprise. Ironically, the regional bodies did not object to this dramatic reduction in their power. It was left to a local politician in the Tyumen district to petition the Constitutional Court claiming a violation of his individual voting rights.[35] The Constitutional Court eventually upheld the law on the appointment of governors, concluding that it simply followed the constitution's demand for a unified system of executive power. According to the court, while nowhere explicitly written in the constitution, Russian governors were subordinate to the president who oversaw the successful coordination of all organs of state power. Thus, the Constitutional Court confirmed the top-down delivery of Russian law, what later became known as Putin's "power vertical." However, in a special opinion, Justice Anatolii Kononov dissented, arguing that by placing the notion of unity above all other constitutional principles, the Court had managed to convert an independent wing of government into a "subdivision of federal structures."[36] Kononov further insisted that the Court had not defended Russia's hierarchy of laws, allowing a mere statute to change the democratic intent of the Russian constitution.

By forging a more unified state—and ending the treaty-making process—Putin had converted regional government, which for better or worse had enjoyed significant autonomy under Yeltsin, into an organ of state power. Putin's reinforcement of the state, however, was still not finished. The 2003 Duma elections represented an overwhelming victory for Putin; his United Russia Party became the largest bloc in the Duma. Rather than assuming control of the legislative agenda, however, United Russia increasingly ceded this initiative to the presidential administration. According to the Russian legal scholar Aleksei Avtonomov, it was useless after 2003 for citizens to appeal to the Duma for legislative action because it did not "do anything without direction from the [presidential] administration."[37] The political scientist Thomas Remington concurred, noting that "presidential control over the parliament, particularly after 2003, resulted both in a large number of laws and a nearly veto-free record of law making."[38] Thus, Putin had taken Russia's nascent representative and judicial institutions, which theoretically held out some possibilities for the division of powers, and converted them to what they historically had always been: organs of state power.

Putin set his sights on one last institution as part of his consolidation of state power: the prosecutor's office. Yet rather than strengthening the procuracy, the state's most reliable ally and longest-running legal institution, Putin chose to divide it. In 2007, he created the Investigative Committee, which, while theoretically still a part of the prosecutor's office, nevertheless assumed independent control over major criminal investigations. This decision represented a dramatic reduction in the procuracy's supervisory powers and its ability to oversee and participate in the pretrial process.[39] The procuracy's primary remaining source of leverage over the Investigative Committee was its ability to reject bringing the investigator's charges to court. This right of rejection subsequently would be employed by prosecutors in several high-profile cases, but it never cast the procuracy—or the Investigative Committee—in a favorable light. On the contrary, such public squabbles only demonstrated how these two institutions worked at cross-purposes with each other to the obvious detriment of Russian justice.

Why Putin chose to weaken an institution that had demonstrated consistent loyalty to him remains a mystery. Admittedly, the idea to separate the procuracy's investigative and prosecutorial functions had circulated since the late Gorbachev period.[40] Putin may have had his own personal reasons for supporting what on paper appeared to be a progressive change. The decision came in the aftermath of several investigations that had implicated the security services and other state agencies in various acts of wrongdoing.[41] Putin possibly wanted to control such probes going forward, especially in politically sensitive cases. In any event, Putin made sure to install a loyalist—his law school classmate Aleksandr Bastrykhin—as head of the Investigative Committee.

The fact that the above reforms occurred in 2007 was not mere happenstance. The 1993 constitution barred Putin from a third consecutive term, and he refused to amend Russia's founding document. Nevertheless, as Putin contemplated his final days as president, he intensified his level of activity, as reflected in the significant increase in the number of decrees issued starting in 2007.[42] Of course, the end of Putin's second term would not turn out to be a natural break in his time in power. If Putin had left the political scene in 2008, however, he might well have been remembered as that unique politician who actually did what he said he was going to do. His 1999 millennium message promised a return to established "state and law" principles, and he never wavered from this goal. He revived the state by abandoning Yeltsin's asymmetrical federalism and imposing a power vertical that could implement the center's laws and decrees in the regions. He further converted the legislature into an organ of state power whereby it ceased to be a check on the president's authority and instead was largely subsumed under the presidential administration. Yet Putin also addressed the gaps in crucial areas of legal regulation—land, criminal procedure, intellectual property—that while far from perfect nevertheless continued Russia's retreat from Soviet law and toward more established civil law principles. Everyday law returned to Russia, but so too did political justice, exposing the duality of Russian law and casting a cloud over its long-term prospects. Russian law, however, was about to move center stage as Putin's chosen successor—Dmitry Medvedev—tread where no Russian leader had gone before. He decided to make legal reform the defining issue of his presidency.

The Medvedev interregnum (2008–2012)

Like Putin, Dmitry Medvedev attended Leningrad State University Law School but at a decidedly different time and with different career aspirations. He began law school in 1982 and graduated with high honors in 1987. Yet unlike Putin, he was not destined for the security services. Instead, he received a postgraduate appointment to study corporate and securities law. He subsequently became a lecturer at his alma mater, but he also was brought into St. Petersburg city government by Anatolii Sobchak, where he worked with Vladimir Putin. Putin brought him to Moscow, where he eventually rose to be first deputy prime minister and then president, thanks to Putin's patronage.

Medvedev made legal reform the central part of his political program. In his "Go Russia" speech of September 2009, Medvedev emphasized the need "to create a modern efficient judiciary, acting in accordance with new legislation on the judicial system and based on contemporary legal principles."[43] He further called on the judicial system "to understand the difference between what it means to act in the public interest or in the selfish interests of a corrupt bureaucrat or businessman."[44] Medvedev concluded by calling for a whole new attitude to the law. "We also have to rid ourselves of the contempt for law and justice, which, as I've said repeatedly, has lamentably become a tradition in this country."[45]

Medvedev backed up his words with targeted changes that addressed substantive parts of civil and criminal law.[46] The list of reforms is impressive, although in light of subsequent events, not overwhelmingly decisive. In civil law, Medvedev eliminated a blatant conflict of interest by ending the appointment of government ministers to state companies (Medvedev himself had previously served as Chairman of the Board of Gazprom). He further attempted to limit the number of repeat business inspections by government agencies that only served to encourage corruption. Medvedev's reforms in criminal law were equally substantial. He decriminalized slander and defamation so that such complaints would only be heard in civil courts and not serve as a means to criminalize free speech. He also streamlined the appeals process, thereby limiting the opportunities to pursue supervisory review in criminal cases. Henceforth, any verdict in the courts of general jurisdiction would be heard by the appeals court *de novo* (i.e., addressing issues of fact and law), with subsequent appeals only allowed for serious breaches of substantive or procedural law. Medvedev further pushed through legislation that sought to "humanize" the worst features of Russian criminal law by encouraging non-custodial alternatives and forbidding jail sentences for non-serious, first-time offenders.

Medvedev presided over major institutional reforms as well. The Higher Commercial Court asserted its independence by declaring that it possessed the right to issue binding precedential decisions and thereby engage in law-creating activities. The Constitutional Court later upheld this right of precedent, although it set specific conditions that had to be met before such binding determinations could be announced.[47] Medvedev also engaged in a very public and constructive dialogue with leading civil society representatives. From 2009 to 2012, Medvedev met seven times with the President's Council for Civil Society and Human Rights. These meetings addressed the major issues of the day, including environmental protection, migration, Russia's multinational principles, corporate raiding, and anti-corruption, as well as cases involving individual human rights abuses. At Medvedev's last meeting with the council in April 2012, he admitted that while it was not always easy to listen to what the council members had to say, their comments were "absolutely sincere, from the heart, and as a rule, very well argued."[48]

Not all of Medvedev's legal reforms can be seen in a progressive light. He limited the scope of jury trials by removing from their jurisdiction cases involving spying, terrorism, and other serious crimes against the state. He further reined in the Constitutional Court by changing the method of selecting the chairman and deputy chairman; instead of the justices themselves electing the head of the court, the president henceforth would nominate the candidates for these positions, to be "confirmed" (i.e., rubber-stamped) by the Federation Council. Finally, Medvedev called for the first fundamental amendment to the 1993 constitution, increasing the terms of office for the president and Duma deputies to six and five years, respectively. Medvedev provided little legal justification for this decision, but it was clear that he or Putin would be the first beneficiary.

The Medvedev presidency now stands as a historical footnote in the long reign of Vladimir Putin. Yet for legal historians, Medvedev remains a compelling figure, not necessarily for his overall record but as a cautionary tale about reforming the Russian legal system. To begin with, he blamed much of Russia's legal predicament not on the state and its policies but on the people themselves. "Russia is a country where people don't like to observe the law. It is, as they say, a country of legal nihilism."[49] Medvedev later commented that Russians must "cultivate a taste of the rule of law," adding that it was "the job of the courts with broad public support to cleanse the country of corruption."[50] Medvedev essentially blamed the people, and not the state, for the country's legal nihilism, even though it was the state that blithely ignored the law whenever it suited its purposes. Retired Constitutional Court Justice Tamara Morshchakova later called Medvedev out on this point; she attributed the country's inability to achieve the rule of law to Putin's counter-reforms, and not the Russian people. According to Morshchakova, neither the "particularities of Russian life, nor the mentalities of our fellow countrymen, are an obstacle to fair justice."[51]

Medvedev first misdiagnosed the cause of Russia's legal nihilism. He then compounded this mistake by overestimating his ability to cure the disease, most notably in the now infamous Magnitsky affair.[52] Russian attorney Sergei Magnitsky investigated a classic case of corporate raiding of a Western investment company and discovered that not only had tax and law enforcement officials stolen the company, they had filed for and received an illegal tax refund of $230 million. Magnitsky, a genuine believer in Russian law, reported the crime to the appropriate authorities. But instead of thanking Magnitsky, the authorities arrested the whistleblower and held him in inhumane conditions. In an effort to coerce false testimony, investigators withheld medical assistance, and after eleven months in detention, Magnitsky died in prison at the age of 37.

The Magnitsky case gathered significant media attention and therefore raised public interest in Medvedev's rule-of-law agenda. Independent commissions interrogated the prison officials and concluded that the conditions of Magnitsky's detention amounted to torture. Medvedev fired twenty prison officials while ending pretrial detention for certain types of economic crimes, including fraud and embezzlement. Medvedev seemed to have Russia's law enforcement agencies on the ropes, yet they successfully waged a counteroffensive that shifted attention away from their criminal actions and paradoxically toward Magnitsky himself. The procuracy chose not to investigate the extravagant spending of the criminal investigators in the case while the Ministry of Interior decided to reward the investigators with public honors. Indeed, the authorities appeared uninterested in probing a tax fraud perpetrated against the Russian state. Thus, the Magnitsky case became emblematic at how powerful state institutions, instead of fighting corruption, protect their own at all costs, and that even the president of the Russian Federation could do nothing about it. Several years later, in a truly Kafkaesque trial, Magnitsky would be tried and convicted posthumously for stealing $230 million.

Medvedev's rule-of-law aspirations never recovered from the Magnitsky affair. Instead, he stood by helplessly as a second carefully orchestrated show trial of Khodorkovskii occurred in 2010. The second proceeding was based on even more dubious charges than the first; the new indictment focused on Khodorkovskii's alleged embezzlement of company funds and of 350 million tons of oil—more than Yukos's entire production during the time period! These fresh charges were legally inconsistent with the first indictment; Khodorkovskii previously had been convicted for not paying taxes, but now he was being accused of stealing the money, which theoretically meant that there had been no revenue on which to evade taxes in the first place. The proceeding also contained numerous procedural irregularities. Despite Medvedev's recently passed legislation allowing entrepreneurs to be released on bail in economic crimes, Khodorkovskii again was denied bail. The trial further raised obvious questions regarding double jeopardy. Finally, the case exposed the divisions within the famed ruling tandem of Putin and Medvedev.[53] On the eve of the second verdict, Putin announced that "a thief should sit in jail," triggering one of Medvedev's few public rebukes against his mentor for issuing a prejudicial statement before the outcome of the trial was announced.[54]

Khodorkovskii not surprisingly was convicted and sentenced to an additional six years in jail, and even though Medvedev would later authorize a special commission under the President's Council for Civil Society and Human Rights to conduct a legal analysis of the Yukos case, Medvedev seems to have been powerless to address the procedural irregularities associated with the case.[55] The second Khodorkovskii decision showed that the rise of everyday law was no obstacle to the selective and political use of justice. On a broader level, the Khodorkovskii proceeding revealed what had always been suspected—that despite Medvedev's elevation to the presidency, Putin remained in charge of the state. Indeed, Medvedev increasingly relied on decrees during his time in office to implement his anti-corruption and rule-of-law agenda, but, since he did not control the state, his orders fell on deaf ears.[56] Thus, the Medvedev presidency confirmed the essential governing reality of the 1993 constitution. While Western commentators focused on its super-presidential aspects, the crucial institution remained the state. As prime minister, Putin never lost control of the central organs of the state, such as the media, the security services, state corporations, and criminal investigations. Thus, Putin simply was able to inform Medvedev on September 24, 2011, that he was returning to the presidency.

Putin cracks down (2012–2018)

Putin's return was anything but triumphant. Thanks to Medvedev's constitutional reforms, Putin could contemplate six, and most likely twelve, more years in power. Such a prospect convinced a wide sector of Russian society—particularly in the major urban areas—to take to the streets and protest. Such a response was unexpected, given that Putin had presided over the very prosperity and stability that had allowed the protesters to enter the ranks of the middle class. Since Putin could not be loved, he decided on the next best thing: to be feared.

Putin pursued this strategy through a pure exercise of state power. He demanded—and the Duma meekly approved—a series of laws that undermined the civil liberties set forth in the Russian constitution. He limited the freedom of assembly by sharply increasing the potential fines for unsanctioned meetings. Freedom of speech was curtailed through a variety of measures, including a new law on blasphemy that covered any statement that might offend the "religious feelings" of believers. Putin further reversed Medvedev and re-criminalized slander with increased penalties in cases involving libel against government officials. He expanded the definition of treason to include any consultation with any foreign state or international organization. Putin also attacked the independence of nongovernmental organizations (NGOs), the cornerstone of civil society, by demanding that groups engaged in political activity register as "foreign agents" if they received funding from abroad. And when the foreign agents law still allowed unwanted NGOs to operate, Putin introduced a law on undesirable organizations that not only prohibited certain designated foreign groups from operating inside Russia but also imposed serious criminal penalties on any Russian NGO that received grants or otherwise cooperated with said undesirable organization.

All of the above statutes contained such broad language so as to provide the state the maximum flexibility in enforcing them. The laws were followed up by a series of political trials to reinforce the message that basic civil liberties should not be used to challenge the state. The trials of the Bolotnaia Square protesters brought a combination of organizers, participants, and a few unlucky bystanders to justice for what was essentially a police riot that occurred the day before Putin's 2012 inauguration. The randomness of these prosecutions and substantial prison sentences served as an overt warning against future demonstrations.[57] In July 2012, the trial of three members of a feminist protest art collective "Pussy Riot" received international attention. The prosecution of three young women for a controversial punk rock art protest in Christ the Savior Church again displayed the impotence of Russian criminal procedure in political cases; to identify the moral damage inflicted by the brief performance in a near-empty church, the government proffered testimony from people who had seen the edited footage on TV but had not witnessed the alleged crime in person.[58] The court eventually found two of the defendants guilty and sentenced them to two years for "hooliganism motivated by religious hatred," a sentence even Prime Minister Medvedev found excessive.[59]

Finally, in 2014, Aleksei Navalny, the anti-corruption crusader and one of the leaders of the opposition, was convicted on trumped-up charges that he had stolen $500,000 of timber while working for the governor of Kirov. Navalny received a suspended sentence in the case while his brother received three-and-a-half years in jail. The conviction meant Navalny could not run for political office, although in an unexpected, and still mysterious, development, Navalny was allowed to run for mayor of Moscow while the verdict was on appeal.[60]

As the above demonstrates, Putin had returned to the long-standing Russian tradition of weaponizing the law to reinforce the power of the state. The above trials gained the most coverage, but they were by no means isolated affairs. The director of Moscow's Ukrainian library was convicted for possessing "extremist" books, a Russian blogger received a three-and-a-half-year suspended sentence under the "blasphemy law" for posting a video of himself playing Pokémon Go in a church, a journalist received more than three years in jail for calling for a change in the Russian constitution via referendum, and an activist was detained for installing a memorial plaque on the home of a victim of Stalin's repressions.[61] Putin further went after the press, the internet, and members of the arts community in order to reassert state control. And after the annexation of Crimea in 2014, Russia closed down the independent Crimean Tatar Assembly (the Mejlis), declaring it an extremist organization.

Putin's second round of political trials differed from the first one; while the Khodorkovskii case had been primarily directed against the economic elite, this new spate of political proceedings was more broadly directed against Russian society or at least that growing segment that wanted a more open, liberal country. Putin admittedly stopped short of resorting to mass repressions; the use of selective justice worked just as well. The 2012 protest movement soon lost its momentum and then disappeared in the patriotic wave that accompanied Crimea's annexation in 2014. Putin further managed to avoid rewriting the constitution to restrict Russia's civil liberties, a much more draconian and controversial action. Such a change technically would have required a constitutional convention. Requests for such a gathering were put forward, particularly to change Article 13(2) that prohibits the establishment of state ideology.[62] Little enthusiasm existed, however, for passing a law to hold a constitutional assembly, and Putin did not need to provoke a constitutional crisis to reassert state power. Instead, he was able to pursue his goals legally, both via legislation and through the courts.

In addition to selective prosecutions, Putin relied on decrees, a compliant judiciary (the outcomes of the above political cases were never in doubt), and a deferential procuracy in order to reassert state power.[63] The procuracy's unquestioned loyalty to the state was on clear display during the implementation of Putin's Foreign Agents Law. The Foreign Agents Law contained no definition of the sanctioned action—"political activity"—in the actual statute. Furthermore, the Ministry of Justice at first did not want to register any NGOs, largely because the Minister of Justice Aleksandr Konovalov did not agree with the legislation.[64] Thus, it fell to the procuracy to force the issue and investigate human rights and other groups to ensure compliance with the law, *de facto* defining the term political activity in the process.[65] The procuracy once again proved its absolute allegiance to the state, and when Putin upped the ante in 2015 by introducing the law on undesirable organizations, he assigned the procuracy (with the agreement of the Ministry of Foreign Affairs) the right to ban any foreign or international organization that threatened the Russian constitutional system, the country's military defense, or the safety of the Russian state.[66]

Yet despite its heightened status, the procuracy's position was not unassailable. It still found itself in conflict with the Investigative Committee over several high-profile indictments. Moreover, human rights groups protested the procuracy's extended investigatory powers under the Foreign Agents Law to the Constitutional Court, contending that they were too broad and violated international legal norms. The Duma's representative to the Constitutional Court rejected such claims, justifying the procuracy's actions, in part, by referring to its historical role as the "eyes of the sovereign." "Prosecutorial supervision (*nadzor*) is necessary," he opined. "This was proven historically, when in the Russian empire the position of general procurator was introduced. If prosecutorial review is abolished, won't we be placing too many obligations on the court?"[67] Yet while upholding the general principle of *nadzor*, the Constitutional Court rejected the government's arguments, demanding that precise rules be adopted to regulate document requests and the investigatory process.[68]

The Constitutional Court nipped around the edges of other government legislation as well, for example, overturning the total ban on ex-convicts seeking political office and reversing the conviction of Ildar Dadin for organizing a series of unsanctioned demonstrations. Dadin had been sentenced to two-and-a-half years in prison under the 2014 law that criminalized the holding of three unsanctioned meetings within a six-month period. Dadin appealed to the Constitutional Court, stating that numerous constitutional rights—including freedom of speech and freedom of assembly—had been violated. The Constitutional Court's February 2017 ruling refrained from declaring the law on meetings unconstitutional.

However, it did call for changes in the underlying statute, saying in part that the law must adequately reflect the potential dangers associated with the demonstration in question. Thus, the Court found that any violation of the law of meetings had to consider whether the gathering actually led to violence or property damage. The Court also noted that Dadin had been subject to administrative penalties for his previous unsanctioned meetings and that such administrative fines could not, by themselves, be evidence of guilt in a criminal proceeding without being cross-examined.[69] In light of the above procedural irregularities and the law's unclear requirements, the Court overturned Dadin's conviction.

As the Dadin ruling showed, the Constitutional Court retained an independent streak, although it was careful not to directly declare Putin's crackdown on Russian civil liberties unconstitutional. More importantly, the Constitutional Court fell into line with one of Putin's highest priorities, namely finding a pretext to reject decisions by the European Court of Human Rights. While the Constitutional Court had, in many ways, facilitated the introduction of European Court decisions into Russian law, its chairman Valerii Zorkin increasingly objected to what he perceived as Strasbourg's judicial activism and expanding interpretation of human rights at the direct expense of national legislation.[70] Other European countries have raised similar objections, but they have quietly found ways to avoid implementing European Court determinations without either undermining the court's legitimacy or asserting the supremacy of their national laws. Yet Putin's third term was focused on affirming Russia's national sovereignty, and in July 2015, the Constitutional Court's review powers were expanded to include the right to overturn European Court rulings if such decisions contravened the Russian constitution.[71] The Constitutional Court has now exercised this prerogative in a limited number of cases, most notably in rejecting the European Court's 1.9 billion euro award to Yukos shareholders for violating the company's rights under the European Convention.[72] As a result, Russia once again found itself diverging with European practices, and the full ramifications of this decision have yet to be revealed.

Putin confronted one final judicial obstacle in his reassertion of state power: the Higher Commercial Court. This tribunal had grown increasingly independent under the chairmanship of Anton Ivanov, not only in terms of asserting the right of legal precedent but also in promoting greater transparency in the judicial process. All *ex parte* communications to the court, for example, were posted on the court's website, as were all judicial opinions in individual cases. Most ominously, however, the state regularly lost cases in the commercial courts, particularly in tax-related matters.[73] To stamp out this assertion of judicial independence, Putin took the drastic step of abolishing the Higher Commercial Court, the most pro-reform judicial institution in Russia, and placing the lower commercial courts under the supervision of the least progressive court, the Supreme Court. As justification, Putin emphasized the need to have uniformity in judicial practice, although procedures already existed that allowed the Supreme Court and the Higher Commercial Court to issue joint opinions on common matters.

Putin's decision to abolish the Higher Commercial Court resulted in the most substantial revision to the 1993 constitution to date. All references to the Higher Commercial Court were removed, and Russia went from having three high courts to two, with a not-too-subtle message that the Constitutional Court could suffer a similar fate if it asserted its independence too aggressively. As part of the amendment process, Putin further snuck in a provision renaming Chapter 7 "Judicial Power and the Procuracy," thus righting Yeltsin's original wrong of failing to recognize the procuracy's unique position within the Russian legal system. These changes further enhanced the president's ability to appoint and dismiss members of the procuracy.[74] The amendments confirmed that the procuracy was not a member of the executive or judicial branch but a specific state institution that only answered to the nation's supreme ruler.

The above reforms buttressed the state's coercive powers, which were already substantial even before Putin's counterreforms. The criminal justice system continued to display a strong accusatorial bias, a sign not necessarily of corruption but deep-rooted inertia.[75] Indeed, despite all the substantive reforms of criminal procedure, the underlying career incentives of Russia's legal practitioners remained consistent with Soviet practices. Prosecutors were evaluated by their conviction rate, and judges were marked down by the number of cases (i.e., acquittals) overturned. Sergei Pashin, the co-author of the 1991 *Conception of Judicial Reform* and later a federal judge, essentially was run out of the profession for an acquittal rate of 7 percent.[76] The procuracy further remained vigilant in its protection of its general supervisory powers. It still reviews millions of civilian complaints every year, thereby continuing to compete directly with the courts over the review of individual disputes. Moreover, when discussions began in 2012 about establishing an ombudsman for business affairs, the procuracy almost immediately stepped in and created its own special division for upholding the rights of entrepreneurs, thereby staking its claim in the oversight of business legislation.[77]

The judiciary also defended its distinct corporate interests. There were repeated calls to expand the talent pool of the judiciary and encourage more members of the *advokatura* to apply, thereby increasing the number of judges with genuine legal practice skills. The judiciary, however, lacked the prestige, and more importantly the appropriate level of compensation, to attract practicing lawyers. Therefore, Russian judges continued to be drawn primarily from the procuracy and legal secretariat, bringing a bureaucratic, and decidedly pro-statist bias to their decision-making.[78] Finally, while the bar produced its fair share of lawyers who bravely defended human rights and Russian civil liberties, the profession's rank and file members still relied on a steady stream of state-appointed criminal cases for their livelihood, and these advocates remain much more hesitant to challenge the status quo. Although a national association of jurists was formed in 2005 that united judges, prosecutors, advocates, and other legal professionals, the three main branches of the legal system retain their own corporate structures specifically designed to defend their narrow professional interests.

Thus, no major legal institution took the lead to reform the criminal justice system. Jury trials did acquit at a higher rate (approximately 15–20 percent), but like other continental legal systems, Russia let prosecutors protest non-guilty verdicts, thereby allowing higher appellate courts to overturn acquittals and send defendants back for a second trial.[79] In one of the most spectacular jury trials, the alleged murderers of the journalist Anna Politkovskaia were first acquitted in a stinging vote of no confidence in the government's evidence, only to have the verdict overturned on appeal and a retrial that found the defendants guilty.[80] Indeed, the main innovation of the 2001 Criminal Procedure Code that seemingly worked as intended was the plea-bargaining provisions. Defendants regularly resorted to such special procedures even if they did not necessarily lead to dramatically reduced sentences; in a criminal justice system with a 99 percent conviction rate, their options were truly limited.

The hopes that Russia's nascent property rights and private law could restrain the state also proved to be misplaced. According to the Russian Anti-monopoly Service, the Russian state went from controlling 35 percent of GDP in 2005 to 70 percent in 2015.[81] These assets were overseen through various state entities, including specifically designated state corporations as well as joint stock companies with majority state ownership. Moreover, while a sizeable proportion of Russians owned their own apartments, over 90 percent of all land (federal, municipal, regional) remained in state hands, an unproductive resource that produced limited financial benefit for the state.[82] In the aftermath of the 2014 recession, economists called for a new round of privatizations to raise additional state revenues, yet low stock prices—as well as the requirement that all major initial public offerings (IPOs) involving Russian companies take place on a Russian exchange—doomed any major sell-off of state assets. Instead, in order to fill the state's coffers, the government ordered all state companies to pay 50 percent of their profits to the state (and private shareholders) as dividends. Such a demand made little economic sense—it sharply limited how much companies could reinvest in their business—but the dividend policy kept the state afloat.

Commercial law was originally conceived by the Yeltsin reformers as a check on the state. Putin did not abandon commercial law, in the sense that the corporate structure was still used to raise capital and to determine the value of an enterprise. Putin just made sure that the state remained the controlling shareholder in those industries that mattered. Thus, he redefined the corporation's original mission and transformed it into the state's primary sponsor. As the journalist Maxim Trudolyubov notes, state-owned enterprises mainly are used "to preserve social stability and are viewed only secondarily as economic units."[83]

Private enterprises continue to operate in Russia, and businesses regularly turn to the courts with their legal disputes, thereby bestowing a degree of legitimacy on the prevailing legal system. The government also regularly loses business-related cases in civil and administrative disputes, demonstrating a degree of judicial independence that is often overlooked when assessing the Russian legal system. Yet at the same time, the legal system still does not provide sufficient protection for business. For example, the business community has long complained about repeat and intrusive state inspections from multiple regulatory bodies (tax investigators, health inspectors, prosecutors, etc.). These repeat visits place a major financial burden on private enterprise.[84] Moreover, many entrepreneurs have found themselves in preliminary detention as a result of these inspections, subject to shakedowns, blackmail, and abusive prison conditions. Putin seemingly recognizes the problem and for several years running has used his annual state-of-the-nation speech to call for changes in the inspection process, yet there have been few signs of improvement.[85] After all, these inspections feed the power vertical and provide local authorities with key supplemental sources of income, thereby ensuring their loyalty to Putin's system and the political status quo.

Corruption remains an intractable problem that delegitimizes law as an independent and impartial arbitrator within Russian society. According to an August 2017 poll conducted by the NAFI Research Center, 49 percent of all Russians believed that it was impossible to conduct business in the country without bribes.[86] Government authorities have tried to deflect the issue by highlighting the prosecutions of low-level corruption among teachers, doctors, and members of the police, as well as the occasional arrest of a prominent government official. The latter detentions, however, are often the result of political in-fighting and a not-so-subtle reminder to toe the party line. The fight against corruption can still rally Russian society in support of a more just and transparent legal system—as evident in March 2017 when Aleksei Navalny organized a major anti-corruption demonstration in Moscow in March 2017 that prompted protests in more than eighty cities across the country.[87] Therefore, much as Putin did with the oligarchs, he was forced to draw a red line on this issue. In the aftermath of the March 2017 protests, Putin emphasized that while people should engage in constructive dialogue on fighting corruption, such discussions should not be used by political forces to promote their own "selfish interests."[88] Such a compartmentalized view of politics accurately reflects the state and law tradition that citizens can exercise their rights up until the point that they intersect with state power and no further.

Conclusion

The restoration of the concept of state and law—along with many of its historical practices—has defined Putin's eighteen years (and counting) in power. Indeed, his very utterances on the subject—"the state is the law"; "the stronger the state, the freer the individual"—echo Korkunov's writings on the Russian state from more than a century ago.[89] Moreover, Putin has relied on basic state and law principles on numerous occasions. For example, Putin allowed the last bilateral treaty with Tatarstan to expire in 2017, thereby bringing to an end the treaty-making process and all the legal irregularities associated with these agreements. Putin's legal policies and the predominance of federal law within the legal system have pushed Russia as close as it has ever been to the ideal of the nation-state. Yet paradoxically, Putin still relies on the flexibility inherent in the notion of the "unified" state to allow certain regions essentially to opt out of Russian law but not out of the Russian Federation. It is widely recognized that Russian legislation does not act in Chechnya, while sharia law is regularly used in Dagestan.[90] A true nation-state would find such a situation intolerable; the Russian state can live with such a contradiction, as long as no region questions Moscow's ultimate sovereignty, and the integrity of the state is preserved.

Putin also has been influenced by state and law principles when confronting ideological questions. While Putin put forward various conservative/nationalist ideas during his third term, he did not go so far as to convert the multinational state into a Russian state. He seemingly played with this idea in October 2016 when he announced the need to enact a law on the Russian nation, although he used the generic term for "Russian" (*rossiiskii*) as opposed to the ethnic term (*russkii*).[91] Nevertheless, by March 2017, government officials had backed away from this controversial suggestion, instead calling for a more neutral law on state nationality policy.[92] The Russian state has always been a multinational state, and any attempt to transform it into a mono-ethnic state is fraught with peril, as Putin well understands.

Finally, the state and law model has provided the foundation for Putin's substantive legal reforms. Indeed, in light of Yeltsin's uneven legislative record—and the longer, more entrenched negative Soviet legacy—the early years of Putin's presidency included several important legal advances. Among his accomplishments, Putin streamlined the appellate process, filled in major legislative gaps in civil and criminal laws, promoted a more equal and unified vision of Russian federalism, and presided over the reestablishment of the principle of *res judicata* (finality of judgments). He further did not overrule Yeltsin's decision to sign up for the European Convention, thereby allowing European human rights law to enter Russian law (albeit with some important recent exceptions). Even after Putin's third-term crackdown, these initial reforms still influenced how Russians understood and used everyday law. According to an April 2017 Levada Center opinion poll, 47 percent of Russians believed that citizens should be allowed to fight for their rights even if they went against the interests of the state.[93] The legal reforms launched by Yeltsin—the birth of constitutional jurisprudence, the expansion of private law, increased transparency through the publication of laws—were not all rolled back by Putin, thereby giving post-Soviet law its own evolutionary potential that cannot be unilaterally dismissed.

Yet the pursuit of legal modernization in Russia, like the theory of state and law itself, has its boundaries, and Putin turns out to be an outstanding representative of these limitations. Thus, even though Putin has acted within a more defined hierarchy of laws, he can still bypass the legislature and issue decrees that carry the force of law. Putin also tolerates a legal duality that defies Western notions of the rule of law, with everyday law operating relatively independently but within a legal system that remains highly politicized when confronted with a real (or even imaginary) opponent. Putin can accept this paradox because like his predecessors, he has successfully compartmentalized law so that private law practices do not impinge on the broad public law powers of the state. Putin also continues to rely on the state's coercive powers to maximum advantage, undermining the 1993 constitution's nascent civil liberties and using the courts to punish his political opponents. Lastly, despite numerous calls to clean up the legal system, Putin has waged a rather lackluster campaign against corruption, in large part because corruption continues to grease the wheels of the state and his political and economic system.

Thus, Putin's legal modernization efforts, while not inconsequential, have nevertheless stopped short of the rule of law. Instead, his reforms have reinforced traditional Russian notions of "state and law" and "legality," with an emphasis on the notion that the organs of state power and Russian citizens should fulfill the law as written. Putin himself has referred to the supremacy of statutes (*gospodstvo zakona*) as opposed to the law-based state (*pravovoe gosudarstvo*) as his ultimate objective.[94] Putin has not veered from his 1999 millennium message and his pro-statist agenda, even under the extreme pressure of the 2014–2016 economic recession. Therefore, as Putin contemplates his fourth term as president, he is unlikely to stray too far from the state and law principles that have brought him this far.

Conclusion

For over 300 years, the state has served as Russia's most prominent and revered national institution. The tsars may have had Orthodoxy on their side, and the Communists may have had history on their side, but the state has outlasted all competing ideologies as Russia's main source of governance, national unity, and inspiration. Historians have long recognized the conflicting characteristics that make up the inner workings of the Russian state: it is both strong and weak, able to punish individual citizens seemingly at will but often unable to transmit basic instructions down to the local level. It is both Russian-centric and multiethnic, run primarily by Russians but still having to satisfy the demands of a multinational population. Most puzzling, the state is both conservative and modernizing, espousing traditional values but acting as the primary instigator of economic and social change. Finally, the Russian state is all or nothing; by concentrating power in one centralized, highly bureaucratic institution, the Russian state invariably fails to invest sufficient resources in other intermediary institutions that build political consensus.

It has been the historic task of Russian law to somehow navigate among these political contradictions, structural weaknesses, and cultural differences and still govern a vast continental empire. Thus, the theory of "state and law" does not lead with such concepts as liberty or equality but with the essential idea of unity. The first article of the 1906 constitution explicitly began with the notion of the "one and indivisible" state, and subsequent constitutions have provided variations on this theme. The "unified" state does not necessarily mean that one law applies to all subjects. After all, the imperial period was marked with a high degree of legal pluralism. Nor does unity always translate into one consistent policy. On the contrary, the Russian government often works at cross-purposes with different interest groups and clans fighting for influence up and down the bureaucratic ladder. The unified state does not eliminate these internal divisions. What it does espouse, however, is a single source of sovereignty that cannot be challenged by any other national group or state institution. The treaty-making process, which facilitated the expansion of the Russian empire and subsequently provided the political foundation for both the Soviet Union and the Russian Federation, invariably reinforced this essential principle of one ruling sovereign. The greatest challenge to the unified state is dual power, which implies two (and usually more) competing sources of sovereignty and which historically has resulted in state collapse, as occurred in 1917 and 1991.

To prevent such a calamity, the unified state requires unlimited power or at least sufficient flexibility to reply decisively to any potential challenge. So while the state theoretically may stand separate from the ruler, Russian law allows the ruler to exercise state power in its purest form without any formal constraints. Indeed, Russia has never embraced a theory of natural law that limits the authority of its designated leader and his or her use of state power. Moreover, as has been highlighted throughout this book, Russian rulers have been endowed with the unique power of decree that allows their very word to become law. While the 1906 and the 1993 constitutions imposed theoretical limits on this authority—most notably that decrees must be enacted without contradicting prevailing law—this hierarchy of laws has never successfully restrained a ruler's discretionary powers. The great irony is that when Russian liberals have gained power— the Provisional Government in 1917 and Boris Yeltsin in 1991—they too have felt compelled to rule by decree, invariably linking them to Russia's statist tradition.

Russia does produce laws, which have received various titles and designations over the centuries to highlight their more general, normative characteristics. Yet with the exception of two notable periods—1906–1917 and 1991–2000—laws have emanated exclusively from the bureaucracy and not from an independent legislature. The situation under Vladimir Putin is only slightly more ambiguous; an elected Duma exists on paper but the legislative agenda largely has been set by the presidential administration and government ministries. In any event, Russian law historically has reflected bureaucratic concerns with no input from society and without the legitimization provided by an independent legislature.

But while "laws" occupy a prominent position in the legal hierarchy, Russia traditionally has contained multiple sources of law within its borders—custom, foreign law, personal decrees, detailed codes, bureaucratic rulings—often delivered in a chaotic and nontransparent fashion. And when Russian officialdom has felt the need for a significant overhaul of the legal system, it simply has borrowed Western legal principles and adapted them to meet domestic needs, with varying degrees of success. Such actions reflect Russia's status as a net importer of law. Its greatest legal innovation— socialist law—fatally broke down at the end, forcing the Russian Federation to reestablish links with the Western legal tradition.

All of the above observations, however, do not render Russia a lawless country. Admittedly, the goal during the Imperial and Soviet periods was never a law-based state or the rule of law, and not surprisingly, neither regime pursued this objective. Instead, the Russian state practiced its own version of "*zakonnost'*" that, while exempting the ruler (and in the Soviet case, the ruling party), nevertheless demanded that certain laws be observed by the state and its subjects alike. Russian legality, or law abidingness, takes two forms. On the one hand, legality is the top-down transmission of rules and regulations from the center to the regions, delivered by the so-designated "organs" of state power, where all parties are expected to fulfill the requirements of the law. These intermediary organs often have proven rather adept at avoiding central commands, thereby creating the basis for arbitrary rule and corruption. Nevertheless, this administrative pursuit of top-down legality dates back to Peter the Great, was first successfully deployed by Catherine the Great, reached its apogee in the Soviet Union, and now finds its modern-day equivalent in Putin's vaunted power vertical. This form of legality also reinforces the bureaucratic nature of Russian law where the goal is to promote order and discipline, not to foster individual rights and liberties.

The second form of legality can be found in the courts and in the more general application of Russian law in ordinary disputes. This book focuses on the two major strands of everyday practice: criminal and civil. Russia has relied on a highly politicized system of criminal justice for centuries. It spans the torture and violence of Peter the Great, the tsarist system of exile, the post-1864 political trials, Stalin's terror, the trials of dissidents, and the selective prosecution of the Putin era. Moreover, since the 1930s, the ability to prove one's innocence in court has steadily shrunk to near impossible odds (less than 1 percent), and the current state has consistently backed away from jury trials, the one credible check on its control of the criminal process.

Yet the harshness of Russian criminal law is contrasted with a surprisingly resilient and at times independent civil justice system. At virtually every stage of Russian history, citizens from all levels of society have turned to the courts to litigate their civil disputes, thereby suggesting a degree of faith in the legal system that is often assumed missing under Russian law. Historians have also discovered a greater degree of procedural regularity under Russian law than originally believed, most notably during the reigns of Peter the Great and Nicholas I as well as in the post-reform peasant courts. Kathryn Hendley further demonstrates that everyday law has enjoyed a considerable revival over the past twenty-five years. Even the Soviet period produced its own practice of everyday law, although the general absence and under-representation of certain essential topics (contracts, torts, corporate law) from the regular court docket ultimately rendered Soviet law incapable of adapting during a time of rapid political and economic change.

The persistence of everyday law under difficult conditions speaks to the duality—and underlying possibility—of Russian law. The civil courts traditionally have educated people about the law and how to exercise their rights, often at the state's expense. At the same time, the basic principles of "state and law" have always made sure that these private law values and procedures do not challenge the overwhelming public law powers of the state. This means that the ruler remains above the law, that the bureaucracy controls the legislative agenda, that commercial law does not allow for significant capital accumulation in private hands, and that all questions of national rights and personal freedom are subordinated to the need to maintain the unity and the integrity of the multinational state.

The distribution of power among the three main legal institutions—the judiciary, procuracy, and the bar—is also heavily biased in favor of the state with the procuracy serving as the "eyes" of the sovereign. The procuracy did not begin as a legal institution; it first exercised administrative and executive functions. And even after almost three centuries, it remains inexorably linked to the state as opposed to a specific branch of government. Historically, the procuracy has not been recognized as a source of law; that domain belongs to the actual statutes, administrative rulings, and (in the tsarist period) legal customs, as well as to judicial practice. Yet at various stages in Russian history, the procuracy has been assigned the power of legislative initiative, and even today, the procuracy enjoys the right to participate in law-creating activities. Its extensive supervisory authority—and right to ensure the uniformity of Russian law—provides it with an additional capacity to shape Russia's rules, regulations, and statutes.

The Judicial Reforms of 1864 and the 1993 constitution represent attempts to provide the judiciary and the *advokatura* with greater autonomy and to create an adversarial system of justice. In both cases, these institutions have used their newfound independence to hold the state accountable, yet equality among the three pillars of justice remains elusive. The modern-day procuracy's power (although notably not the state's power) has been reduced by separating the investigation and prosecution functions. Nevertheless, the procuracy's legacy has proven to be more deep-rooted than many Western rule-of-law experts recognize and stands out as one of the key institutional factors that distinguishes Russian law from its foreign counterparts.

The concepts of "state and law" and "legality" have now governed Russia for more than three centuries and under three distinct ideological regimes, an impressive record of continuity interrupted only by stunning moments of absolute collapse. How Russia might get from *zakonnost'* to the rule of law remains the final, and as yet, unanswered question. The courts naturally can serve an important forum in transforming public attitudes toward law, and sufficient examples can be found in Russia's distant and recent past to confirm that such change is possible. But while the duality of Russian law persists, it remains unlikely that the practices of everyday law could not only neutralize the highly politicized nature of Russian justice but also overcome top-down legality (i.e., the power vertical), the elevated status of the procuracy within Russia's legal hierarchy, entrenched corruption among political and economic elites, and the president's unimpeded exercise of state power.

Thus, absent a major crisis, any attempt to overhaul the Russian legal system will demand a political decision by the Russian state. The risks of legal reform have been highlighted throughout this book. Future reformers will have to balance the desire to expand individual rights and regional autonomy with the need to preserve state integrity, with the example of Yeltsin's messy treaty-making process still present in their minds. No Russian ruler who loses national territory, one should hasten to add, has ever been considered a success. Similarly, any renewed attempt at economic modernization would require a legal modernization that inevitably would raise questions about the status of private law and the state's willingness to accept a more vibrant and independent commercial sector.

A major renovation of Russian law would have to wring out other concessions from the country's political establishment as well. State power would have to give way to a real separation of powers, informal controls over the judiciary would have to be dropped, and the supervisory powers of the procuracy would have to be reined in. In other words, the last remnants of Soviet law would have to be abandoned and the historic promise of the Judicial Reforms of 1864 restored. Finally, the Russian ruler would have to be held accountable to the law, sacrificing the last bastion of state power that has been essential in holding an empire and (post-1991) a multinational country together.

No one should underestimate the challenges associated with such a transformation. The pursuit of legal reform and evolutionary change can quickly overflow its banks, as past rulers—notably Alexander II, Nicholas II, and Mikhail Gorbachev—have learned. Nevertheless, legal reform remains at the top of the agenda as to what needs to be done to make Russia a more stable and competitive nation in the twenty-first century. Thus, Russian law does not stand at the periphery of present-day developments or Russian history. On the contrary, it has always been an integral part of the reform process and a major catalyst for political, economic, and social change. No one can predict how long Putin's power vertical and unified state will last, but the pendulum no doubt will swing, and when it does, Russian law will again take center stage as a critical factor in any future political transition.

NOTES

Introduction

1. Harold J. Berman, *Justice in the U.S.S.R.: An Interpretation of Soviet Law* (Cambridge, MA: Harvard University Press, 1963), 188.
2. Kathryn Hendley, *Everyday Law in Russia* (Ithaca and London: Cornell University Press, 2017), 5–15.
3. Ibid., 225–27.
4. Marc Szeftel, *The Russian Constitution of April 23, 1906: Political Institutions of the Duma Monarchy* (Brussels: Editions de la Librarie encyclopédique, 1976), 151; 171; V. I. Vlasov, G. B. Vlasova, and S. V. Denisenko, *Teoriia gosudarstva i prava* (Rostov-on-Don: Feniks, 2017), 341–42.
5. Richard Wortman, "Russian Monarchy and the Rule of Law: New Considerations of the Court Reform of 1864," *Kritika: Explorations in Russian and Eurasian History* 6, no. 1 (2005), 148.

Chapter 1

1. Richard Hellie, "Early Modern Russian Law: The *Ulozhenie* of 1649," *Russian History* 15, nos. 2–4 (1988), 164–65.
2. Ibid., 160.
3. Nancy Shields Kollmann, *The Russian Empire: 1450–1801* (Oxford: Oxford University Press, 2017), 168–69.
4. Those convicted of the most serious crimes were branded and disfigured to ensure easy recognition if they tried to escape. Ibid., 170–71.
5. Hellie, "Early Modern Russian Law," 179. For an additional evaluation of the Law Code of 1649, see: George G. Weickhardt, "Due Process and Equal Justice in the Muscovite Codes," *Russian Review* 51, no. 4 (1992), 473–79.
6. Richard Hellie, "Russian Law from Oleg to Peter the Great," in *The Laws of Rus'—Tenth to Fifteenth Centuries*, trans. and ed. Daniel H. Kaiser (Salt Lake City: Charles Schlacks, Jr., 1993), xxxviii.
7. Kollmann, *The Russian Empire*, 139.
8. Hellie, "Early Modern Russian Law," 177.
9. Nancy Shields Kollmann, *Crime and Punishment in Early Modern Russia* (Cambridge: Cambridge University Press, 2012), 169; Nancy Shields Kollmann,

By Honor Bound: State and Society in Early Modern Russia (Ithaca: Cornell University Press, 1999), 116–19.

10. Valerie Kivelson, *Cartographies of Tsardom: The Land and Its Meanings in Seventeenth-Century Russia* (Ithaca and London: Cornell University Press, 2006), 53.

11. Ibid., 46–47.

12. Hellie, "Early Modern Russian Law," 166.

13. Kollmann, *Crime and Punishment*, 104–12.

14. Serhii Plokhy, *The Gates of Europe: A History of Ukraine* (New York: Basic Books, 2015), 105.

15. Ibid., 107.

16. Kollmann, *Crime and Punishment*, 426.

17. Oleg Kharkhordin, "What Is the State? The Russian Concept of *Gosudarstvo* in the European Context," *History and Theory* 40 (May 2001), 218–20. For an overview of the Russian state's historical evolution, see: David McDonald, "1991 and the History of Russian *Gosudarstvennost'*," *Ab Imperio* 3 (2011), 223–37.

18. Cited in M. A. Isaev, *Istoriia rossiiskogo gosudarstva i prava* (Moscow: Statut, 2012), 209.

19. Ibid., 210. See Chapter 3 for an in-depth discussion of Korkunov's legal theory.

20. Evgenii V. Anisimov, *The Reforms of Peter the Great: Progress through Coercion in Russia*, trans. John T. Alexander (Armonk, NY and London: M. E. Sharpe, 1993), 227–29.

21. Ibid., 240–41.

22. Lindsey Hughes, *Russia in the Age of Peter the Great* (New Haven, CT and London: Yale University Press, 1998), 197.

23. As quoted in Gordon B. Smith, *Reforming the Russian Legal System* (Cambridge and New York: Cambridge University Press, 1996), 1.

24. Simon Dixon, *The Modernisation of Russia 1676–1825* (Cambridge: Cambridge University Press, 1999), 51–52.

25. Richard Pipes, *Property and Freedom* (New York: Alfred A. Knopf, 1999), 187. Peter's law on single inheritance provoked strong opposition within the nobility and was subsequently repealed in 1731. Dixon, *The Modernisation of Russia 1676–1825*, 94.

26. Anisimov, *The Reforms of Peter the Great*, 192.

27. Ibid., 75–77.

28. Richard Pipes, "Was There Private Property in Muscovite Russia?" *Slavic Review* 53, no. 2 (1994), 529–30.

29. Berman, *Justice in the U.S.S.R.*, 203.

30. Hughes, *Russia in the Age of Peter the Great*, 132.

31. Berman, *Justice in the U.S.S.R.*, 179–80. Harold J. Berman, *Law and Revolution: The Formation of the Western Legal Tradition* (Cambridge, MA: Harvard University Press, 1983), 85–119.

32 Hughes, *Russia in the Age of Peter the Great*, 125.
33 Kollmann, *Crime and Punishment*, 183–84.
34 Ibid., 191–94.
35 Kollmann, *By Honor Bound*, 234.
36 Kollmann, *Crime and Punishment*, 190.
37 N. P. Karpichenko and V. N. Ambarov, *Istoriia otechestvennogo gosudarstva i prava* (Moscow: Moskovskii gumanitarnyi institut im. E. R. Dashkovoi, 2014), 71.
38 Kollmann, *Crime and Punishment*, 196–97.
39 Ibid., 262.
40 Ibid., 182; Anisimov, *The Reforms of Peter the Great*, 164.
41 Anisimov, *The Reforms of Peter the Great*, 218.
42 Sergei M. Kazantsev, "The Judicial Reform of 1864 and the Procuracy in Russia," in *Reforming Justice in Russia, 1864–1996: Power, Culture, and the Limits of the Legal Order*, ed. Peter H. Solomon, Jr. (Armonk, NY: M. E. Sharpe, 1997), 46.
43 A. G. Zviagintsev, *Istoriia prokuratury Rossii* (Moscow: Iuniti, 2010), 106.
44 D. O. Serov, *Sudebnaia reforma Petra I: Istoriko-pravovoe issledovanie* (Moscow: Zertsalo, 2009), 93.
45 Ibid.
46 Ibid., 70–71; 94.
47 Kollmann, *Crime and Punishment*, 415.
48 Ibid., 199.
49 Hughes, *Russia in the Age of Peter the Great*, 120–21.
50 As quoted in ibid., 122.
51 Richard Wortman, *The Development of a Russian Legal Consciousness* (Chicago: University of Chicago Press, 1976), 9.

Chapter 2

1 Isabel de Madariaga, *Russia in the Age of Catherine the Great* (New Haven, CT, and London: Yale University Press, 1981), 152.
2 Ibid., 153–54.
3 *The Nakaz of Catherine the Great: Collected Texts*, ed. William E. Butler and Vladimir A. Tomsinov (Clark, NJ: The Lawbook Exchange, 2010), 364.
4 Butler and Tomsinov, *The Nakaz of Catherine the Great*, Article 178.
5 de Madariaga, *Russia in the Age of Catherine the Great*, 182–83.
6 Ekaterina Pravilova, *A Public Empire: Property and the Quest for the Common Good in Imperial Russia* (Princeton, NJ: Princeton University Press, 2014), 25.

7 Ibid., 29.

8 John P. LeDonne, *Ruling Russia: Politics and Administration in the Age of Absolutism, 1762–1796* (Princeton, NJ: Princeton University Press, 1984), 69.

9 Marc Raeff, *The Well-ordered Police State: Social and Institutional Change through Law in the Germanies and Russia 1600–1800* (New Haven, CT and London: Yale University Press, 1983), 228.

10 de Madariaga, *Russia in the Age of Catherine the Great*, 282–83.

11 LeDonne, *Ruling Russia*, 145–46.

12 Pipes, *Property and Freedom*, 194.

13 de Madariaga, *Russia in the Age of Catherine the Great*, 299–301.

14 Daniel Field, *The End of Serfdom: Nobility and Bureaucracy in Russia, 1855–1861* (Cambridge, MA: Harvard University Press, 1976), 14–15.

15 David Moon, "Reassessing Russian Serfdom," *European History Quarterly* 26, no. 4 (1996), 511.

16 Tracy Dennison, *The Institutional Framework of Russian Serfdom* (Cambridge: Cambridge University Press, 2011), 120–23.

17 de Madariaga, *Russia in the Age of Catherine the Great*, 283.

18 Janet M. Hartley, "Catherine's Conscience Court—An English Equity Court?" in *Russia and the West in the Eighteenth Century*, ed. A. G. Cross (Newtonville, MA: Oriental Research Partners, 1983), 311–14.

19 Jane Burbank, "An Imperial Rights Regime: Law and Citizenship in the Russian Empire," *Kritika: Explorations in Russian and Eurasian History* 7, no. 3 (2006), 397–403.

20 Dixon, *The Modernisation of Russia*, 143. See also: A. H. Brown, "The Father of Russian Jurisprudence: The Legal Thought of S. E. Desnitskii," in *Russian Law: Historical and Political Perspectives*, ed. William E. Butler (Leyden: A. W. Sijthoff, 1977), 117–41.

21 Kazantsev, "The Judicial Reform," 49.

22 S. M. Kazantsev, *Istoriia tsarskoi prokuratury* (St. Petersburg: Sankt-Peterburgskogo Universiteta, 1993), 81.

23 Kazantsev, "The Judicial Reform," 50; Kazantsev, *Istoriia*, 99.

24 N. A. Kolokolov, ed., *Istoriia sudebnoi sistemy v Rossii* (Moscow: Iuniti-Dana, 2009), 188.

25 LeDonne, *Ruling Russia*, 183.

26 Michael Khodarkovsky, *Bitter Choices: Loyalty and Betrayal in the Russian Conquest of the North Caucasus* (Ithaca and London: Cornell University Press, 2011), 18–19.

27 Zenon Kohut, *Russian Centralism and Ukrainian Autonomy: Imperial Absorption of the Hetmanate 1760s–1830s* (Cambridge, MA: Harvard Ukrainian Research Institute, 1998), 213–18.

28 Ibid., 235–36; 286–87.

29 Karpichenko and Ambarov, *Istoriia otechestvennogo gosudarstva i prava*, 100.

30 Marc Raeff, *Michael Speransky: Statesman of Imperial Russia, 1772–1839* (The Hague: Martinus Nijhoff, 1957), 198.

31 Ibid., 35–36. Janet M. Hartley, *Alexander I (Profiles in Power)* (London and New York: Longman, 1994), 30–44.

32 Raeff, *Michael Speransky*, 42.

33 M. M. Rassolov and S. A. Batova, eds., *Ministerstvo iustitsii Rossii za 200 let (1802–2002): Istoriko-pravovoi ocherk* (Moscow: NORMA, 2002), 12.

34 Wortman, *The Development of a Russian Legal Consciousness*, 37. For a more positive view on the State Council, see: Victor Leontovitsch, *The History of Liberalism in Russia*, trans. Parmen Leontovitsch (Pittsburgh: University of Pittsburgh Press, 2012), 44–45.

35 Rassolov and Batova, *Ministerstvo iustitsii Rossii za 200 let*, 14.

36 S. M. Kazantsev, *Dorevoliutsionnye iuristy o prokurature* (St. Petersburg: Iuridicheskii Tsentr Press, 2001), 17; Rassolov and Batova, *Ministerstvo*, 19.

37 Kazantsev, "The Judicial Reform," 51.

38 Ibid., F. I. Gredinier, "Prokurorskii nadzor za piat'desiat let, istekshikh so vremeni ego preobrazovaniia po Sudebnym Ustavam Imperatora Aleksandra II," in *Sudebnye Ustavy 20 noiabria 1864 g. za piat'desiat let*, vol. 2 (Petrograd: Senatskaia tipografiia, 1914), 204–05.

39 Kazantsev, *Dorevoliutsionnye iuristy*, 17.

40 N. N. Efremova, *Ministerstvo Iustitsii Rossiiskoi Imperii: 1802–1917gg*. (Moscow: Nauka, 1983), 50–51.

41 Daniel T. Orlovsky, *The Limits of Reform: The Ministry of Internal Affairs in Imperial Russia, 1802–1881* (Cambridge, MA and London: Harvard University Press, 1981), 36–37.

42 Ibid., 37.

43 Janet M. Hartley, "The 'Constitutions' of Finland and Poland in the Reign of Alexander I: Blueprints for Reform in Russia," in *Finland and Poland in the Russian Empire: A Comparative Study*, eds. Michael Branch, Janet Hartley, and Antoni Maczak (London: School of Slavonic and East European Studies, University of London, 1995), 46–48.

44 Ibid., 50; Norman Davies, *God's Playground: A History of Poland*, vol. II (New York: Columbia University, 1982), 307–09.

45 Hartley, "The 'Constitutions' of Finland and Poland," 49–54.

46 Audrey L. Altstadt, *The Azerbaijani Turks: Power and Identity under Russian Rule* (Stanford: Hoover Institution Press, 1992), 17–19; Ronald Grigor Suny, *The Making of the Georgian Nation* (Bloomington: Indiana University Press, 1988), 58–59; 72–73; Nikolas K. Gvosdev, *Imperial Politics and Perspectives towards Georgia, 1760–1819* (New York: St. Martin's Press, 2000), 118–20; Austin Jersild, *Orientalism and Empire: North Caucasus Mountain Peoples and the Georgian Frontier, 1845–1917* (Montreal: McGill-Queen's University Press, 2002), 89–109.

47 Cited in Samuel Kucherov, *Courts, Lawyers, and Trials under the Last Three Tsars* (Westport: Greenwood Press, 1953), 115.

48 Raeff, *Michael Speransky*, 164–68; David Christian, "The Political Ideals of Michael Speransky," *The Slavonic and East European Review* 54, no. 2 (1976), 192–213; John Gooding, "The Liberalism of Michael Speransky," *The Slavonic and East European Review* 64, no. 3 (1986), 401–24.

49 Dixon, *The Modernisation of Russia*, 136.

50 M. M. Vinaver, *Iz oblasti tsivilistiki* (St. Petersburg: Tipografiia A. G. Rozena, 1908), 1–78. See also: Tatiana Borisova, "Russian National Legal Tradition: *Svod* versus *Ulozhenie* in Nineteenth Century Russia," *Review of Central and East European Law* 33, no. 3 (2008), 334–38.

51 William E. Butler, "Book Review: *A Woman's Kingdom: Noblewomen and the Control of Property in Russia, 1700–1861; Pravovoe regulirovanie imushchestvennykh otnoshenii v Rossii vo vtoroi polovine XVIII veka*; and *In Search of Legality: Michael Speranskii and the Codification of Russian Law*," *Kritika: Explorations in Russian and Eurasian History* 7, no. 2 (2006), 659.

52 Raeff, *Michael Speransky*, 339–40.

53 George L. Yaney, *The Systematization of Russian Government: Social Evolution in the Domestic Administration of Imperial Russia, 1711–1905* (Urbana: University of Illinois Press, 1973), 195–96; 254–56; 261–65.

54 Thomas C. Owen, *The Corporation under Russian Law, 1800–1917* (Cambridge: Cambridge University Press, 1991), 18–19.

55 Jonathan W. Daly, *Autocracy under Siege: Security Police and Opposition in Russia, 1866–1905* (DeKalb: Northern Illinois University Press, 1998), 13.

56 Orlovsky, *The Limits of Reform*, 31.

57 Raeff, *Michael Speransky*, 340–42.

58 Ibid., 342.

59 Virginia Martin, *Law and Custom in the Steppe: The Kazakhs of the Middle Horde and Russian Colonialism in the Nineteenth Century* (Richmond, UK: Curzon Press, 2001), 34–59.

60 Tatiana Borisova, "The Digest of Laws of the Russian Empire: The Phenomenon of Autocratic Legality," *Law and History Review* 30, no. 3 (2012), 912.

61 Ibid., 914.

62 Ibid., 916–17.

63 Pravilova, *A Public Empire*, 44–45.

64 Wortman, *The Development of a Russian Legal Consciousness*, 45–46.

65 Ibid., 223.

66 Girish N. Bhat, "The Consensual Dimension of Late Imperial Russian Criminal Procedure: The Example of Trial by Jury," in *Reforming Justice in Russia, 1864–1996: Power, Culture, and the Limits of the Legal Order*, ed. Peter H. Solomon, Jr. (Armonk, NY: M. E. Sharpe, 1997), 62–63.

67 Wortman, *The Development of a Russian Legal Consciousness*, 239–40.

68 Sergei Antonov, *Bankrupts and Usurers of Imperial Russia: Debt, Property, and the Law in the Age of Dostoevsky and Tolstoy* (Cambridge, MA and London: Harvard University Press, 2016), 206.

69 Ibid., 308.

70 Michelle Lamarche Marrese, *A Woman's Kingdom: Noblewomen and the Control of Property in Russia, 1700–1861* (Ithaca and London: Cornell University Press, 2002), 238–40.

71 Antonov, *Bankrupts and Usurers*, 296–302.

72 Roberta Thompson Manning, *The Crisis of the Old Order in Russia: Gentry and Government* (Princeton, NJ: Princeton University Press, 1982), 43.

73 Yaney, *The Systematization of Russian Government*, 30.

74 Orlovsky, *The Limits of Reform*, 10–11; Yaney, *The Systematization of Russian Government*, 223–24. An in-depth review of the major works on the Russian state as a governing institution is beyond the scope of this book. For an authoritative overview of this topic, see: Ronald Grigor Suny, "Rehabilitating Tsarism: The Imperial Russian State and Its Historians," *Comparative Studies in Society and History* 31, no. 1 (1989), 168–79. Historians have also begun to examine the state from a functional perspective, as opposed to focusing on social backgrounds and institutional debates. See: Susanne Schattenberg and Christopher Gilley, "Max Weber in the Provinces: Measuring Imperial Russia by Modern Standards," *Kritika: Explorations in Russian and Eurasian History* 13, no. 4 (2012), 889–902; Geoffrey Hosking, "Patronage and the Russian State," *The Slavonic and East European Review* 78, no. 2 (2000), 301–20.

75 Yaney, *The Systematization of Russian Government*, 83.

Chapter 3

1 Wortman, *The Development of a Russian Legal Consciousness*, 254–57.

2 Isaev, *Istoriia rossiiskogo gosudarstva i prava*, 468.

3 Wortman, *The Development of a Russian Legal Consciousness*, 260–61.

4 N. Depp, "O znachenie advokatov v grazhdanskom protsese," *Zhurnal Ministerstva Iustitsii* no. 12 (1861), 444.

5 Isaev, *Istoriia rossiiskogo gosudarstva i prava*, 494. For an overview of the justice of the peace courts, see: Joan Neuberger, "Popular Legal Cultures: The St. Petersburg mirovoi sud," in *Russia's Great Reforms, 1855–1881*, eds. Ben Eklof, John Bushnell, and Larissa Zakharova (Bloomington: Indiana University Press, 1994), 231–43.

6 Kucherov, *Courts, Lawyers, and Trials*, 86.

7 Corinne Gaudin, *Ruling Peasants: Village and State in Late Imperial Russia* (DeKalb: Northern Illinois Press, 2007), 18.

8 Ibid., 123.

9 Wortman, *The Development of a Russian Legal Consciousness*, 270–75; Orlovsky, *The Limits of Reform*, 80–84.

10 E. N. Berendts, *Sviaz sudebnoi reformy s drugimi reformami Imperatora Aleksandra II i vliianie ee na gosudarstvennyi i obshchestvennyi byt Rossii* (Petrograd: Senatskaia Tipografiia 1915), 122.

11 As quoted in Orlovsky, *The Limits of Reform*, 176.

12 Ibid., 172.

13 Wortman, "Russian Monarchy and the Rule of Law," 152–56. Wortman's observations were made in the context of reviewing Ekaterina Pravilova's book on prerevolutionary administrative law. Pravilova concludes that while the theoretical principles of administrative law resonated among prominent jurists, the necessary practical steps were not taken to transform state administration and hold it legally accountable. E. A. Pravilova, *Zakonnost' i prava lichnosti; administrativnaia iustitsiia v Rossii (vtoraia polovina XIX v.–oktiabr' 1917 g.)* (St. Petersburg: Izdatel'stvo SEAGS, 2000), 251–52.

14 Daniel Beer, *The House of the Dead: Siberian Exile under the Tsars* (New York: Alfred A. Knopf, 2017), 187.

15 Ibid., 346.

16 Richard Pipes, *Russia under the Old Regime*, 2nd ed. (New York: Collier Books, 1992), 302.

17 Ibid., 313.

18 Daly, *Autocracy under Siege*, 36–37.

19 Abraham Ascher, *P. A. Stolypin: The Search for Stability in Late Imperial Russia* (Stanford: Stanford University Press, 2001), 316–18.

20 The second half of the nineteenth century witnessed the further expansion of Russian law into the central parts of the empire (Kazan, Crimea, the Caucasus, Central Asia, and Siberia). At the same time, strong pockets of Islamic law and custom remained, often acting in open violation of Russian statutory law. See: Robert D. Crews, *For Prophet and Tsar: Islam and Empire in Russia and Central Asia* (Cambridge, MA: Harvard University Press, 2006), 268–70. For an excellent overview of the historiography on legal pluralism during the Russian empire, see: Stefan B. Kirmse, "Law and Society in Imperial Russia," *InterDisciplines: Journal of History and Sociology* 3, no. 2 (2012), 103–34.

21 Edward C. Thaden, ed., *Russification in the Baltic Provinces and Finland, 1855–1914* (Princeton, NJ: Princeton University Press, 1981), 86–87.

22 Yanni Kotsonis, *States of Obligation: Taxes and Citizenship in the Russian Empire and Early Soviet Republic* (Toronto: University of Toronto Press, 2014), 130.

23 The famous Russian historian Nikolai Karamzin questioned the need for uniformity in Russian law. Writing in 1811, Karamzin argued that Russians should study the local civil statutes of Finland, Poland, and the western provinces but not replace them if such action would lead to "great and lasting disaster." Richard Pipes, *Karamzin's Memoir on Ancient and Modern Russia* (New York: Atheneum, 1969), 189–90.

24 Bhat, "The Consensual Dimension of Late Imperial Russian Criminal Procedure," 62–63.

25 William G. Wagner, *Marriage, Property, and Law in Late Imperial Russia* (Oxford: Clarendon Press, 1994), 351–64.

26 Ibid., 216–20.

27 Wortman, *The Development of a Russian Legal Consciousness*, 266–67.

28 Alexander K. Afanas'ev, "Jurors and Jury Trials in Imperial Russia, 1866–1885," in *Russia's Great Reforms, 1855–1881*, eds. Ben Eklof, John Bushnell, and Larissa Zakharova (Bloomington: Indiana University Press, 1994), 225.

29 Ibid., 226.

30 Louise McReynolds, *Murder Most Russian: True Crime and Punishment in Late Imperial Russia* (Ithaca and London: Cornell University Press, 2013), 89.

31 Girish N. Bhat, "The Moralization of Guilt in Late Imperial Russian Trial by Jury: The Early Reform Era," *Law and History Review* 15, no. 1 (1997), 82–83; Afanas'ev, "Jurors and Jury Trials," 228; Jörg Baberowski, "Law, the Judicial System and the Legal Profession," in *The Cambridge History of Russia, Volume II: Imperial Russia, 1689–1917*, ed. Dominic Lieven (Cambridge: Cambridge University Press, 2006), 348–54.

32 McReynolds, *Murder Most Russian*, 110.

33 Kucherov, *Courts, Lawyers, and Trials*, 63.

34 Baberowski, "Law, the Judicial System and the Legal Profession," 351.

35 McReynolds, *Murder Most Russian*, 82.

36 William E. Pomeranz, "The Practice of Law and the Promise of Rule of Law: The *Advokatura* and the Civil Process in Tsarist Russia," *Kritika: Explorations in Russian and Eurasian History* 16, no. 2 (2015), 238–39.

37 Gaudin, *Ruling Peasants*, 88–89; Jane Burbank, *Russian Peasants Go to Court: Legal Culture in the Countryside, 1905–1917* (Bloomington: Indiana University Press, 2004), 82–118.

38 The autocracy created a second type of advocate, the private attorney, in 1874 largely to address the shortage of licensed lawyers. Private attorneys were required to obtain a license from the local court, but there were no educational requirements for joining the profession. Private attorneys further did not form their own corporate body to represent their interests. Although the creation of the private profession was viewed as a temporary measure, private attorneys practiced until the end of the tsarist period. William E. Pomeranz, "'Profession or Estate'? The Case of the Russian Pre-revolutionary *Advokatura*," *The Slavonic and East European Review* 77, no. 2 (1999), 257–62.

39 Pomeranz, "The Practice of Law," 244–54.

40 William E. Pomeranz, "Justice from Underground: The History of the Underground *Advokatura*," *The Russian Review* 52, no. 3 (1993), 321–40. Joan Neuberger, "'Shysters' or Public Servants? Uncertified Lawyers and Legal Aid for the Poor in Late Imperial Russia," *Russian History/Histoire Russe* 23, nos. 1–4 (1996), 295–310.

41 William E. Pomeranz, "Legal Assistance in Tsarist Russia: The St. Petersburg Consultation Bureaus," *Wisconsin International Law Journal* 14, no. 3 (1996), 586–610.

42 Ibid., 604–06.

43 Gaudin, *Ruling Peasants*, 18.

44 Pomeranz, "Justice from Underground," 333–35.

45 Gaudin, *Ruling Peasants*, 94.

46 Burbank, *Russian Peasants Go to Court*, 247.

47 Stefan B. Kirmse, "Law and Empire in Late Tsarist Russia: Muslim Tatars Go to Court." *Slavic Review* 72, no. 4 (2013), 778–801.

48 Burbank, *Russian Peasants Go to Court*, 268–71.

49 Gaudin, *Ruling Peasants*, 130–31; Stephen P. Frank, *Crime, Cultural Conflict, and Justice in Rural Russia, 1856–1914* (Berkeley: University of California Press, 1999), 243–75; Gareth Popkins, "Code versus Custom? Norms and Tactics in Volost Court Appeals, 1889–1917," *The Russian Review* 59, no. 3 (2000), 424.

50 Cathy A. Frierson, "'I Must Always Answer to the Law…' Rules and Responses in the Reformed *Volost'* Court," *Slavonic and East European Review* 75, 2 (1997), 334.

51 Stephen F. Williams, *The Reformer: How One Liberal Fought to Preempt the Russian Revolution* (New York and London: Encounter Books, 2017), 209–12.

52 The development of private law was just one manifestation of the rise of civil society during the late tsarist period. See: Joseph Bradley, *Voluntary Associations in Tsarist Russia: Science, Patriotism, and Civil Society* (Cambridge, MA: Harvard University Press, 2009); Adele Lindenmeyr, *Poverty Is Not a Vice: Charity, Society, and the State in Imperial Russia* (Princeton, NJ: Princeton University Press, 1996).

53 Owen, *The Corporation under Russian Law*, 118–32.

54 Kotsonis, *States of Obligation*, 109–11; 198–203.

55 Ibid., 80–81; 148–50; Pomeranz, "The Practice of Law," 242.

56 Pravilova, *A Public Empire*, 257–69.

57 Vinaver, *Iz oblasti tsivilistiki*, 335.

58 Ibid.

59 The professionalization and rationalization of Russia's criminal process included other measures as well, such as a greater reliance on medical expertise. See: Elisa M. Becker, *Medicine, Law, and the State in Imperial Russia* (Budapest and New York: Central European University Press, 2011).

60 Kazantsev, "The Judicial Reform," 55–56.

61 Pomeranz, "The Practice of Law," 254–56. The procuracy acquired other administrative functions during the latter part of the nineteenth and early twentieth centuries that reinstated some of its supervisory powers but never to the extent that existed in the pre-reform era. Gredinier, "Prokurorskii nadzor za piat'desiat let," 215–24.

62 Kazantsev, "The Judicial Reform," 56–58.

63 G. B. Sliozberg, *Dela minuvshikh dnei: Zapiski russkago evreia*, 1 (Paris: Pascal, 1933), 245.

64 Andrzej Walicki, *Legal Philosophies of Russian Liberalism* (Notre Dame and London: University of Notre Dame Press, 1992), 133–39; 155–64.

65 Ibid., 312–19.

66 Ibid., 213–90.

67 The most complete summary of Korkunov's theory in English is George L. Yaney, "Bureaucracy and Freedom: N. M. Korkunov's Theory of State," *The American Historical Review* 71, no. 2 (1966), 468–86.

68 N. M. Korkunov, *Russkoe gosudarstvennoe pravo* (St. Petersburg: M. M. Stasiulevich, 1901), 209.

69 Ibid., 33.

70 Ibid., 177–78.

71 Ibid., 206–07.

72 Ibid., 209–10.

73 Ibid., 179–200.

74 Ibid., 211.

75 Ibid., 444–45.

76 President Dmitry Medvedev cited Korkunov during his first state-of-the-nation speech in 2008, when he criticized the corruption among government bureaucrats and other organs of state power. As the great prerevolutionary theorist Korkunov noted, Medvedev proclaimed, "The establishment of legality is always felt as a restraint on the arbitrary rule of the powerful." http://kremlin.ru/events/president/transcripts/1968. See also: Alexander M. Yakovlev, *Striving for Law in a Lawless Land: Memoirs of a Russian Reformer* (Armonk, NY and London: M. E. Sharpe, 1996), 22–23; 100–01; Isaev, *Istoriia rossiiskogo gosudarstva i prava*, 210–12; 453–54.

77 G. F. Shershenevich, *Nauka grazhdanskogo prava v Rossii* (Kazan, 1893, reprinted by Moscow: Statut, 2003), 206–19. For additional analysis of Muromtsev's political and theoretical activities, see: D. V. Aronov, *Pervyi Spiker: Opyt nauchnoi biografii Sergeia Andreevicha Muromtseva* (Moscow: IG Iurist, 2006); V. D. Zorkin, *Muromtsev: Iz istorii politicheskoi i pravovoi mysli* (Moscow:Iuridicheskaia literatura, 1979).

78 Peter Holquist, "The Russian Empire as a 'Civilized State': International Law as Principle and Practice in Imperial Russia, 1874–1878" (Washington, DC: NCEEER, 2004), 1–27; Jeffrey Kahn, "'Protection and Empire': The Martens Clause, State Sovereignty, and Individual Rights," *Virginia Journal of International Law 56*, no. 1 (2016), 1–48.

79 Walicki, *Legal Philosophies*, 343–402; see also: Susan Heuman, *Kistiakovsky: The Struggle for National and Constitutional Rights in the Last Years of Tsarism* (Cambridge, MA: Harvard Ukrainian Research Institute, 1998), 59–92.

80 Bogdan Kistiakovskii, "In the Defense of Law," in *Landmarks: A Collection of Essays of the Russian Intelligentsia-1909*, eds. Boris Shragin and Albert Todd, trans. Marian Schwartz (New York: Karz Howard, 1977), 113.

81 Ibid., 120–21.

82 Ibid., 118.

83 Richard Wortman, "Property Rights, Populism, and Russian Political Culture," in *Civil Rights in Imperial Russia*, eds. Olga Crisp and Linda Edmondson (Oxford: Clarendon Press, 1989), 14.

84 Barbara Alpern Engel, *Breaking the Ties That Bound: The Politics of Marital Strife in Late Imperial Russia* (Ithaca and London: Cornell University Press, 2011), 18–19; 238–41; 268–69; Eric Lohr, *Russian Citizenship: From Empire to Soviet Union* (Cambridge, MA and London: Harvard University Press,

2012), 53–82; Paul W. Werth, *The Tsar's Foreign Faiths: Toleration and the Fate of Religious Freedom in Imperial Russia* (Oxford: Oxford University Press, 2014), 224–56; 263–64.

Chapter 4

1 Harold J. Berman, "The Rule of Law and the Law-based State with Special Reference to the Soviet Union," in *Toward the "Rule of Law" in Russia: Political and Legal Reform in the Transition Period*, ed. Donald D. Barry (Armonk, NY and London: M. E. Sharpe, 1992), 44–47.

2 M. M. Vinaver, *Nedavnee* (Paris: M. O. Volf', 1926), 14.

3 V. D. Spasovich, *Zastol'nye rechi, 1873–1901* (Leipzig: E. L. Karpovich, 1903), 5; Fyodor Dostoevsky, *A Writer's Diary: Volume One, 1873–1876*, trans. Kenneth Lantz (Evanston: Northwestern University Press, 1993), 356–84.

4 As quoted in N. A. Troitskii, *Tsarizm pod sudom progressivnoi obshchestvennosti, 1866–1895gg* (Moscow: Mysl', 1979), 188.

5 For an in-depth analysis of Vera Zasulich's early years and involvement in the revolutionary movement, see: Ana Siljak, *Angel of Vengeance: The "Girl Assassin," The Governor of St. Petersburg, and Russia's Revolutionary World* (New York: St. Martin's Press, 2008).

6 Kucherov, *Courts, Lawyers, and Trials*, 220.

7 Ibid., 221.

8 William C. Fuller, Jr., *Civil-Military Conflict in Imperial Russia, 1881–1914* (Princeton, NJ: Princeton University Press, 1985), 119–20.

9 Ibid., 120–21.

10 I. V. Gessen, *Istoriia russkoi advokatury*, vol. 1 (Moscow, 1914, republished by Moscow: Iurist,1997), 303–19.

11 Baberowski, "Law, the Judicial System and the Legal Profession," 362–64.

12 N. A. Troitskii, *Advokatura v Rossii i politicheskie protsessy: 1866–1904* (Tula: Avtograf, 2000), 393.

13 Karabchevskii spoke highly of Stolypin in his memoirs, noting that it was Stolypin who brought order in the aftermath of the 1905 Revolution. N. P. Karabchevskii, *Chto glaza moi videli*, vol. 2 (Berlin: Izdanie Ol'gi Diakovoi i ko.,1921), 54.

14 Kucherov, *Courts, Lawyers, and Trials*, 228.

15 Ibid., 230.

16 Karabchevskii, *Chto glaza moi videli*, vol. 2, 68.

17 Ibid., 121–22.

18 T. A. Ugrimova and A. G. Volkov,"*Stoi v zavete svoem…*" *Nikolai Konstantinovich Murav'ev: Advokat i obshchestvennyi deiatel'* (Moscow: AMA Press, 2004), 191–201.

19 Ibid., 79. See also: Troitskii, *Advokatura v Rossii i politicheskie protsessy, 1866–1904*, 322; 343.

20 Ugrimova and Volkov, "*Stoi v zavete svoem…*," 23.

21 Troitskii, *Advokatura v Rossii*, 359. For a discussion of the evolving concept of civil rights in tsarist Russia, see: W. E. Butler, "Civil Rights in Russia: Legal Standards in Gestation," and Linda Edmondson, "Was There a Movement for Civil Rights in Russia in 1905?" in Crisp and Edmondson, *Civil Rights in Imperial Russia*, 1–12; 263–85.

22 Ugrimova and Volkov, "*Stoi v zavete svoem…*," 45.

23 N. A. Troitskii, *Korifei rossiiskoi advokatury* (Moscow: Tsentrpoligraf, 2006), 292.

24 In 1904, Murav'ev represented the worker Stepan Loginov, who had shot and lightly wounded a foreign-born factory director. No one has the right to kill a man, Murav'ev recognized from the start. Nevertheless, he used his closing argument to describe the "great unhappiness" of Loginov's life, arguing that Loginov shot the director out of suffering, not out of a premeditated plan to commit murder. Murav'ev ended his speech by quoting a poignant letter from Loginov to his mother, an emotional appeal that clearly worked on the jury, which acquitted Loginov of the charges. Ugrimova and Volkov, "*Stoi v zavete svoem…*," 45–57.

25 Ugrimova and Volkov, "*Stoi v zavete svoem…*," 15.

26 Pomeranz. "The Practice of Law," 258–62.

27 S. M. Shakrai and K. P. Krakovskii, *Iuristi i revoliutsiia: Pro et Contra* (Moscow: Kuchkovo pole, 2017).

28 As quoted in Kucherov, *Courts, Lawyers and Trials*, 312. Gruzenberg recounts his major cases in his memoirs. See: O. O. Gruzenberg, *Yesterday: Memoirs of a Russian-Jewish Lawyer*, trans. Don C. Rawson and Tatiana Tipton (Berkeley: University of California Press, 1981).

29 For a full translation of the Fundamental Laws, see: Szeftel, *The Russian Constitution of April 23, 1906*, 84–108.

30 B. E. Nolde, *Ocherki russkogo gosudarstvennogo prava* (St. Petersburg: Pravda, 1911), 278.

31 Peter Holquist, "Dilemmas of a Progressive Administrator: Baron Boris Nolde," *Kritika: Explorations in Russian and Eurasian History* 7, no. 2 (2006), 267.

32 Richard Wortman, "The 'Integrity' (*Tselost'*) of the State in Imperial Russian Representation," *Ab Imperio* 2 (2011), 20–39.

33 Fundamental Laws, Article 105.

34 Ibid., Article 4.

35 Ibid., Article(s) 20; 24.

36 Szeftel, *The Russian Constitution*, 218; 309–11.

37 Isaev, *Istoriia rossiiskogo gosudarstva i prava*, 370–81; 452–55; 460–61.

38 Fundamental Laws, Article(s) 72, 73.

39 Szeftel, *The Russian Constitution*, 197–98.
40 Geoffrey Hosking, *The Russian Constitutional Experiment: Government and Duma, 1907–1914* (Cambridge: Cambridge University Press, 1973), 243–51.
41 Szeftel, *The Russian Constitution*, 198.
42 Ascher, *P. A. Stolypin*, 205–06.
43 Szeftel, *The Russian Constitution*, 152; 303.
44 Ibid., 147–49.
45 Aronov, *Pervyi Spiker*, 121–37.
46 Robert P. Browder and Alexander F. Kerensky, *The Russian Provisional Government, 1917: Documents*, vol. 1 (Stanford: Stanford University Press, 1961), 135.
47 For an overview of the commission's activities, see: William E. Pomeranz, "The Provisional Government and the Law-based State," in *Russia's Home Front in War and Revolution, 1914–22*, Book 4, eds. Adele Lindenmeyr, Christopher Read, Peter Waldron (Bloomington: Slavica Publishers, forthcoming). See also: Leonard Shapiro, "The Political Thought of the First Provisional Government," in *Revolutionary Russia*, ed. Richard Pipes (Cambridge, MA: Harvard University Press, 1968), 106.
48 N. K. Murav'ev, "O rabote Chrezvychainoi sledstvennoi komissii. Doklad na Pervom Vserossiiskom s"ezde Rabochikh i Soldatskikh Deputatov (Petrograd, June 16, 1917)," reprinted in Ugrimova and Volkov, "*Stoi v zavete svoem...,*" 204.
49 Ibid., 206–07.
50 Ibid., 209.
51 Ibid., 211.
52 Ibid., 211–12.
53 Ibid., 214.
54 I. V. Varfolomeev, *Zakon i trepet: Ocherk deiatel'nosti Chrezvychainoi sledstvennoi kommissii Vremennogo pravitel'stva* (Saratov: Nauchnaia kniga, 2006), 205–12.
55 P. E. Shchegolev, ed., *Padenie tsarskogo rezhima, stenograficheskie otchety doprosov i pokazanii, dannykh v 1917 g. v Chrezvychainoi Sledstvennoi Kommissii Vremennogo Pravitel'stva*, vol. 2 (Leningrad: Gosudarstvennoe Izdatel'stvo, 1925), 344. Available online: http://militera.lib.ru/docs/da/padenie/index.html.
56 Ibid., 351.
57 Varfolomeev, *Zakon i trepet*, 149.
58 M. I. Kupriianov and N. A. Kovalenko, *Chrezvychainaia sledstvennaia komissiia Vremennogo pravitel'stva (mart-oktiabr' 1917 g.)* (Moscow: MAKS Press, 2009), 175–78.
59 Varfolomeev, *Zakon i trepet*, 253–54; Kupriianov and Kovalenko, *Chrezvychainaia sledstvennaia komissiia*, 111–16; 191–92.

Chapter 5

1. Robert Service, *Lenin: A Political Life, The Strengths of Contradiction*, vol. 1 (Bloomington: Indiana University Press, 1985), 32.
2. I. B. Sternik, *V. I. Lenin—Iurist* (Tashkent: Uzbekistan, 1969), 225–54.
3. Cited in Jane Burbank, "Lenin and the Law in Revolutionary Russia," *Slavic Review* 54, no. 1 (1995), 29.
4. Cited in Darrell P. Hammer, "The Dictatorship of the Proletariat," in *Lenin and Leninism: State, Law, and Society*, ed. Bernard W. Eissenstat (Lexington, MA, Toronto, and London: Lexington Books, 1971), 34.
5. Ibid., 39.
6. Robert Service, *Lenin: A Political Life, Worlds in Collision*, vol. 2 (Bloomington and Indianapolis: Indiana University Press, 1991), 217.
7. Ibid., 218.
8. V. I. Lenin, *State and Revolution* (New York: International Publishers, 1932), 44.
9. Service, *Lenin: A Political Life*, vol. 2, 226.
10. Lenin, *State and Revolution*, 84.
11. Peter H. Solomon, Jr., *Soviet Criminal Justice under Stalin* (Cambridge: Cambridge University Press, 1996), 21–24.
12. *Konstitutsiia Rossiiskoi Sotsialisticheskoi Federativnoi Sovetskoi Respubliki*, July 10, 1918. Available online: http://constitution.garant.ru/history/ussr-rsfsr/1918/. Available online in English at: http://www.departments.bucknell.edu/russian/const/1918toc.html
13. Ibid., Article 31.
14. Ibid., Article(s) 32–33.
15. Ibid., Article(s) 38, 40.
16. Ibid., Article 13.
17. Ibid., Article 6.
18. Ibid., Article(s) 3, 20.
19. Marc Jansen, *A Show Trial under Lenin: The Trial of the Socialist Revolutionaries, Moscow 1922*, trans. Jean Sanders (The Hague, Boston, and London: Martinus Nijhoff, 1982), 72.
20. Karpichenko and Ambarov, *Istoriia otechestvennogo gosudarstva i prava*, 198.
21. Ibid., 199.
22. Isaev, *Istoriia Rossiiskogo gosudarstva i prava*, 712–13.
23. Ivo Lapenna, "Lenin, Law, and Legality," in *Lenin: The Man, the Theorist, the Leader: A Reappraisal*, eds. Leonard Schapiro and Peter Reddaway (New York: Frederick A. Praeger, 1967), 262.
24. Solomon, *Soviet Criminal Justice*, 28.

25 Gordon B. Smith, *The Soviet Procuracy and the Supervision of Administration* (Leiden: Sijthoff & Noordhoff, 1978), 14.

26 Ibid.

27 Eugene Huskey, *Russian Lawyers and the Soviet State: The Origins and Development of the Soviet Bar, 1917–1939* (Princeton, NJ: Princeton University Press, 1986), 90.

28 Ibid., 138–40.

29 Solomon, *Soviet Criminal Justice*, 31–32.

30 N. V. Mikhailova et al., *Istoriia otechestvennogo gosudarstva i prava* (Moscow: Iuniti-Dana, 2014), 288–89.

31 Alan M. Ball, *Russia's Last Capitalists: The Nepmen, 1921–1929* (Berkeley: University of California Press, 1987), 154–60.

32 Tracy McDonald, *Face to the Village: The Riazan Countryside under Soviet Rule, 1921–1930* (Toronto: University of Toronto Press, 2011), 90–91; 97–98.

33 Solomon, *Soviet Criminal Justice*, 50–52.

34 Richard Pipes, *The Formation of the Soviet Union: Communism and Nationalism, 1917–1923* (Cambridge, MA: Harvard University Press, 1954), 246–47; 253–55.

35 Ibid., 249.

36 Merle Fainsod, *How Russia Is Ruled* (Cambridge, MA: Harvard University Press, 1956), 308.

37 Pipes, *The Formation of the Soviet Union*, 265.

38 *Konstitutsiia Soiuza Sovetskikh Sotsialisticheskikh Respublik*, January 31, 1924. Available online: http://constitution.garant.ru/history/ussr-rsfsr/1924/.

39 Ibid., Article(s) 4, 6.

40 Ibid., Article 26.

41 Ibid., Article(s) 45, 46.

42 For a recent reassessment of Pashukanis, see: Scott Newton, *Law and the Making of the Soviet World: The Red Demiurge* (Oxford: Routledge, 2015), 100–27.

43 Berman, *Justice in the U.S.S.R.*, 42.

44 Robert Sharlet, "Stalinism and Soviet Legal Culture," in *Stalinism: Essays in Historical Interpretation*, ed. Robert C. Tucker (New York and London: W. W. Norton & Company, 1977), 162.

45 Golfo Alexopoulos, *Stalin's Outcasts: Aliens, Citizens, and the Soviet State, 1926–1936* (Ithaca and London: Cornell University Press, 2003), 22.

46 Sharlet, "Stalinism and Soviet Legal Culture," 164.

47 Alexopoulos, *Stalin's Outcasts*, 26–42.

48 Solomon, *Soviet Criminal Justice*, 149. For an excellent overview of criminal law under Stalin from 1928–36, see: Jonathan Daly, *Crime and Punishment in Russia: A Comparative History from Peter the Great to Vladimir Putin* (London: Bloomsbury, 2018), 104–14.

49 Sheila Fitzpatrick, *Everyday Stalinism: Ordinary Life in Extraordinary Times: Soviet Russia in the 1930s* (Oxford and New York: Oxford University Press, 1999), 7.

50 Smith, *Reforming the Russian Legal System*, 35–38.

51 Solomon, *Soviet Criminal Justice*, 232.

52 Elizabeth A. Wood, *Performing Justice: Agitation Trials in Early Soviet Russia* (Ithaca and London: Cornell University Press, 2005), 92–93; 114–18; 122–27; 170–71.

53 Julie A. Cassiday, *The Enemy on Trial: Early Soviet Courts on Stage and Screen* (DeKalb: Northern Illinois University Press, 2000), 115.

54 Ibid., 171.

55 Cited in Wood, *Performing Justice*, 209.

56 Robert Conquest, *The Great Terror: Stalin's Purge of the Thirties* (New York: Collier Books, 1973), 179–80.

57 Ibid., 573.

58 Solomon, *Soviet Criminal Justice*, 157.

59 Berman, *Justice in the U.S.S.R.*, 54.

60 Sharlet, "Stalinism and Soviet Legal Culture," 170–78. For a detailed analysis of early Soviet family law, see: Wendy Z. Goldman, *Women, the State, and Revolution: Soviet Family Policy and Social Life, 1917–1936* (Cambridge: Cambridge University Press, 1993).

61 *Konstitutsiia Soiuza Sovetskikh Sotsialisticheskikh Respublik*, December 5, 1936. Available online: http://constitution.garant.ru/history/ussr-rsfsr/1936/red_1936/3958676/. Available in English at: http://www.departments.bucknell.edu/russian/const/1936toc.html

62 Ibid., Article 49(b).

63 Ibid., Article(s) 16–17.

64 Ibid., Article(s) 119–123.

65 Berman, *Justice in the U.S.S.R.*, 56–57.

66 Huskey, *Russian Lawyers and the Soviet State*, 218–19.

67 Ibid., 227.

68 Smith, *Reforming the Russian Legal System*, 33.

69 For an analysis of early Soviet nationality policy, see: Francine Hirsch, *Empire of Nations: Ethnographic Knowledge and the Making of the Soviet Union* (Ithaca and London: Cornell University Press, 2005); Terry Martin, *The Affirmative Action Empire: Nations and Nationalism in the Soviet Union, 1923–1939* (Ithaca and London; Cornell University Press 2001).

70 Solomon, *Soviet Criminal Justice*, 191.

71 Yuri Slezkine, *The House of Government: A Saga of the Russian Revolution* (Princeton, NJ: Princeton University Press, 2017), 951–53.

72 Solomon, *Soviet Criminal Justice*, 457–58.

73 Ibid., 158.

74 Peter H. Solomon, Jr., "The Bureaucratization of Criminal Justice under Stalin," in *Reforming Justice in Russia, 1864–1996: Power, Culture, and the Limits of the Legal Order*, ed. Peter H. Solomon, Jr. (Armonk, NY: M. E. Sharpe, 1997), 228–55.

75 Daly, *Crime and Punishment*, 124.

Chapter 6

1 Miriam Dobson, *Khrushchev's Cold Summer: Gulag Returnees, Crime, and the Fate of Reform after Stalin* (Ithaca and London: Cornell University Press, 2009), 27.

2 Berman, *Justice in the U.S.S.R.*, 70–71.

3 Dobson, *Khrushchev's Cold Summer*, 37.

4 Ibid., 51–53.

5 Ibid., 61.

6 Ibid., 50.

7 Kathleen E. Smith, *Moscow 1956: The Silenced Spring* (Cambridge, MA: Harvard University Press, 2017), 55–81.

8 Beer, *The House of the Dead*, 351.

9 Ibid., 357.

10 Ibid., 346.

11 James Heinzen, *The Art of the Bribe: Corruption under Stalin, 1943–53* (New Haven, CT and London: Yale University Press, 2016), 35.

12 Dobson, *Khrushchev's Cold Summer*, 184.

13 William E. Butler, *Soviet Law* (London: Butterworths, 1983) 277; 292–93.

14 Khrushchev also introduced more informal local practices to policing, most notably by creating volunteer people's patrols (*druzhiny*) in 1958 to enforce public order. The people's patrols enjoyed considerable extralegal authority—including the right to demand identification papers—but existed outside any formal government structures and instead were under the direction of the Communist Party. Berman, *Justice in the U.S.S.R.*, 286–88.

15 Butler, *Soviet Law*, 128.

16 George Feifer, *Justice in Moscow* (Lincoln, NE: Authors Guild Backprint.Com Edition, 2000), 127.

17 Yoram Gorlizki, "Delegalization in Russia: Soviet Comrades' Courts in Retrospect," *The American Journal of Comparative Law* 46, no. 3 (1998), 409–17.

18 Berman, *Justice in the U.S.S.R.*, 291.

19 Gorlizki, "Delegalization in Russia," 422.

20 Feifer, *Justice in Moscow*, 154–56.

21 Ibid., 69.

22 Smith, *The Soviet Procuracy*, 19–20.

23 Ibid., 20.

24 Gordon B. Smith, "The Struggle over the Procuracy," in *Reforming Justice in Russia, 1864–1996: Power, Culture, and the Limits of the Legal Order*, ed. Peter H. Solomon, Jr. (Armonk, NY: M. E. Sharpe, 1997), 350.

25 Pamela A. Jordan, *Defending Rights in Russia: Lawyers, the State, and Legal Reform in the Post-Soviet Era* (Vancouver: UBC Press, 2005), 39.

26 Yuri Feofanov, "The Trial of Ian Rokotov," in *Politics and Justice in Russia: Major Trials of the Post-Stalin Era*, eds. Yuri Feofanov and Donald D. Barry (Armonk, NY and London: M. E. Sharpe, 1996), 26–29.

27 Ibid., 31.

28 Max Haywood, ed. and trans., *On Trial: The Soviet State versus "Abram Tertz" and "Nikolai Arzhak"* (New York: Harper & Row, 1966), 175–76.

29 Benjamin Nathans, "The Dictatorship of Reason: Aleksandr Vol'pin and the Idea of Rights under 'Developed Socialism'," *Slavic Review* 66, no. 4 (2007), 631–32; 659–61.

30 Dina Kaminskaya, *Final Judgment: My Life as a Soviet Defense Attorney* (New York: Simon and Schuster, 1982), 38.

31 Ibid., 190.

32 Ibid., 194.

33 Ibid., 202.

34 Ibid., 203.

35 Butler, *Soviet Law*, 344–45.

36 Yuri Orlov, *Dangerous Thoughts: Memoirs of a Russian Life* (New York: William Morrow and Company, 1991), 222–24.

37 Ibid., 227–30.

38 Todd Foglesong, "The Reform of Criminal Justice and Evolution of Judicial Dependence in Late Soviet Russia," in *Reforming Justice in Russia, 1864–1996: Power, Culture, and the Limits of the Legal Order*, ed. Peter H. Solomon, Jr. (Armonk, NY: M. E. Sharpe, 1997), 294.

39 For a discussion of the links between socialist law and civil law practices, see: John Quigley, "Socialist Law and the Civil Law Tradition," *The American Journal of Comparative Law* 37, no. 4 (1989), 781–808.

40 *Konstitutsiia Soiuza Sovetskikh Sotsialisticheskikh Respublik*, October 7, 1977. Available online: http://constitution.garant.ru/history/ussr-rsfsr/1977/red_1977/5478732/. Available online in English: http://www.departments.bucknell.edu/russian/const/1977toc.html

41 An additional clause within Article 6 stipulated that party organizations must act within the framework of the 1977 constitution, suggesting the possibility of certain constitutional restraints on the party's activities. Yet Article 6 only imposed this theoretical limitation on party organizations, leaving the party itself in an unassailable position as the sole political force responsible for overseeing and implementing the constitution. Viktor Sheinis, *Vlast' i zakon:*

Politika i konstitutsii v Rossii v XX–XXI vekakh (Moscow: Mysl', 2014), 322–23.

42 Benjamin Nathans, "Soviet Rights-Talk in the Post-Stalin Era, " in *Human Rights in the Twentieth Century*, ed. Stefan-Ludwig Hoffman (Cambridge: Cambridge University Press, 2011), 189.

43 Butler, *Soviet Law*, 39–46; 48–51.

44 Ibid., 46–48; 53–54.

45 Thomas F. Remington, *Presidential Decrees in Russia: A Comparative Perspective* (Cambridge: Cambridge University Press, 2014), 62.

46 Butler, *Soviet Law*, 55; Berman, *Justice in the U.S.S.R.*, 76.

47 Butler, *Soviet Law*, 53.

48 Ronald Grigor Suny, *The Revenge of the Past: Nationalism, Revolution, and the Collapse of the Soviet Union* (Stanford: Stanford University Press, 1993), 120.

49 1977 Constitution, Art. 159.

50 Jordan, *Defending Rights in Russia*, 40–43.

51 Donald D. Barry and Harold J. Berman, "The Soviet Legal Profession," *Harvard Law Review* 82, no. 1 (1968), 1–41.

52 Bernard Rudden, "Scientific Socialism and Soviet Private Law," *Notre Dame Law Review* 61, no. 2 (1986), 159–62.

53 Robert Rand, *Comrade Lawyer: Inside Soviet Justice in an Era of Reform* (Boulder: Westview Press, 1991), 1; 11.

54 Smith, *The Soviet Procuracy*, 61–74.

55 Smith, "The Struggle over the Procuracy," 353.

56 William E. Pomeranz, "Supervisory Review and Finality of Judgments under Russian Law," *Review of Central and East European Law* 34, no. 1 (2009), 17–18.

57 Alena Ledeneva, "Telephone Justice in Russia," *Post-Soviet Affairs* 24, no. 4 (October–December 2008), 326–27.

58 Peter H. Solomon, Jr., "The Case of the Vanishing Acquittal: Informal Norms and the Practice of Soviet Criminal Justice," *Soviet Studies* 39, no. 4 (1987), 538–46.

59 For an overview of late Soviet criminal law, see: Daly, *Crime and Punishment*, 134–46.

60 Kathryn Hendley, *Trying to Make Law Matter: Legal Reform and Labor Law in the Soviet Union* (Ann Arbor: The University of Michigan Press, 1996), 33.

61 Alena V. Ledeneva, *Russia's Economy of Favors: Blat, Networking and Informal Exchange* (Cambridge: Cambridge University Press, 1998), 35–37; 39–47.

62 Ibid., 37.

63 Ibid., 37; 68.

64 Ibid., 42–47.

65 Heinzen, *The Art of the Bribe*, 258.
66 Konstantin M. Simis, *USSR: The Corrupt Society: The Secret World of Soviet Capitalism* (New York: Simon and Schuster, 1982), 299.
67 Hendley, *Trying to Make Law Matter*, 172.
68 Ibid., 170.
69 Ibid., 167.
70 Ibid.
71 Ibid., 170.
72 Berman, *Justice in the U.S.S.R.*, 203.
73 Aleksandr Makovskii, "Uroki reformirovaniia Grazhdanskogo kodeksa Rossii (2008–13)," *The Senate Readings*, April 12, 2013. Available online: http://www.ksrf.ru/ru/Info/Reading/Pages/PerformanceMakovskii.aspx
74 Kistiakovskii, "In the Defense of Law," 128.
75 Isaev, *Istoriia rossiiskogo gosudarstva i prava*, 705.
76 Ibid., 693.
77 Ibid.

Chapter 7

1 Mikhail Gorbachev, *Memoirs* (New York: Doubleday, 1996), 53.
2 John N. Hazard, "Soviet Law Takes a Fresh Breath," *Bulletin of the Australian Society of Legal Philosophy* 17, no. 1 (1992), 12–14; Martin McCauley, *Gorbachev* (London and New York: Longman, 1998), 68–70.
3 Marshall I. Goldman, *What Went Wrong with Perestroika* (New York and London: W. W. Norton & Company, 1992), 115.
4 Berman, "The Rule of Law and the Law-based State," 43–48.
5 Eugene Huskey, "From Legal Nihilism to *Pravovoe Gosudarstvo*: Soviet Legal Development, 1917–1990," in *Toward the "Rule of Law" in Russia: Political and Legal Reform in the Transition Period*, ed. Donald D. Barry (Armonk, NY and London: M. E. Sharpe, 1992), 33–39.
6 Robert Sharlet, *Soviet Constitutional Crisis: From De-Stalinization to Disintegration* (Armonk, NY and London: M. E. Sharpe, 1992), 86.
7 Archie Brown, *The Gorbachev Factor* (Oxford: Oxford University Press, 1996), 180.
8 Jane Henderson, "The 1988 Soviet Constitutional Reforms and Sources of Law," *The King's College Law Journal* 1, no. 1 (1990–91), 64–66.
9 Smith, *Reforming the Russian Legal System*, 73–75.
10 Kathleen E. Smith, *Remembering Stalin's Victims: Popular Memory and the End of the USSR* (Ithaca and London: Cornell University Press, 1996), 41–62.
11 Brown, *The Gorbachev Factor*, 262–64.

12 Ibid., 267–69.
13 Ibid., 202–05.
14 McCauley, *Gorbachev*, 165.
15 Sharlet, *Soviet Constitutional Crisis*, 95.
16 Ibid.
17 Brown, *The Gorbachev Factor*, 280–81; William Taubman, *Gorbachev: His Life and Times* (New York and London: W. W. Norton & Company, 2017), 576–77.
18 John Russell, "Improbable Unions: The Draft Union Treaties in the USSR, 1990–1991," *Review of Central and East European Law* 22, no. 4 (1996), 396.
19 On May 29, 1990, Boris Yeltsin was elected the chairman of the presidium of the RSFSR Supreme Soviet. Timothy J. Colton, *Yeltsin: A Life* (New York: Basic Books, 2008), 182.
20 Taubman, *Gorbachev*, 580.
21 Russell, "Improbable Unions," 401–02.
22 Sharlet, *Soviet Constitutional Crisis*, 113.
23 Victoria E. Bonnell, Ann Cooper, and Gregory Freidin, eds., *Russia at the Barricades: Eyewitness Accounts of the August 1991 Coup* (Armonk, NY and London: M. E. Sharpe, 1994), 35.
24 Ibid., 171.
25 Russell, "Improbable Unions," 399.
26 Plokhy, *The Gates of Europe*, 321.
27 Leon Aron, *Yeltsin: A Revolutionary Life* (New York: St. Martin's Press, 2000), 132–33.
28 Ibid., 203–05.
29 Ibid., 220; Taubman, *Gorbachev*, 336.
30 Colton, *Yeltsin*, 157–58.
31 Aron, *Yeltsin*, 318.
32 The primary exception to this rule was the Karelo-Finnish Union Republic that existed from 1940 to 1956 and bordered Finland. In 1956, however, the Karelo-Finnish SSR was incorporated into the RSFSR and became the Karelian Autonomous Soviet Socialist Republic.
33 William E. Pomeranz, "The Russian Constitutional Court's Interpretation of Federalism: Balancing Center-Regional Relations," *The Parker School Journal of East European Law* 4, no. 4 (1997), 412–13.
34 Remington, *Presidential Decrees in Russia*, 72–73.
35 Aron, *Yeltsin*, 495–96.
36 For a discussion of the role of corporate law during Russian privatization, see: Katharina Pistor, "Company Law and Corporate Governance in Russia," in *The Rule of Law and Economic Reform in Russia*, eds. Jeffrey D. Sachs and Katharina Pistor (Boulder: Westview Press, 1997), 165–87.

37 Colton, *Yeltsin*, 230–31.
38 Remington, *Presidential Decrees in Russia*, 71.
39 Aron, *Yeltsin*, 496.
40 Ibid., 503.
41 Alexei Trochev, *Judging Russia: The Constitutional Court in Russian Politics, 1990–2006* (Cambridge: Cambridge University Press, 2008), 105; Herman Schwartz, *The Struggle for Constitutional Justice in Post-Communist Europe* (Chicago and London: University of Chicago Press, 2000), 118–22.
42 Trochev, *Judging Russia*, 195–97; Schwartz, *The Struggle for Constitutional Justice*, 122–25.
43 The Communist Party case revolved around Yeltsin's decrees that ordered the party to cease activity and hand over its property to the government. The Communist Party appealed to the Constitutional Court and organized a spirited defense that highlighted the accomplishments of the party. Yeltsin's lawyers responded by arguing that the party had routinely violated the constitution while in power and that it had not atoned for its past mistakes. The Constitutional Court ultimately tried to split the difference by banning the party's leadership structures but allowing the party to organize on a regional level. The Court's decision was never enforced, and the Communist Party remained the prime opposition party during the 1990s. For an overview of the trial, see: Kathleen E. Smith, *Mythmaking in the New Russia: Politics and Memory during the Yeltsin Era* (Ithaca and London: Cornell University Press, 2002), 18–28.
44 Smith, *Reforming Russia*, 91.
45 William E. Pomeranz, "Judicial Review and the Russian Constitutional Court: The Chechen Case," *Review of Central and East European Law* 23, no. 1 (1997), 12–13.
46 Aron, *Yeltsin*, 512.
47 Robert B. Ahdieh, *Russia's Constitutional Revolution: Legal Consciousness and the Transition to Democracy, 1985–1996* (University Park: The Pennsylvania State University Press, 1997), 51.
48 Aron, *Yeltsin*, 511.
49 Ibid., 513.
50 Remington, *Presidential Decrees in Russia*, 100–01.
51 Isaev, *Istoriia rossiiskogo gosudarstva i prava*, 717.
52 Aron, *Yeltsin*, 516–17.
53 Ibid., 517.
54 Ibid., 517–18.
55 Colton, *Yeltsin*, 279.
56 Smith, *Reforming Russia*, 102.
57 Ibid.
58 Leonid Batkin, "The Minefield of Russian Constitutionalism: Before and after October 1993," in *Remaking Russia: Voices from Within*, ed. Heyward Isham (Armonk, NY and London: M. E. Sharpe, 1995), 114.

59 *The Russian Constitution at Fifteen: Assessments and Current Challenges to Russia's Legal Development*, ed. F. Joseph Dresen and William E. Pomeranz (Washington, DC: Kennan Institute Occasional Paper no. 304, 2009), 50.

60 Ibid.

Chapter 8

1 Robert Sharlet, "Legal Transplants and Political Mutations: The Reception of Constitutional Law in Russia and the Newly Independent States," *East European Constitutional Review* 7, no. 4 (1998), 60.

2 Ibid., 64.

3 For a more detailed analysis of the Russian constitution, see: Jane Henderson, *The Constitution of the Russian Federation: A Contextual Analysis* (Oxford and Portland, OR: Hart Publishing, 2011), 81–104.

4 *Konstitutsiia Rossiskoi Federatsii* (with amendments). Available online: http://www.ksrf.ru/ru/INFO/LEGALBASES/CONSTITUTIONRF/Pages/default.aspx. Available online in English: http://www.ksrf.ru/en/INFO/LEGALBASES/CONSTITUTIONRF/Pages/default.aspx.

5 T. N. Rad'ko, V. V. Lazarev, and L. A. Morozova, *Teoriia gosudarstva i prava* (Moscow: Prospekt, 2014), 443–47.

6 V. D. Perevalov et al., *Teoriia gosudarstva i prava* (Moscow: NORMA, 2008), 53.

7 V. V. Komarova, *Konstitutsionnaia zakonnost' v realizatsii printsipa razdeleniia vlastei po primere Rossiiskoi Federatsii* (Moscow: Prospekt, 2014), 49–53. See also: M. V. Baglai and B. N. Gabrichidze, *Konstitutsionnoe pravo Rossiiskoi Federatsii* (Moscow: INFRA·M—KODEKS, 1996), 290–312; L. A. Okun'kov, ed., *Kommentarii k Konstitutsii Rossiiskoi Federatsii* (Moscow, BEK, 1996), 43.

8 Anatolii Lyskov, "Sud—eto organ gosudarstvennoi vlasti," *Kommersant Vlast'* 27 (July 13, 2009), 23–25.

9 1993 Constitution, Article 117.

10 Ibid., Article(s) 105, 106.

11 Ibid., Article 125(2.a).

12 Ibid., Article(s) 5(2); 68(2).

13 Ibid., Article 13.

14 Ibid., Article 55. Article 29 did include an implied limitation on freedom of speech by banning propaganda that might instigate social, racial, national, or religious hatred and strife.

15 These provisions include innocent until proven guilty, no retroactive application of justice, and the basic protections against self-incrimination, double jeopardy, and illegally obtained evidence. The constitution further upheld the right to be represented by an attorney, who would be provided free-of-charge in cases so specified under law. The right to consult with a lawyer began from the moment of being taken into custody. Ibid., Article(s) 48–51; 54.

16 Ibid., Article(s) 20; 47.

17 The constitution provides an extra layer of protection for the fundamental rights listed in Chapters 1 and 2. Pursuant to Article 135, Chapters 1 and 2 (along with Chapter 9) cannot be revised by parliament; instead, if parliament votes by 3/5th majority to amend these sections, Russia would have to call a constitutional assembly. In contrast, pursuant to Article 135, other parts of the constitution can be amended via federal constitutional law.

18 Batkin, "The Minefield of Russian Constitutionalism," 116.

19 The 1993 constitution only provided a general description of the other two high courts and their respective jurisdictions. The Supreme Court was designated as the supreme judicial body for civil, criminal, administrative, and other cases under the jurisdiction of the common courts. The Higher Commercial Court received similar status over economic cases examined by the *arbitrazh* courts with its primary focus being commercial disputes between business enterprises. Both courts were empowered to engage in supervisory functions to be defined later in law, as well as to provide "explanations" on the issues of court proceedings. Whether such explanations rose to the level of "precedent" remained undefined in the constitution. Russian Constitution, Article(s) 126, 127.

20 The constitution identified five broad areas of review and further indicated when (and under what circumstances) institutions could appeal to the Constitutional Court. To highlight the complexity of this jurisdiction, under Article 125(5), certain institutions (the president, the legislature, the government, and regional legislatures) were given the right to ask the Court for an interpretation of the constitution. Individual citizens were not given this general right. Instead, citizen petitions to the court were only allowed under Article 125(4) in concrete (or pending) cases involving violations of federal law. Thus, normative and nonnormative decrees by the president, the government, or any public authority could not be appealed by individuals to the Constitutional Court.

21 Gordon B. Smith, "The Procuracy: Constitutional Questions Deferred," in *Russia and Its Constitution: Promise and Political Reality*, ed. Gordon B. Smith and Robert Sharlet (Leiden: Koninklijke Brill, 2008), 106.

22 The procuracy was not named as one of the designated government bodies with this privilege under Article 104.

23 Gordon B. Smith, "The Procuracy, Putin, and the Rule of Law in Russia," in *Russia, Europe, and the Rule of Law*, ed. Ferdinand Feldbrugge (Leiden and Boston: Martinus Nijhoff, 2007), 7.

24 M. Steven Fish, *Democracy Derailed in Russia: The Failure of Open Politics* (Cambridge: Cambridge University Press, 2005), 224–44; Stephen Holmes, "Superpresidentialism and Its Problems," *East European Constitutional Review* 2/3, nos. 4/1 (1993/94), 123–26.

25 Colton, *Yeltsin*, 285.

26 Jeffrey Kahn, *Federalism, Democratization, and the Rule of Law in Russia* (Oxford: Oxford University Press, 2002), 235.

27 Pomeranz, "The Russian Constitutional Court's Interpretation of Federalism," 414–16.

28 Pomeranz, "Judicial Review and the Russian Constitutional Court," 25–42.

29 Ibid., 47–48.

30 The Constitutional Court later objected to the attempts by the Supreme Court and Higher Commercial Court to engage in constitutional review. This assertion of exclusive jurisdiction created tension between the three high courts and further suffered from being a legal overstretch, since the 1993 constitution did not grant the Constitutional Court the sole right of judicial review over all constitutional disputes. William Burnham and Alexei Trochev, "Russia's War between the Courts: The Struggle over the Jurisdictional Boundary between the Constitutional Court and Regular Courts," *The American Journal of Comparative Law* 55, no. 3 (2007), 381–452.

31 Pomeranz, "The Russian Constitutional Court's Interpretation of Federalism," 434–37; Trochev, *Judging Russia*, 245–46.

32 The passage of Part I and Part II of the Russian Civil Code has a unique legislative history. In both cases, the Federation Council, the upper house of the Russian legislature, failed to ratify the code. It actually rejected Part I, but not within the required time period, thereby allowing President Yeltsin to sign the code into law. Moreover, the Federation Council never even voted on Part II of the Civil Code, again allowing the law to come into existence after the appropriate time period had elapsed. Thus, Russia's most important pieces of economic legislation were never ratified by the full parliament. Christopher Osakwe, "Anatomy of the 1994 Civil Codes of Russia and Kazakhstan: A Biopsy of the Economic Constitutions of Two Post-Soviet Republics," *Notre Dame Law Review* 73, no. 5 (1998), 1442.

33 Ibid., 1416. The Russian Civil Code was not an entirely foreign document; commentators identified links to the 1991 USSR Fundamental Principles of Civil Procedure, and even some elements from the 1964 RSFSR Civil Code survived, particularly in the administration of state property. Ibid., 1425–27.

34 Ibid., 1437.

35 Colton, *Yeltsin*, 426. The Federal Assembly also overrode Yeltsin's veto on several occasions. See: Aron, *Yeltsin*, 714.

36 Ibid., 674.

37 Remington, *Presidential Decrees in Russia*, 137–140.

38 Cheryl W. Gray and Kathryn Hendley, "Developing Commercial Law in Transition Economies: Examples from Hungary and Russia," in *The Rule of Law and Economic Reform in Russia*, eds. Jeffrey D. Sachs and Katharina Pistor (Boulder: Westview Press, 1997), 157–60; Kathryn Hendley, "The Spillover Effects of Privatization on Russian Legal Culture," *Transnational Law & Contemporary Problems* 5, no. 1 (Spring, 1995), 58–62.

39 David E. Hoffman, *The Oligarchs: Wealth and Power in the New Russia* (New York: Public Affairs, 2002), 193.

40 Ibid., 234–35.

41 Vadim Volkov, *Violent Entrepreneurs: The Use of Force in the Making of Russian Capitalism* (Ithaca and London: Cornell University Press, 2002), 29–49.

42 Ibid., 134–54; 191.

43 Hoffman, *The Oligarchs*, 308–20.

44 Ibid., 243–45.
45 Ibid., 259–60.
46 Karen Dawisha, *Putin's Kleptocracy: Who Owns Russia?* (New York: Simon & Schuster, 2014), 106–17.
47 Anders Aslund, *Russia's Capitalist Revolution: Why Market Reform Succeeded and Democracy Failed* (Washington, DC: Peter G. Peterson Institute for International Economics, 2007), 194–97. See also: Neela Banerjee, "Russia's Embryos of Enterprise: A New Breed of Small Entrepreneurs Springs from the Financial Chaos," *New York Times*, July 20, 1999. Available online: http://www.nytimes.com/1999/07/20/business/russia-s-embryos-enterprise-new-breed-small-entrepreneurs-springs-financial.html?pagewanted=all.
48 Peter H. Solomon, Jr. and Todd S. Foglesong, *Courts and Transition in Russia: The Challenge of Judicial Reform* (Boulder: Westview Press, 2000), 10–12.
49 Stephen C. Thaman, "The Resurrection of Trial by Jury in Russia," *Stanford Journal of International Law* 31, no. 61 (1995), 80–82.
50 Stephan C. Thaman, "Jury Trial and Adversary Procedure in Russia: Reform of Soviet Inquisitorial Procedure or Democratic Window Dressing?" in *Russia and Its Constitution: Promise and Political Reality*, eds. Gordon B. Smith and Robert Sharlet (Leiden: Koninklijke Brill, 2008), 144–45.
51 Volkov, *Violent Entrepreneurs*, 180.
52 Kathryn Hendley, "Remaking an Institution: The Transition in Russia from State *Arbitrazh* to *Arbitrazh* Courts," *American Journal of Comparative Law* 46, no. 1 (Winter, 1998), 125–27.
53 Solomon and Foglesong, *Courts and Transition in Russia*, 13.
54 Ibid., 47–49.
55 Ibid., 33–35.
56 Smith, "The Procuracy: Constitutional Questions Deferred," 107; Smith, "The Procuracy, Putin, and the Rule of Law in Russia," 2–3; V. G. Bessarabov and D. R. Pashtov, *Uchastie prokuratury v zakonotvorcheskoi deiatel'nosti organov gosudarstvennoi vlasti sub"ektov Rossiiskoi Federatsii* (Moscow: Iurlitinform, 2016), 57–59.
57 Smith, "The Procuracy, Putin, and the Rule of Law in Russia," 3–6.
58 Steven Lee Myers, *The New Tsar: The Rise and Reign of Vladimir Putin* (New York: Vintage Books, 2015), 142.
59 Jordan, *Defending Rights in Russia*, 74–78.
60 Ibid., 78–79.
61 Ibid., 11–13.
62 Stanislaw Pomorski, "Justice in Siberia: A case study of a lower criminal court in the city of Krasnoyarsk," *Communist and Post-Communist Studies* 34 (2001), 455–68.
63 Ibid., 476.
64 Yeltsin's farewell address can be found online at: http://www.nytimes.com/2000/01/01/world/yeltsin-resigns-in-boris-yeltsin-s-words-i-have-made-a-decision.html.

Chapter 9

1. Vladimir Putin et al., *First Person: An Astonishingly Frank Self-Portrait*, trans. Catherine A. Fitzpatrick (New York: Public Affairs, 2000), 40–41.
2. Myers, *The New Tsar*, 58.
3. Fiona Hill and Clifford G. Gaddy, *Mr. Putin: Operative in the Kremlin* (Washington, DC: Brookings Institution Press, 2015), 117–18.
4. Myers, *The New Tsar*, 50.
5. Ibid., 108–11.
6. Vladimir Putin, "Rossiia na rubezhe tysiacheletii," *Nezavisimaia gazeta*, December 30, 1999. Available at: http://www.ng.ru/politics/1999-12-30/4_millenium.html. Available in English at: http://pages.uoregon.edu/kimball/Putin.htm.
7. Ibid.
8. Ibid.
9. Kotsonis, *States of Obligation*, 80–81.
10. Putin, "Rossiia na rubezhe tysiacheletii."
11. Kahn, *Federalism*, 240–45.
12. Ibid., 245–48.
13. Smith, "The Procuracy: Constitutional Questions Deferred," 109–13.
14. Gordon M. Hahn, "The Impact of Putin's Federative Reforms on Democratization in Russia," *Post-Soviet Affairs* 19, no. 2 (2003), 117.
15. Kahn, *Federalism*, 257–60.
16. Henderson, *The Constitution of the Russian Federation*, 100.
17. The introduction of the Russian Land Code was not without its problems. For example, the statute implementing the Land Code called on enterprises to purchase the land underneath their factories, which had remained under state ownership even after the 1990s privatization process. Regional governments inflated the sales price to the point that the owners objected to what essentially amounted to a second privatization, and the government was forced to delay these implementing regulations. William E. Pomeranz, "Russian Land Reform Revisited: Proposed Amendments to the Russian Land Code," *Russia/Eurasia Executive Guide*, September 15, 2003, 3–4; 12–13.
18. William Burnham and Jeffrey Kahn, "Russia's Criminal Procedure Code Five Years Out," *Review of Central and East European Law* 33 (2008), 34–39.
19. Peter H. Solomon, Jr., "The Criminal Procedure Code of 2001: Will It Make Russian Justice More Fair?" in *Ruling Russia: Law, Crime, and Justice in a Changing Society*, ed. William Alex Pridemore (Lanham, MD: Rowman & Littlefield, 2005), 84.
20. Peter H. Solomon, Jr., "Plea Bargaining Russian Style," *Demokratizatsiya* 20, no. 3 (2012), 289.
21. Jeffrey D. Kahn, "Russia's 'Dictatorship of Law' and the European Court of Human Rights," *Review of Central and East European Law* 29, no. 1 (2004),

4–5; Alexei Trochev, "All Appeals Lead to Strasbourg? Unpacking the Impact of the European Court of Human Rights on Russia," *Demokratizatsiya* 17, no. 2 (2009), 145–78.

22 William E. Pomeranz, "Uneasy Partners: Russia and the European Court of Human Rights," *Human Rights Brief* 19, no. 3 (2012), 20.

23 Pomeranz "Supervisory Review and Finality of Judgments under Russian Law," 19–28.

24 Between 2000 and 2010, the number of civil cases before the courts of general jurisdiction doubled. During that same time period, the commercial courts experienced a 70 percent rise in the number of cases. Kathryn Hendley, "The Puzzling Non-consequences of Societal Distrust of Courts: Explaining the Use of Russian Courts," *Cornell International Law Journal* 45, no. 3 (2012), 523.

25 Hendley, *Everyday Law*, 58–133; 151–54.

26 Ibid., 173–78.

27 Thomas Firestone "Criminal Corporate Raiding in Russia," *The International Lawyer* 42, no. 4 (2008), 1210–18.

28 Hoffman, *The Oligarchs*, 479–89.

29 Ibid., 445–57.

30 Richard Sakwa, *Putin and the Oligarch: The Khodorkovsky-Yukos Affair* (London and New York: I. B. Tauris, 2014), 49–50; 57–58.

31 Ibid., 62.

32 Ibid., 96–97.

33 Ibid., 99.

34 Myers, *The New Tsar*, 255–59.

35 William E. Pomeranz, "President Medvedev and the Contested Constitutional Underpinnings of Russia's Power Vertical," *Demokratizatsiya* 17, no. 2 (2009), 181–82.

36 Ibid., 185.

37 Dresen and Pomeranz, "The Russian Constitution at Fifteen," 20.

38 Remington, *Presidential Decrees in Russia*, 109.

39 In 2011, the Investigative Committee became an independent organization outside the formal structures of the prosecutor's office, cutting the last institutional links between the two organizations. The head of the Investigative Committee is appointed by, and reports directly to, the president.

40 Smith, *Reforming the Russian Legal System*, 113.

41 Ethan S. Burger, and Mary S. Holland, "Law as Politics: The Russian Procuracy and its Investigative Committee," *New York University Public Law and Legal Theory Working Papers*, no. 108 (2008), 183.

42 Remington, *Presidential Decrees in Russia*, 103.

43 Dmitry Medvedev, "Go Russia," September 10, 2009. Available online: http://en.kremlin.ru/events/president/news/5413.

44 Ibid.

45 Ibid.

46 For an overview of Medvedev's reforms, see: Peter H. Solomon, Jr., "Courts, Law and Policing under Medvedev: Many Reforms, Modest Change, New Voices," in *Russia after 2012: From Putin to Medvedev to Putin—Continuity, Change, or Revolution?* ed. J. L. Black and Michael Johns (London and New York: Routledge, 2013), 19–41.

47 William E. Pomeranz and Max Gutbrod, "The Push for Precedent in Russia's Judicial System," *Review of Central and East European Law* 37, no. 1 (2012), 15–18.

48 *Sovet pri Prezidente Rossiiskoi Federatsii po razvitiiu grazhdanskogo obshchestva i pravam cheloveka*, 2009–2012 (Moscow: BEST Print, 2012), 17.

49 Lionel Barber, Neil Buckley, and Catherine Belton, "Laying Down the Law: Medvedev Vows War on Russia's 'Legal Nihilism'," *Financial Times*, December 24, 2008. Available online: https://www.ft.com/content/e46ea1d8-c6c8-11dd-97a5-000077b07658

50 Medvedev, "Go Russia."

51 Tamara Morshchakova, "Eti predlozheniia absoliutno realizuemy," *Kommersant Vlast'*, no. 25 (2009). Available online: https://www.kommersant.ru/doc/1192668. For a more detailed refutation of Medvedev's argument, see: Kathryn Hendley, "Who Are the Legal Nihilists in Russia?" *Post-Soviet Affairs* 28, no. 2 (2012), 149–86.

52 For an overview of the Magnitsky affair, see: William E. Pomeranz, "The Magnitsky Case and the Limits of Russian Legal Reform," *Russian Analytical Digest*, no. 92 (2011), 12–15.

53 Sakwa, *Putin and the Oligarch*, 132–43.

54 Ibid., 141.

55 Ibid., 211–15.

56 Remington, *Presidential Decrees in Russia*, 145–46.

57 Myers, *The New Tsar*, 410–11.

58 Ibid., 410–11; 414–17.

59 Richard Sakwa, *Putin Redux: Power and Contradiction in Contemporary Russia* (London and New York: Routledge, 2014), 184.

60 Ibid., 164–67; 212–13.

61 Daria Litvinova, "Russian Court Convicts 'Extremist' Ukraine Library Director," *The Moscow Times*, June 8, 2017. Available online: https://themoscowtimes.com/articles/russian-court-convicts-exremist-ukraine-library-director-58170; Elena Cresci, "Russian YouTuber Convicted for Playing Pokémon Go in Church," *The Guardian*, May 11, 2017. Available online: https://www.theguardian.com/technology/2017/may/11/pokemon-go-russian-youtuber-convicted-playing-church-ruslan-sokolovsky;"Russian Journalist Sokolov Jailed for Extremism after Calling for Referendum," *The Moscow Times*, August 10, 2017. Available online: https://themoscowtimes.com/articles/russian-journalist-sokolov-jailed-for-extremism-after-calling-for-referendum-58629; "Russian Activist

Charged over Gulag Memorial Plaque," *The Moscow Times*, August 15, 2017. Available online: https://themoscowtimes.com/news/russian-activist-charged-over-gulag-memorial-plaque-58658.

62 Juliana Demesheva, "State Ideology May Return to Russia," *Institute of Modern Russia*, October 28, 2014. Available online: https://imrussia.org/en/analysis/law/2065-state-ideology-may-return-to-russia.

63 On April 5, 2016, Putin issued a decree establishing a National Guard, a bald assertion of state power that essentially created Putin's own security service of approximately 350,000 people. "Russia's National Guard to Engage in Information Warfare," *Meduza*, October 4, 2016. Available online: https://meduza.io/en/news/2016/10/04/russia-s-national-guard-to-engage-in-information-warfare.

64 Maksim Ivanov, "Miniust ne otkazyvaetsia ot slezhki za 'inostrannymi agentami'," *Kommersant*, February 22, 2013. Available online at: http://www.kommersant.ru/doc/2134015; Grigorii Tumanov, "Miniust privodiat v sootvetstvie s zakonom ob NKO," *Kommersant*, July 4, 2013. Available online: http://www.kommersant.ru/doc/2225624.

65 Grigorii Tumanov, "Prokuratura rasshiriaet agenturnuiu set'," *Kommersant*, April 24, 2013. Available online: http://www.kommersant.ru/doc/2177426.

66 Mariia Karpenko, "Pravozashchitniki prosiat ob"iasnit' mekhanizm ispolneniia zakona o nezhelatel'nykh NKO," *Kommersant*, August 17, 2015. Available online: http://www.kommersant.ru/doc/2780647; Gabrielle Tetrault-Farber, "'Undesirable Organizations' Bill to Tighten Kremlin's Grip on Civil Society," *The Moscow Times*, May 19, 2015. Available online: http://www.themoscowtimes.com/news/article/undesirable-organizations-bill-to-tighten-kremlins-grip-on-civil-society/520922.html.

67 Anna Pushkarskaia, "Konstitutsionnyi sud rassmotrel nadzor," *Kommersant*, January 23, 2015. Available online: http://www.kommersant.ru/doc/2651448.

68 William E. Pomeranz and Kathleen Smith, "Russia, Repression and the Rule of Law," *The Mark News*, February 26, 2015. Available online: http://www.themarknews.com/2015/02/26/russia-repression-and-the-rule-of-law/; Sergei Goriashko, "Proverki NKO prokuraturoi priznali besporiadochnymi," *Kommersant*, February 17, 2015. Available online: http://www.kommersant.ru/doc/2669737.

69 *Postanovlenie Konstitutsionnogo suda Rossiiskoi Federatsii po delu o proverke konstitutsionnosti polozhenii stat'i 212.1 Ugolovnogo kodeksa Rossiiskoi Federatsii v sviazi s zhaloboi grazhdanina I. I. Dadina*, February 10, 2017, 1–43.

70 Valerii Zorkin, "Rossiia i Strasburg: Problemy realizatsii Konventsii o pravakh cheloveka," *Rossiiskaia gazeta*, October 21, 2015. Available online: https://rg.ru/2015/10/21/zorkin.html.

71 Ekaterina Mishina, "Sensatsiia, kotoroi ne bylo," *Institute of Modern Russia*, July 23, 2015. Available online: https://www.imrussia.org/ru/analitika/pravo/2357.

72 Anna Pushkarskaia, "Konstitutsionnyi sud razreshil ne ispolniat resheniia ESPCh," *Kommersant*, July 14, 2015. Available online: https://www.kommersant.ru/doc/2767837.

73 Alexei Trochev, "Suing Russia at Home," *Problems of Post-Communism* 59, no. 5 (2012), 22.

74 I. V. Tkachev, "Novye vekhi razvitiia prokuratury Rossii," *Ostrasli prava*, May 16, 2015. Available online: http://xn—-7sbbaj7auwnffhk.xn–p1ai/article/4150; I. V. Tkachev, "Prokuratura kak gosudarstvennyi organ s osobym statusom," *Predprinimatel'stvo i pravo*, December 3, 2014. Available online: http://lexandbusiness.ru/view-article.php?id=4555.

75 Peter H. Solomon, Jr., "Understanding Russia's Low Rate of Acquittal: Pretrial Screening and the Problem of Accusatorial Bias," *Review of Central and East European Law* 40, no. 1 (2015), 26. Commercial court judges have made greater strides toward independence. See: Kathryn Hendley, "Are Russian Judges Still Soviet?" *Post-Soviet Affairs* 23, no. 3 (July–September 2007), 240–74.

76 Viktoriia Voloshina, "Opravdyvaia podsudimogo, ty ssorishs'ia s pravokhranitel'mymi organami," *Moskovskie Novosti*, January 18, 2013. Available online: http://www.mn.ru/society/rights/85558.

77 Nikolai Sergeev, "Iurii Chaika ustanovil nadzor za biznesom," *Kommersant*, May 25, 2012. Available online: http://www.kommersant.ru/doc/1942419.

78 *Diagnostika raboty sudebnoi sistemy v sfere ugolovnogo sudoproizvodstva i predlozheniia po ee reformirovaniiu, Chast' I*, eds. Arina Dmitrieva et al., The Institute for the Rule of Law (St. Petersburg: 2016), 46–51. Available online: http://www.enforce.spb.ru/products/other-publications/6731-6731-i.

79 Kristi O'Malley, "Not Guilty until the Supreme Court Finds You Guilty: A Reflection on Jury Trials in Russia," *Demokratizatsiya* 14, no. 1 (2006), 42–53.

80 For a detailed analysis of the first trial, see: Keith Gessen, "The Accused," *The New Yorker*, March 23, 2009, 42–53.

81 Yekaterina Mereminskaia, "Russian Anti-monopoly Service: State Doubles Presence over Past Decade," *The Moscow Times*, September 29, 2016. Available online: https://themoscowtimes.com/articles/russian-state-doubles-economy-presence-over-past-decade-55529.

82 Nadezhda Krasnushkina, "Zemliu predlozhili otdat' khoroshim liudiam," *Kommersant*, July 28, 2017. Available online: https://www.kommersant.ru/doc/3368430.

83 Maxim Trudolyubov, *The Tragedy of Property: Private Life, Ownership and the Russian State*, trans. Arch Tait (Cambridge, UK and Bedford, MA: Polity Press, 2018), 174. I am grateful to Max for sharing the page proofs of his book with me.

84 Jordan Gans-Morse, "Threats to Property Rights in Russia: From Private Coercion to State Aggression," *Post Soviet Affairs* 28, no. 3 (2012), 283–87. See also: the Russian business ombudsman's 2016 report to the president for a discussion of the inspection problem. *Kniga zhalob i predlozhenii rossuskogo biznesa* (2016), 13–15. Available online: http://doklad.ombudsmanbiz.ru/pdf/zhaloby16.pdf.

85 Aleksandra Prokopenko and Margarita Papchenkova, "Putin potrebuet ot zakonodatelei pomoch' biznesu," *Vedomosti*, December 2, 2015. Available online: https://www.vedomosti.ru/economics/articles/2015/12/03/619402-

putin-pomoch-biznesu. Putin specifically was asked about the repeat inspection problem at his December 2017 press conference. He admitted that law enforcement—and not a business—was responsible for these excessive number of inspections and that he had not seen any real progress toward solving this perpetual problem. "Glavnye tezisy prezidenta," *Kommersant*, December 14, 2017. Available online: https://www.kommersant.ru/doc/3496154.

86 Daria Nikolaeva, "Polovina rossiian ne verit v biznes bez vziatok," *Kommersant*, August 4, 2017. Available online: https://www.kommersant.ru/doc/3374349.

87 Multiple arrests followed these anti-corruption demonstrations, and several protesters ultimately received significant prison sentences, although without the same public reaction as occurred after the Bolotnaia protests. Anastasiia Kurilova, "Osuzhden shestoi figurant 'dela 26 marta'," *Kommersant*, December 7, 2017. Available online: https://www.kommersant.ru/doc/3488976.

88 Neil MacFarquhar, "Vladimir Putin, in First Remarks on Russian Protests, Warns of Potential Chaos," *The New York Times*, March 30, 2017. Available online: https://www.nytimes.com/2017/03/30/world/europe/putin-russia-protests.html.

89 Kahn, *Federalism*, 238–39; 245.

90 "Chechen Leader Kadyrov Says Human Rights Work 'Won't Fly' in His Region," *The Moscow Times*, January 18, 2018. Available online: https://themoscowtimes.com/news/chechen-leader-kadyrov-says-human-rights-work-wont-fly-in-his-region-60214; "Vnutrenniaia imperiia Chechnia," *Vedomosti*, June 30, 2015. Available online: https://www.vedomosti.ru/opinion/articles/2015/06/30/598580-vnutrennyaya-imperiya-chechnya; Zakir Magomedov, "Pochemu v Dagestane stanoviatsia populiarnymi shariatskie sudy," *Kavkaz.Realii*, January 25, 2017. Available online: https://www.kavkazr.com/a/vmesto-suda-shariat/28256797.html.

91 Tom Balmforth, "Putin Calls for Law on 'Russian Nation' Ahead of Unity Day," *RFE/RL*, November 1, 2016. Available online: https://www.rferl.org/a/russia-putin-law-on-russian-nation-ahead-unity-day/28089153.html.

92 Natal'ia Gorodetskaia, "Edinstvo natsii ne vyderzhalo kritiki," *Kommersant*, March 7, 2017. Available online: https://www.kommersant.ru/doc/3235995.

93 "'Levada-tsentr': 47% rossiian schitaiut svoi prava vazhnee interesov gosudarstva," *Kommersant*, April 3, 2017. Available online: https://www.kommersant.ru/doc/3260618.

94 Hendley, *Everyday Law*, 229.

BIBLIOGRAPHY

Afanas'ev, Alexander K. "Jurors and Jury Trials in Imperial Russia, 1866–1885." In *Russia's Great Reforms, 1855–1881*, edited by Ben Eklof, John Bushnell, and Larissa Zakharova, 214–23. Bloomington: Indiana University Press, 1994.

Ahdieh, Robert B. *Russia's Constitutional Revolution: Legal Consciousness and the Transition to Democracy, 1985–1996*. University Park: The Pennsylvania State University Press, 1997.

Alexopoulos, Golfo. *Stalin's Outcasts: Aliens, Citizens, and the Soviet State, 1926–1936*. Ithaca and London: Cornell University Press, 2003.

Altstadt, Audrey L. *The Azerbaijani Turks: Power and Identity under Russian Rule*. Stanford: Hoover Institution Press, 1992.

Anisimov, Evgenii V. *The Reforms of Peter the Great: Progress through Coercion in Russia*. Translated by John T. Alexander. Armonk, NY and London: M. E. Sharpe, 1993.

Antonov, Sergei. *Bankrupts and Usurers of Imperial Russia: Debt, Property, and the Law in the Age of Dostoevsky and Tolstoy*. Cambridge, MA and London: Harvard University Press, 2016.

Aron, Leon. *Yeltsin: A Revolutionary Life*. New York: St. Martin's Press, 2000.

Aronov, D. V. *Pervyi Spiker: Opyt nauchnoi biografii Sergeia Andreevicha Muromtseva*. Moscow: IG Iurist, 2006.

Ascher, Abraham. *P. A. Stolypin: The Search for Stability in Late Imperial Russia*. Stanford: Stanford University Press, 2001.

Aslund, Anders. *Russia's Capitalist Revolution: Why Market Reform Succeeded and Democracy Failed*. Washington, DC: Peter G. Peterson Institute for International Economics, 2007.

Baberowski, Jörg. "Law, the Judicial System and the Legal Profession." In *The Cambridge History of Russia, Volume II: Imperial Russia, 1689–1917*, edited by Dominic Lieven, 344–68. Cambridge: Cambridge University Press, 2006.

Baglai M. V. and B. N. Gabrichidze. *Konstitutsionnoe pravo Rossiiskoi Federatsii*. Moscow: INFRA·M—KODEKS, 1996.

Ball, Alan M. *Russia's Last Capitalists: The Nepmen, 1921–1929*. Berkeley: University of California Press, 1987.

Barry, Donald D. and Harold J. Berman. "The Soviet Legal Profession." *Harvard Law Review* 42, no. 1 (1968): 1–41.

Batkin, Leonid. "The Minefield of Russian Constitutionalism: Before and after October 1993." In *Remaking Russia: Voices from Within*, edited by Heyward Isham, 107–27. Armonk, NY and London: M. E. Sharpe, 1995.

Becker, Elisa M. *Medicine, Law, and the State in Imperial Russia*. Budapest and New York: Central European University Press, 2011.

Beer, Daniel. *The House of the Dead: Siberian Exile under the Tsars.* New York: Alfred A. Knopf, 2017.
Berendts, E. N. *Sviaz sudebnoi reformy s drugimi reformami Imperatora Aleksandra II i vliianie ee na gosudarstvennyi i obshchestvennyi byt Rossii.* Petrograd: Senatskaia Tipografiia, 1915.
Berman, Harold J. *Justice in the U.S.S.R.: An Interpretation of Soviet Law.* 2nd ed. Cambridge, MA and London: Harvard University Press, 1963.
Berman, Harold J. *Law and Revolution: The Formation of the Western Legal Tradition.* Cambridge, MA: Harvard University Press, 1983.
Berman, Harold J. "The Rule of Law and the Law-based State with Special Reference to the Soviet Union." In *Toward the "Rule of Law" in Russia: Political and Legal Reform in the Transition Period*, edited by Donald D. Barry, 43–60. Armonk, NY and London: M. E. Sharpe, 1992.
Bessarabov, V. G. and D. R. Pashtov. *Uchastie prokuratury v zakonotvorcheskoi deiatel'nosti organov gosudarstvennoi vlasti sub"ektov Rossiiskoi Federatsii.* Moscow: Iurlitinform, 2016.
Bhat, Girish N. "The Consensual Dimension of Late Imperial Russian Criminal Procedure: The Example of Trial by Jury." In *Reforming Justice in Russia, 1864–1996: Power, Culture, and the Limits of the Legal Order*, edited by Peter H. Solomon, Jr., 61–81. Armonk, NY: M. E. Sharpe, 1997.
Bhat, Girish N. "The Moralization of Guilt in Late Imperial Russian Trial by Jury: The Early Reform Era." *Law and History Review* 15, no. 1 (1997): 77–113.
Bonnell, Victoria E., Ann Cooper, and Gregory Freidin, eds. *Russia at the Barricades: Eyewitness Accounts of the August 1991 Coup.* Armonk, NY and London: M. E. Sharpe, 1994.
Borisova, Tatiana. "The Digest of Laws of the Russian Empire: The Phenomenon of Autocratic Legality." *Law and History Review* 30, no. 3 (2012): 901–25.
Borisova, Tatiana. "Russian National Legal Tradition: *Svod* versus *Ulozhenie* in Nineteenth Century Russia." *Review of Central and East European Law* 33, no. 3 (2008): 295–301.
Boshno, S. V. *Teoriia gosudarstva i prava.* Moscow: Eksmo, 2007.
Bradley, Joseph. *Voluntary Associations in Tsarist Russia: Science, Patriotism, and Civil Society.* Cambridge, MA: Harvard University Press, 2009.
Brown, A. H. "The Father of Russian Jurisprudence: The Legal Thought of S. E. Desnitskii." In *Russian Law: Historical and Political Perspectives*, edited by William E. Butler, 117–41. Leyden: A. W. Sijthoff, 1977.
Brown, A. H. *The Gorbachev Factor.* Oxford: Oxford University Press, 1996.
Burbank, Jane. "An Imperial Rights Regime: Law and Citizenship in the Russian Empire." *Kritika: Explorations in Russian and Eurasian History* 7, no. 3 (2006): 397–431.
Burbank, Jane. "Legal Culture, Citizenship, and Peasant Jurisprudence: Perspectives from the Early Twentieth Century." In *Reforming Justice in Russia, 1864–1996: Power, Culture, and the Limits of the Legal Order*, edited by Peter H. Solomon, Jr., 82–106. Armonk, NY: M. E. Sharpe, 1997.
Burbank, Jane. "Lenin and the Law in Revolutionary Russia." *Slavic Review* 54, no. 1 (1995): 23–44.
Burbank, Jane. *Russian Peasants Go to Court: Legal Culture in the Countryside, 1905–1917.* Bloomington and Indianapolis: Indiana University Press, 2004.

Burbank, Jane and Frederick Cooper. *Empires in World History: Power and the Politics of Difference*. Princeton, NJ and Oxford: Princeton University Press, 2010.

Burbank, Jane, Mark Von Hagan, and Anatolyi Remnev, eds. *Russian Empire: Space, People, Power, 1700–1930*. Bloomington and Indianapolis: Indiana University Press, 2007.

Burger, Ethan S. and Mary Holland. "Law as Politics: The Russian Procuracy and Its Investigative Committee." *New York University Public Law and Legal Theory Working Papers*, no. 108 (2008): 142–93.

Burnham, William and Jeffrey Kahn. "Russia's Criminal Procedure Code Five Years Out." *Review of Central and East European Law* 33, no. 1 (2008): 1–93.

Burnham, William and Alexei Trochev. "Russia's War between the Courts: The Struggle over the Jurisdictional Boundary between the Constitutional Court and Regular Courts." *The American Journal of Comparative Law* 55, no. 3 (2007): 381–452.

Butler, William E. *Russian Law*. Oxford: Oxford University Press, 1999.

Butler, William E. *Soviet Law*. London: Butterworths, 1983.

Butler, William E. and Vladimir A. Tomsinov, eds. *The Nakaz of Catherine the Great: Collected Texts*. Clark, NJ: The Lawbook Exchange, 2010.

Cassiday, Julie A. *The Enemy on Trial: Early Soviet Courts on Stage and Screen*. DeKalb: Northern Illinois University Press, 2000.

Colton, Timothy J. *Yeltsin: A Life*. New York: Basic Books, 2008.

Conquest, Robert. *The Great Terror: Stalin's Purge of the Thirties*. New York: Collier Books, 1973.

Crews, Robert. *For Prophet and Tsar: Islam and Empire in Russia and Central Asia*. Cambridge, MA and London: Harvard University Press, 2006.

Daly, Jonathan W. *Autocracy under Siege: Security Police and Opposition in Russia, 1866–1905*. DeKalb: Northern Illinois University Press, 1998.

Daly, Jonathan W. *Crime and Punishment in Russia: A Comparative History from Peter the Great to Vladimir Putin*. London: Bloomsbury, 2018.

Daly, Jonathan W. *The Watchful State: Security Police and Opposition in Russia, 1906–1917*. DeKalb: Northern Illinois University Press, 2004.

Davies, Norman. *God's Playground: A History of Poland*. Vol. 2. New York: Columbia University Press, 1982.

Dawisha, Karen. *Putin's Kleptocracy: Who Owns Russia?* New York: Simon & Schuster, 2014.

De Madariaga, Isabel. *Russia in the Age of Catherine the Great*. New Haven, CT and London: Yale University Press, 1981.

Dennison, Tracy. *The Institutional Framework of Russian Serfdom*. Cambridge: Cambridge University Press, 2011.

Dixon, Simon. *The Modernization of Russia 1676–1825*. Cambridge: Cambridge University Press, 1999.

Dobson, Miriam. *Khrushchev's Cold Summer: Gulag Returnees, Crime, and the Fate of Reform after Stalin*. Ithaca and London: Cornell University Press, 2009.

Dowler, Wayne. *Russia in 1913*. DeKalb: Northern Illinois University Press, 2010.

Edmondson, Linda. "Was There a Movement for Civil Rights in Russia in 1905?" In *Civil Rights in Imperial Russia*, edited by Olga Crisp and Linda Edmondson, 264–85. Oxford: Clarendon Press, 1989.

Efremova, N. N. *Ministerstvo Iustitsii Rossiiskoi Imperii: 1802–1917gg.* Moscow: Nauka, 1983.

Engel, Barbara Alpern. *Breaking the Ties That Bound: The Politics of Marital Strife in Late Imperial Russia.* Ithaca and London: Cornell University Press, 2011.

Fainsod, Merle. *How Russia Is Ruled.* Cambridge, MA: Harvard University Press, 1956.

Feifer, George. *Justice in Moscow.* Lincoln, NE: Authors Guild Backprint.Com Edition, 2000.

Feofanov, Yuri. "The Trial of Ian Rokotov." In *Politics and Justice in Russia: Major Trials of the Post-Stalin Era*, edited by Yuri Feofanov and Donald D. Barry, 22–31. Armonk, NY and London: M. E. Sharpe, 1996.

Field, Daniel. *The End of Serfdom: Nobility and Bureaucracy in Russia, 1855–1861.* Cambridge, MA: Harvard University Press, 1976.

Firestone, Thomas. "Armed Injustice: Abuse of the Law and Complex Crime in Post-Soviet Russia." *Denver Journal of International Law and Policy* 38, no. 4 (2009): 555–80.

Firestone, Thomas. "Criminal Corporate Raiding in Russia." *The International Lawyer* 42, no. 4 (2008): 1207–29.

Fish, M. Steven. *Democracy Derailed in Russia: The Failure of Open Politics.* New York: Cambridge University Press, 2005.

Fitzpatrick, Sheila. *Everyday Stalinism: Ordinary Life in Extraordinary Times: Soviet Russia in the 1930s.* Oxford and New York: Oxford University Press, 1999.

Foglesong, Todd. "The Reform of Criminal Justice and Evolution of Judicial Dependence in Late Soviet Russia." In *Reforming Justice in Russia, 1864–1996: Power, Culture, and the Limits of the Legal Order*, edited by Peter H. Solomon, Jr., 282–324. Armonk, NY: M. E. Sharpe, 1997.

Frank, Stephen P. *Crime, Cultural Conflict, and Justice in Rural Russia, 1856–1914.* Berkeley: University of California Press, 1999.

Frierson, Cathy A. "'I Must Always Answer to the Law … ' Rules and Responses in the Reformed *Volost'* Court." *Slavonic and East European Review* 75, no. 2 (1997): 308–34.

Frierson, Cathy A. "Rural Justice in Russia: The Volost' Court Debate, 1861–1912." *Slavonic and East European Review* 64, no. 4 (1986): 526–45.

Frye, Timothy. *Property Rights and Wrongs: How Power, Institutions, and Norms Shape Economic Conflict in Russia.* Cambridge: Cambridge University Press, 2017.

Fuller, William C., Jr. *Civil-Military Conflict in Imperial Russia, 1881–1914.* Princeton, NJ: Princeton University Press, 1985.

Gans-Morse, Jordan. "Threats to Property Rights in Russia: From Private Coercion to State Aggression." *Post-Soviet Affairs* 28, no. 3 (2012): 263–95.

Gaudin, Corinne. *Ruling Peasants: Village and State in Late Imperial Russia.* Dekalb: Northern Illinois University Press, 2007.

Gessen, I. V. *Istoriia russkoi advokatury.* Vol. 1. Republished by Moscow: Iurist, 1997.

Goldman, Marshall I. *What Went Wrong with Perestroika.* New York and London: W. W. Norton & Company, 1992.

Goldman, Wendy Z. *Women, the State, and Revolution: Soviet Family Policy and Social Life, 1917–1936.* Cambridge: Cambridge University Press, 1993.

Gorbachev, Mikhail. *Memoirs*. New York: Doubleday, 1996.
Gorlizki, Yoram. "Delegalization in Russia: Soviet Comrades' Courts in Retrospect." *The American Journal of Comparative Law* 46, no. 3 (1998): 403–25.
Gray, Cheryl W. and Kathryn Hendley. "Developing Commercial Law in Transition Economies: Examples from Hungary and Russia." In *The Rule of Law and Economic Reform in Russia*, edited by Jeffrey D. Sachs and Katharina Pistor, 139–64. Boulder: Westview Press, 1997.
Gredinier, F. I. "Prokurorskii nadzor za piat'desiat let, istekshikh so vremeni ego preobrazovaniia po Sudebnym Ustavam Imperatora Aleksandra II." In *Sudebnye Ustavy 20 noiabria 1864 g. za piat'desiat let*, vol. 2, 197–249. Petrograd: Senatskaia tipografiia, 1914.
Gruzenberg, O. O. *Yesterday: Memoirs of a Russian-Jewish Lawyer*. Translated by Don C. Rawson and Tatiana Tipton. Berkeley: University of California Press, 1981.
Guk, P. A. *Sudebnyi pretsedent: teoriia i praktika*. Moscow: Iurlitinform, 2009.
Gvosdev, Nikolas K. *Imperial Politics and Perspectives towards Georgia, 1760–1819*. New York: St. Martin's Press, 2000.
Hahn, Gordon M. "The Impact of Putin's Federative Reforms on Democratization in Russia." *Post-Soviet Affairs* 19, no. 2 (2003): 114–53.
Hammer, Darrell P. "The Dictatorship of the Proletariat." In *Lenin and Leninism: State, Law, and Society*, edited by Bernard W. Eissenstat, 25–42. Lexington, MA, Toronto, and London: Lexington Books, 1971.
Hartley, Janet M. *Alexander I (Profiles in Power)*. London and New York: Longman, 1994.
Hartley, Janet M. "Catherine's Conscience Court—An English Equity Court?" In *Russia and the West in the Eighteenth Century*, edited by A. G. Cross, 306–18. Newtonville, MA: Oriental Research Partners, 1983.
Hartley, Janet M. "The 'Constitutions' of Finland and Poland in the Reign of Alexander I: Blueprints for Reform in Russia." In *Finland and Poland in the Russian Empire: A Comparative Study*, edited by Michael Branch, Janet Hartley, and Antoni Maczak, 41–59. London: School of Slavonic and East European Studies, University of London, 1995.
Haywood, Max, ed. and trans. *On Trial: The Soviet State versus "Abram Tertz" and "Nikolai Arzhak."* New York: Harper & Row, 1966.
Hazard, John N. "Soviet Law Takes a Fresh Breath." *Bulletin of the Australian Society of Legal Philosophy* 17, no. 1 (1992): 1–20.
Heinzen, James. *The Art of the Bribe: Corruption under Stalin, 1943–53*. New Haven, CT and London: Yale University Press, 2016.
Hellie, Richard. "Early Modern Russian Law: The *Ulozhenie* of 1649." *Russian History* 15, no. 2–4 (1988): 155–80.
Hellie, Richard. "Russian Law from Oleg to Peter the Great." In *The Laws of Rus'—Tenth to Fifteenth Centuries*, edited and translated by D. Kaiser, xi–xl. Salt Lake City: Charles Schlacks, Jr., 1993.
Henderson, Jane. *The Constitution of the Russian Federation: A Contextual Analysis*. Oxford and Portland, OR: Hart Publishing, 2011.
Henderson, Jane. "The 1988 Soviet Constitutional Reforms and Sources of Law." *The King's College Law Journal* 1, no. 1 (1990–91): 59–77.

Hendley, Kathryn. "Are Russian Judges Still Soviet?" *Post-Soviet Affairs* 23, no. 3 (July–September 2007): 240–74.
Hendley, Kathryn. "Assessing the Rule of Law in Russia." *Cardozo Journal of International and Comparative Law* 14, no. 2 (2006): 347–91.
Hendley, Kathryn. "Business Litigation in the Transition: A Portrait of Debt Collection in Russia." *Law and Society Review* 31, no. 1 (2004): 305–47.
Hendley, Kathryn. "Enforcing Judgments in Russian Economic Courts." *Post-Soviet Affairs* 20, no. 1 (2004): 46–82.
Hendley, Kathryn. *Everyday Law in Russia*. Ithaca and London: Cornell University Press, 2017.
Hendley, Kathryn. "The Puzzling Non-consequences of Societal Distrust of Courts: Explaining the Use of Russian Courts." *Cornell International Law Journal* 45, no. 3 (2012): 517–67.
Hendley, Kathryn. "Remaking an Institution: The Transition in Russia from State *Arbitrazh* to *Arbitrazh* Courts." *American Journal of Comparative Law* 46, no. 1 (Winter, 1998): 93–127.
Hendley, Kathryn. "The Spillover Effects of Privatization on Russian Legal Culture." *Transnational Law & Contemporary Problems* 5, no. 1 (Spring, 1995): 40–64.
Hendley, Kathryn. "'Telephone Law' and the 'Rule of Law': The Russian Case." *Hague Journal on the Rule of Law* 1, no. 2 (2009): 241–62.
Hendley, Kathryn. *Trying to Make Law Matter: Legal Reform and Labor Law in the Soviet Union*. Ann Arbor: The University of Michigan Press, 1996.
Hendley, Kathryn. "Who Are the Legal Nihilists in Russia?" *Post-Soviet Affairs* 28, no. 2 (2012): 149–86.
Heuman, Susan. *Kistiakovsky: The Struggle for National and Constitutional Rights in the Last Years of Tsarism*. Cambridge, MA: Harvard Ukrainian Research Institute, 1988.
Hill, Fiona and Clifford G. Gaddy. *Mr. Putin: Operative in the Kremlin*. Washington, DC: Brookings Institution Press, 2015.
Hirsch, Francine. *Empire of Nations: Ethnographic Knowledge and the Making of the Soviet Union*. Ithaca and London: Cornell University Press, 2005.
Hoffman, David E. *The Oligarchs: Wealth and Power in the New Russia*. New York: Public Affairs, 2002.
Holmes, Stephen. "Superpresidentialism and Its Problems." *East European Constitutional Review* 2/3, nos. 4/1 (1993/94): 123–26.
Holquist, Peter. "Dilemmas of a Progressive Administrator: Baron Boris Nolde." *Kritika: Explorations in Russian and Eurasian History* 7, no. 2 (2006): 241–73.
Holquist, Peter. "The Russian Empire as a 'Civilized State': International Law as Principle and Practice in Imperial Russia, 1874–1878." *The National Council for Eurasian and East European Research* (2004): 1–27.
Hosking, Geoffrey. *The First Socialist Society: A History of the Soviet Union from Within*. 2nd ed. Cambridge, MA: Harvard University Press, 1992.
Hosking, Geoffrey. "Patronage and the Russian State." *The Slavonic and East European Review* 78, no. 2 (2000): 301–20.
Hosking, Geoffrey. *Russia: People and Empire, 1552–1917*. Cambridge, MA: Harvard University Press, 1997.
Hosking, Geoffrey. *The Russian Constitutional Experiment: Government and Duma, 1907–1914*. Cambridge: Cambridge University Press, 1973.

Hughes, Lindsey. *Russia in the Age of Peter the Great*. New Haven, CT and London: Yale University Press, 1998.
Huskey, Eugene. "From Legal Nihilism to *Pravovoe Gosudarstvo*: Soviet Legal Development, 1917–1990." In *Toward the "Rule of Law" in Russia? Political and Legal Reform in the Transition Period*, edited by Donald D. Barry, 23–42. Armonk, NY and London: M. E. Sharpe, 1992.
Huskey, Eugene. *Russian Lawyers and the Soviet State: The Origins and Development of the Soviet Bar, 1917–1939*. Princeton, NJ: Princeton University Press, 1986.
Isaev, M. A. *Istoriia rossiiskogo gosudarstva i prava*. Moscow: Statut, 2012.
Jersild, Austin. *Orientalism and Empire: North Caucasus Mountain Peoples and the Georgian Frontier, 1845–1917*. Montreal: McGill-Queen's University Press, 2002.
Jordan, Pamela A. *Defending Rights in Russia: Lawyers, the State, and Legal Reform in the Post-Soviet Era*. Vancouver: UBC Press, 2005.
Kahn, Jeffrey. *Federalism, Democratization, and the Rule of Law in Russia*. Oxford: Oxford University Press, 2002.
Kahn, Jeffrey. "Russia's 'Dictatorship of Law' and the European Court of Human Rights." *Review of Central and East European Law* 29, no. 1 (2004): 1–14.
Kahn, Jeffrey. "'Protection and Empire': The Martens Clause, State Sovereignty, and Individual Rights." *Virginia Journal of International Law* 56, no. 1 (2016): 1–48.
Kahn, Jeffrey. "The Search for the Rule of Law in Russia." *Georgetown Journal of International Law* 37, no. 2 (2006): 353–409.
Kaminskaya, Dina. *Final Judgment: My Life as a Soviet Defense Attorney*. New York: Simon & Schuster, 1982.
Karabchevskii, N. P. *Chto glaza moi videli*. Vol. 2. Berlin: Izdanie Ol'gi Diakovoi i ko., 1921.
Karpichenko, N. P. and V. N. Ambarov. *Istoriia otechestvennogo gosudarstva i prava*. Moscow: Moskovskii gumanitarnyi institut im. E. R. Dashkovoi, 2014.
Kazantsev, S. M. *Dorevoliutsionnye iuristy o prokurature*. St. Petersburg: Iuridicheskii Tsentr Press, 2001.
Kazantsev, S. M. *Istoriia tsarskoi prokuratury*. St. Petersburg: Sankt-Peterburgskogo Universiteta, 1993.
Kazantsev, S. M. "The Judicial Reform of 1864 and the Procuracy in Russia." In *Reforming Justice in Russia, 1864–1996: Power, Culture, and the Limits of the Legal Order*, edited by Peter H. Solomon, Jr., 44–60. Armonk, NY: M. E. Sharpe, 1997.
Kharkhordin, Oleg. "What Is the State? The Russian Concept of Gosudarstvo in the European Context." *History and Theory* 40, no. 2 (May 2001): 206–40.
Khodarkovsky, Michael. *Bitter Choices: Loyalty and Betrayal in the Russian Conquest of the North Caucasus*. Ithaca and London: Cornell University Press, 2011.
Kirmse, Stefan B. "Dealing with Crime in Late Tsarist Russia: Muslim Tatars and the Imperial Legal System." In *One Law for All? Western Models and Local Practices in (Post-) Imperial Contexts*, edited by Stefan B. Kirmse, 208–41. Frankfurt and New York: Campus, 2012.
Kirmse, Stefan B. "Law and Empire in Late Tsarist Russia: Muslim Tatars Go to Court." *Slavic Review* 72, no. 4 (2013): 778–801.

Kirmse, Stefan B. "Law and Society in Imperial Russia." *InterDisciplines: Journal of History and Sociology* 3, no. 2 (2012): 103–34.

Kistiakovskii, Bogdan. "In the Defense of Law." In *Landmarks: A Collection of Essays of the Russian Intelligentsia-1909*, edited by Boris Shragin and Albert Todd, translated by Marian Schwartz, 112–13. New York: Karz Howard, 1977.

Kivelson, Valerie. *Cartographies of Tsardom: The Land and Its Meanings in Seventeenth-Century Russia*. Ithaca and London: Cornell University Press, 2006.

Kohut, Zenon. *Russian Centralism and Ukrainian Autonomy: Imperial Absorption of the Hetmanate 1760s–1830s*. Cambridge, MA: Harvard Ukrainian Research Institute, 1998.

Kollmann, Nancy Shields. *By Honor Bound: State and Society in Early Modern Russia*. Ithaca and London: Cornell University Press, 1999.

Kollmann, Nancy Shields. *Crime and Punishment in Early Modern Russia*. Cambridge: Cambridge University Press, 2012.

Kollmann, Nancy Shields. *The Russian Empire: 1450–1801*. Oxford: Oxford University Press, 2017.

Kolokolov, N. A., ed. *Istoriia sudebnoi sistemy v Rossii*. Moscow: Iuniti-Dana, 2009.

Komarova, V. V. *Konstitutsionnaia zakonnost' v realizatsii printsipa razdeleniia vlastei po primere Rossiiskoi Federatsii*. Moscow: Prospekt, 2014.

Korkunov, N. M. *Russkoe gosudarstvennoe pravo*. St. Petersburg: M. M. Stasiulevich, 1901.

Kotsonis, Yanni. *States of Obligation: Taxes and Citizenship in the Russian Empire and Early Soviet Republic*. Toronto: University of Toronto Press, 2014.

Kucherov, Samuel. *Courts, Lawyers, and Trials under the Last Three Tsars*. Westport: Greenwood Press, 1953.

Kupriianov, M. I. and N. A. Kovalenko. *Chrezvychainaia sledstvennaia komissiia Vremennogo pravitel'stva (mart-oktiabr' 1917 g.)*. Moscow: MAKS Press, 2009.

Kuritsyn, V. M. *Istoriia gosudarstva i prava Rossii, 1929–1940*. Moscow: Mezhdunarodnye otnosheniia, 1998.

Lapenna, Ivo. "Lenin, Law, and Legality." In *Lenin: The Man, the Theorist, the Leader: A Reappraisal*, edited by Leonard Schapiro and Peter Reddaway, 235–62. New York: Frederick A. Praeger, 1967.

Ledeneva, Alena V. *Russia's Economy of Favors: Blat, Networking and Informal Exchange*. Cambridge: Cambridge University Press, 1998.

Ledeneva, Alena V. "Telephone Justice in Russia." *Post-Soviet Affairs* 24, no. 4 (October–December 2008): 324–50.

LeDonne, John P. *Ruling Russia: Politics and Administration in the Age of Absolutism 1762–1796*. Princeton, NJ: Princeton University Press, 1984.

Lenin, V. I. *State and Revolution*. New York: International Publishers, 1932.

Leontovitsch, Victor. *The History of Liberalism in Russia*. Translated by Parmen Leontovitsch. Pittsburgh: University of Pittsburgh Press, 2012.

Levin-Stankevich, Brian L. "The Transfer of Legal Technology and Culture: Legal Professionals in Tsarist Russia." In *Russia's Missing Middle Class: The Professions in Russian History*, edited by Harley D. Balzer, 223–50. Armonk, NY and London: M. E. Sharpe, 1996.

Liadashcheva-Il'icheva, M. N. *Grazhdanskoe zakonodatel'stvo v Rossii v 1649 – oktiabre 1917 goda: formirovanie i razvitie*. Moscow: Iurlitinform, 2016.

Lindenmeyr, Adele. *Poverty Is Not a Vice: Charity, Society, and the State in Imperial Russia*. Princeton, NJ: Princeton University Press, 1996.
Lohr, Eric. *Russian Citizenship: From Empire to Soviet Union*. Cambridge, MA and London: Harvard University Press, 2012.
Maggs, Peter B., Olga Schwartz, and William Burnham. *Law and the Legal System of the Russian Federation*. 6th ed. New York: Juris Publishing, 2015.
Manning, Roberta Thompson. *The Crisis of the Old Order in Russia: Gentry and Government*. Princeton, NJ: Princeton University Press, 1982.
Marchenko, M. N. *Istochniki prava*. Moscow: Prospekt, 2009.
Marchenko, M. N. *Sudebnoe pravotvorchestvo i sudeiskoe pravo*. Moscow: Prospekt, 2011.
Marchenko, M. N. *Teoriia gosudarstva i prava*. 2nd ed. Moscow: Prospekt, 2014.
Marrese, Michelle Lamarche. *A Woman's Kingdom: Noblewomen and the Control of Property in Russia, 1700–1861*. Ithaca and London: Cornell University Press, 2002.
Martin, Terry. *The Affirmative Action Empire: Nations and Nationalism in the Soviet Union, 1923–1939*. Ithaca and London: Cornell University Press, 2001.
Martin, Virginia. *Law and Custom in the Steppe: The Kazakhs of the Middle Horde and Russian Colonialism in the Nineteenth Century*. Richmond, UK: Curzon Press, 2001.
McCauley, Martin. *Gorbachev*. London and New York: Longman, 1998.
McDonald, David. "1991 and the History of Russian *Gosudarstvennost'*." *Ab Imperio* 2011, no. 3 (2011): 223–37.
McDonald, Tracy. *Face to the Village: The Riazan Countryside under Soviet Rule, 1921–1930*. Toronto: University of Toronto Press, 2011.
McReynolds, Louise. *Murder Most Russian: True Crime and Punishment in Late Imperial Russia*. Ithaca and London: Cornell University Press, 2013.
Mendras, Marie. *Russian Politics: The Paradox of a Weak State*. New York: Columbia University Press, 2012.
Merezhko, Aleksandr. *Psikhologicheskaia shkola prava L. I. Petrazhitskogo: istoki, soderzhanie, vliianie*. Odessa: Feniks, 2016.
Mikhailova, N. V. and G. Iu. Kurskova, eds. *Istoriia otechestvennogo gosudarstva i prava*. Moscow: Unity, 2014.
Moon, David. "Reassessing Russian Serfdom." *European History Quarterly* 26, no. 4 (1996): 483–526.
Myers, Steven Lee. *The New Tsar: The Rise and Reign of Vladimir Putin*. New York: Vintage Books, 2015.
Nathans, Benjamin. "The Dictatorship of Reason: Aleksandr Vol'pin and the Idea of Rights under 'Developed Socialism'." *Slavic Review* 66, no. 4 (2007): 630–63.
Nathans, Benjamin. "Soviet Rights-Talk in the Post-Stalin Era." In *Human Rights in the Twentieth Century*, edited by Stefan-Ludwig Hoffman, 166–90. Cambridge: Cambridge University Press, 2011.
Neuberger, Joan. "Popular Legal Cultures: The St. Petersburg mirovoi sud." In *Russia's Great Reforms, 1855–1881*, edited by Ben Eklof, John Bushnell, and Larissa Zakharova, 231–46. Bloomington: Indiana University Press, 1994.
Neuberger, Joan. "'Shysters' or Public Servants? Uncertified Lawyers and Legal Aid for the Poor in Late Imperial Russia." *Russian History* 23, nos. 1–4 (1996): 295–310.

Newton, Scott. *Law and the Making of the Soviet World: The Red Demiurge.* Oxford: Routledge, 2015.
Nolde, B. E. *Ocherki russkogo gosudarstvennogo prava.* St. Petersburg: Pravda, 1911.
Oksamytnyi, V. V. *Obshchaia teoriia gosudarstva i prava.* Moscow: Unity, 2015.
Okun'kov, L. A., ed. *Kommentarii k Konstitutsii Rossiiskoi Federatsii.* Moscow: BEK, 1996.
O'Malley, Kristi. "Not Guilty until the Supreme Court Finds You Guilty: A Reflection on Jury Trials in Russia." *Demokratizatsiya* 14, no. 1 (2006): 42–53.
Orlov, Yuri. *Dangerous Thoughts: Memoirs of a Russian Life.* New York: William Morrow & Company, 1991.
Orlovsky, Daniel T. *The Limits of Reform: The Ministry of Internal Affairs in Imperial Russia, 1802–1881.* Cambridge, MA and London: Harvard University Press, 1981.
Osakwe, Christopher. "Anatomy of the 1994 Civil Codes of Russia and Kazakstan: A Biopsy of the Economic Constitutions of Two Post-Soviet Republics." *Notre Dame Law Review* 73, no. 5 (1998): 1413–514.
Owen, Thomas. *The Corporation under Russian Law, 1800–1917: A Study in Tsarist Economic Policy.* Cambridge: Cambridge University Press, 1991.
Partlett, William. "The Dangers of Constitution-Making." *Brooklyn Journal of International Law* 28, no. 1 (2012): 193–238.
Perevalov, V. D., ed. *Teoriia gosudarstva i prava.* Moscow: NORMA, 2008.
Pipes, Richard. *The Formation of the Soviet Union: Communism and Nationalism, 1917–1923.* Cambridge, MA: Harvard University Press, 1954.
Pipes, Richard. *Karamzin's Memoir on Ancient and Modern Russia.* New York: Atheneum, 1969.
Pipes, Richard. *Property and Freedom.* New York: Alfred A. Knopf, 1999.
Pipes, Richard. *Russia under the Old Regime.* 2nd ed. New York: Collier Books, 1992.
Pipes, Richard. "Was There Private Property in Muscovite Russia?" *Slavic Review* 53, no. 2 (1994): 524–30.
Pistor, Katherine. "Company Law and Corporate Governance in Russia." In *The Rule of Law and Economic Reform in Russia*, edited by Jeffrey D. Sachs and Katharina Pistor, 165–87. Boulder: Westview Press, 1997.
Plokhy, Serhii. *The Gates of Europe: A History of Ukraine.* New York: Basic Books, 2015.
Pomeranz, William E. "Judicial Review and the Russian Constitutional Court: The Chechen Case." *Review of Central and East European Law* 23, no. 1 (1997): 9–48.
Pomeranz, William E. "Justice from Underground. The History of the Underground *Advokatura.*" *Russian Review* 52, no. 3 (1993): 321–40.
Pomeranz, William E. "Legal Assistance in Tsarist Russia: The St. Petersburg Consultation Bureaus." *Wisconsin International Law Journal* 14, no. 3 (1996): 586–610.
Pomeranz, William E. "Legal Reform through the Eyes of Russia's Leading Jurists: The *Vlast* Debate on the Russian Judiciary." *Problems of Post-Communism* 57, no. 3 (May/June 2010): 3–10.
Pomeranz, William E. "The Magnitsky Case and the Limits of Russian Legal Reform." *Russian Analytical Digest*, no. 92 (2011): 12–15.

Pomeranz, William E. "The Practice of Law and the Promise of Rule of Law: The *Advokatura* and the Civil Process in Tsarist Russia." *Kritika: Explorations in Russian and Eurasian History* 15, no. 2 (2015): 235–62.

Pomeranz, William E. "President Medvedev and the Contested Constitutional Underpinnings of Russia's Power Vertical." *Demokratizatsiya* 17, no. 2 (2009): 179–92.

Pomeranz, William E. "'Profession or Estate'? The Case of the Russian Pre-revolutionary *Advokatura*." *Slavonic and East European Review* 77, no. 2 (1999): 240–68.

Pomeranz, William E. "The Provisional Government and the Law-based State." In *Russia's Home Front in War and Revolution, 1914–22*, Book 4, edited by Adele Lindenmeyr, Christopher Read, and Peter Waldron. Bloomington: Slavica Publishers, forthcoming.

Pomeranz, William E. "The Russian Constitutional Court's Interpretation of Federalism." *Parker School Journal of East European Law* 4, no. 4 (1997): 401–43.

Pomeranz, William E. "Russian Protectionism and the Strategic Sectors Law." *American University International Law Review* 25, no. 2 (2010): 213–24.

Pomeranz, William E. "Supervisory Review and Finality of Judgments under Russian Law." *Review of Central and East European Law* 34, no. 1 (2009): 15–36.

Pomeranz, William E. "Uneasy Partners: Russia and the European Court of Human Rights." *Human Rights Brief* 19, no. 3 (2012): 17–21.

Pomeranz, William E. and Max Gutbrod. "The Push for Precedent in Russia's Judicial System." *Review of Central and East European Law* 37, no. 1 (2012): 1–30.

Pomorski, Stanislaw. "Justice in Siberia: A case study of a lower criminal court in the city of Krasnoyarsk." *Communist and Post-Communist Studies* 34, no. 4 (2001): 447–78.

Popkins, Gareth. "Code versus Custom? Norms and Tactics in Volost Court Appeals, 1889–1917." *The Russian Review* 59, no. 3 (2000): 408–24.

Pravilova, Ekaterina. *A Public Empire: Property and the Quest for the Common Good in Imperial Russia*. Princeton, NJ: Princeton University Press, 2014.

Pravilova, Ekaterina. *Zakonnost' i prava lichnosti: administrativnaia iustitsiia v Rossii (vtoraia polovina XIX v.–oktiabr' 1917 g.)*. St. Petersburg: Izdatel'stvo SEAGS, 2000.

Putin, Vladimir, Nataliya Gevorkyan, Natalya Timakova, and Andrei Kolesnikov. *First Person: An Astonishingly Frank Self-Portrait*. Translated by Catherine A. Fitzpatrick. New York: Public Affairs, 2000.

Quigley, John. "Socialist Law and the Civil Law Tradition." *The American Journal of Comparative Law* 37, no. 4 (1989): 781–808.

Rad'ko, T. N., V. V. Lazarev, and L. A. Morozova. *Teoriia gosudarstva i prava*. Moscow: Prospekt, 2014.

Raeff, Marc. *Michael Speransky: Statesman of Imperial Russia, 1772–1839*. The Hague: Martinus Nijhoff, 1957.

Raeff, Marc. *Understanding Imperial Russia: State and Society in the Old Regime*. Translated by Arthur Goldhammer. New York: Columbia University Press, 1984.

Raeff, Marc. *The Well-ordered Police State: Social and Institutional Change through Law in the Germanies and Russia, 1600–1800*. New Haven, CT and London: Yale University Press, 1983.
Rand, Robert. *Comrade Lawyer: Inside Soviet Justice in an Era of Reform*. Boulder: Westview Press, 1991.
Rassolov, M. M. and S. A. Batova, eds. *Ministerstvo iustitsii Rossii za 200 let (1802–2002): Istoriko-pravovoi ocherk*. Moscow: NORMA, 2002.
Remington, Thomas F. *Presidential Decrees in Russia: A Comparative Perspective*. Cambridge: Cambridge University Press, 2014.
Rendle, Matthew. "Revolutionary Tribunals and the Origins of Terror in Early Soviet Russia." *Historical Research* 84, no. 226 (2011): 694–721.
Rudden, Bernard. "Scientific Socialism and Soviet Private Law." *Notre Dame Law Review* 61, no. 2 (1986): 151–66.
Russell, John. "Improbable Unions: The Draft Union Treaties in the USSR, 1990–1991." *Review of Central and East European Law* 22, no. 4 (1996): 389–416.
Sakwa, Richard. "The Dual State in Russia." *Post-Soviet Affairs* 26, no. 3 (2010): 185–206.
Sakwa, Richard. *Putin and the Oligarch: The Khodorkovsky-Yukos Affair*. London and New York: I. B. Tauris, 2014.
Sakwa, Richard. *Putin Redux: Power and Contradiction in Contemporary Russia*. London and New York: Routledge, 2014.
Schattenberg, Susanne and Christopher Gilley. "Max Weber in the Provinces: Measuring Imperial Russia by Modern Standards." *Kritika: Explorations in Russian and Eurasian History* 13, no. 4 (2012): 889–902.
Schwartz, Herman. *The Struggle for Constitutional Justice in Post-Communist Europe*. Chicago and London: University of Chicago Press, 2000.
Serov, D. O. *Sudebnaia reforma Petra I: Istoriko-pravovoe issledovanie*. Moscow: Zertsalo, 2009.
Service, Robert. *Lenin: A Political Life, The Strengths of Contradiction*. Vol. 1. Bloomington: Indiana University Press, 1985.
Service, Robert. *Lenin: A Political Life, Worlds in Collision*. Vol. 2. Bloomington: Indiana University Press, 1991.
Shakrai, S. M. and K. P. Krakovskii. *Iuristi i revoliutsiia: Pro et Contra*. Moscow: Kuchkovo pole, 2017.
Shapiro, Leonard. "The Political Thought of the First Provisional Government." In *Revolutionary Russia*, edited by Richard Pipes, 87–113. Cambridge, MA: Harvard University Press, 1968.
Sharlet, Robert. "Legal Transplants and Political Mutations: The Reception of Constitutional Law in Russia and the Newly Independent States." *East European Constitutional Review* 7, no. 4 (1998): 59–68.
Sharlet, Robert. *Soviet Constitutional Crisis: From De-Stalinization to Disintegration*. Armonk, NY and London: M. E. Sharpe, 1992.
Sharlet, Robert. "Stalinism and Soviet Legal Culture." In *Stalinism: Essays in Historical Interpretation*, edited by Robert C. Tucker, 155–79. New York and London: W. W. Norton & Company, 1977.
Shchegolev, P. E., ed. *Padenie tsarskogo rezhima, stenograficheskie otchety doprosov i pokazanii, dannykh v 1917 g. Chrezvychainoi Sledstvennoi Kommissii Vremennogo Pravitel'stva*. 7 vols. Leningrad: Gosudarstvennoe Izdatel'stvo, 1925.

Sheinis, Viktor. *Vlast i zakon: politika i konstitutsii v Rossii v XX-XXI vekakh*. Moscow: Mysl', 2014.
Shershenevich, G. F. *Nauka grazhdanskogo prava v Rossii*. Kazan, 1893, reprinted by Moscow: Statut, 2003.
Siljak, Ana. *Angel of Vengeance: The "Girl Assassin," The Governor of St. Petersburg, and Russia's Revolutionary World*. New York: St. Martin's Press, 2008.
Simis, Konstantin M. *USSR: The Corrupt Society: The Secret World of Soviet Capitalism*. New York: Simon & Schuster, 1982.
Slezkine, Yuri. *The House of Government: A Saga of the Russian Revolution*. Princeton, NJ and Oxford: Princeton University Press, 2017.
Sliozberg, G. B. *Dela minuvshikh dnei: Zapiski russkago evreia*. Vol. 1. Paris: Pascal, 1933.
Smith, Gordon B. "The Procuracy: Constitutional Questions Deferred." In *Russia and Its Constitution: Promise and Political Reality*, edited by Gordon B. Smith and Robert Sharlet, 105–22. Leiden: Koninklijke Brill, 2008.
Smith, Gordon B. "The Procuracy, Putin, and the Rule of Law in Russia." In *Russia, Europe, and the Rule of Law*, edited by Ferdinand Feldbrugge, 1–14. Leiden and Boston: Martinus Nijhoff, 2007.
Smith, Gordon B. *Reforming the Russian Legal System*. Cambridge and New York: Cambridge University Press, 1996.
Smith, Gordon B. *The Soviet Procuracy and the Supervision of Administration*. Leiden: Sijthoff & Noordhoff, 1978.
Smith, Gordon B. "The Struggle over the Procuracy." In *Reforming Justice in Russia, 1864–1996: Power, Culture, and the Limits of the Legal Order*, edited by Peter H. Solomon, Jr., 348–73. Armonk, NY: M. E. Sharpe, 1997.
Smith, Kathleen E. *Moscow 1956: The Silenced Spring*. Cambridge, MA: Harvard University Press, 2017.
Smith, Kathleen E. *Mythmaking in the New Russia: Politics and Memory during the Yeltsin Era*. Ithaca and London: Cornell University Press, 2002.
Smith, Kathleen E. *Remembering Stalin's Victims: Popular Memory and the End of the USSR*. Ithaca and London: Cornell University Press, 1996.
Solomon, Peter H., Jr. "The Bureaucratization of Criminal Justice under Stalin." In *Reforming Justice in Russia, 1864–1996: Power, Culture, and the Limits of the Legal Order*, edited by Peter H. Solomon, Jr., 228–55. Armonk, NY: M. E. Sharpe, 1997.
Solomon, Peter H., Jr. "Courts, Law and Policing under Medvedev: Many Reforms, Modest Change, New Voices." In *Russia after 2012: From Putin to Medvedev to Putin—Continuity, Change, or Revolution?* edited by J. L. Black and Michael Johns, 19–41. London and New York: Routledge, 2013.
Solomon, Peter H Jr., "The Criminal Procedure Code of 2001: Will It Make Russian Justice More Fair?" In *Ruling Russia: Law, Crime, and Justice in a Changing Society*, edited by William Alex Pridemore, 77–98. Lanham, MD: Rowman & Littlefield, 2005.
Solomon, Peter H. Jr., "Informal Practices in Russian Justice: Probing the Limits of Post-Soviet Reform." In *Russia, Europe, and the Rule of Law*, edited by Ferdinand Feldbrugge, 79–92. Leiden: Nijhoff, 2007.
Solomon, Peter H. Jr., "Plea Bargaining Russian Style." *Demokratizatsiya* 20, no. 3 (2012): 282–99.

Solomon, Peter H., Jr. *Soviet Criminal Justice under Stalin*. Cambridge: Cambridge University Press, 1996.

Solomon, Peter H., Jr. and Todd S. Foglesong. *Courts and Transition in Russia: The Challenge of Judicial Reform*. Boulder: Westview Press, 2000.

Spasovich, V. D. *Zastol'nye rechi, 1873–1901*. Leipzig: E. L. Karpovich, 1903.

Sternik, I. B. *V. I. Lenin – Iurist*. Tashkent: Izdatel'stvo Uzbekistan, 1969.

Suny, Ronald Grigor. *The Making of the Georgian Nation*. Bloomington: Indiana University Press, 1988.

Suny, Ronald Grigor. Rehabilitating Tsarism: The Imperial Russian State and Its Historians." *Comparative Studies in Society and History* 31, no. 1 (1989): 168–79.

Suny, Ronald Grigor. *The Revenge of the Past: Nationalism, Revolution, and the Collapse of the Soviet Union*. Stanford: Stanford University Press, 1993.

Szeftel, Marc. *The Russian Constitution of April 23, 1906: Political Institutions of the Duma Monarchy*. Brussels: Editions de la Librarie encyclopédique, 1976.

Taubman, William. *Gorbachev: His Life and Times*. New York and London: W. W. Norton & Company, 2017.

Thaden, Edward C. "The Russian Government." In *Russification in the Baltic Provinces and Finland, 1855–1914*, edited by Edward C. Thaden, 15–88. Princeton, NJ: Princeton University Press, 1981.

Thaman, Stephen C. "Jury Trial and Adversary Procedure in Russia: Reform of Soviet Inquisitorial Procedure or Democratic Window Dressing?" In *Russia and Its Constitution: Promise and Political Reality*, edited by Gordon B. Smith and Robert Sharlet, 141–80. Leiden: Koninklijke Brill, 2008.

Thaman, Stephen C. "The Resurrection of Trial by Jury in Russia." *Stanford Journal of International Law* 31, no. 1 (1995): 61–141.

Tissier, Michel. "Local Laws and the Workings of Legal Knowledge in Late Imperial Russia." *Ab Imperio* 2012, no. 4 (2012): 211–44.

Trochev, Alexei. "All Appeals Lead to Strasbourg? Unpacking the Impact of the European Court of Human Rights on Russia." *Demokratizatsiya* 17, no. 2 (2009): 145–78.

Trochev, Alexei. *Judging Russia: The Constitutional Court in Russian Politics, 1990–2006*. Cambridge: Cambridge University Press, 2008.

Trochev, Alexei. "Suing Russia at Home." *Problems of Post-Communism* 59, no. 5 (2012): 18–34.

Troitskii, N. A. *Advokatura v Rossii i politicheskie protsessy, 1866–1904*. Tula: Avtograf, 2000.

Troitskii, N. A. *Tsarizm pod sudom progressivnoi obshchestvennosti, 1866–1895gg*. Moscow: Mysl', 1979.

Trudolyubov, Maxim. *The Tragedy of Property: Private Life, Ownership, and the Russian State*. Translated by Arch Tait. Cambridge and Bedford, MA: Polity Press, 2018.

Ugrimova, T. A. and A. G. Volkov. *"Stoi v zavete svoem ... " Nikolai Konstantinovich Murav'ev: Advokat i obshchestvennyi deiatel'*. Moscow: AMA Press, 2004.

Vaksburg, Arkady. *Stalin's Prosecutor: The Life of Andrei Vyshinsky*. Translated by Jan Butler. New York: Grove Weidenfeld, 1990.

Varfolomeev, Iu. V. *Nikolai Konstantinovich Murav'ev: advokat, politik, chelovek*. Saratov: Nauka, 2007.

Varfolomeev, Iu. V. *Zakon i trepet: Ocherk deiatel'nosti Chrezvychainoi sledstvennoi kommissii Vremennogo pravitel'stva*. Saratov: Nauchnaia kniga, 2006.
Vaskovskii, E. V. *Uchebnik grazhdanskago protsessa*. Moscow: Br. Bashmakovykh, 1914.
Vereshchagin, Alexander. *Judicial Law-making in Post-Soviet Russia*. Oxford: Routledge-Cavendish, 2007.
Vinaver, M. M. "Advokatura i pravovoe gosudarstvo." *Pravo*, no. 13 (1905): 972–90.
Vinaver, M. M. *Iz oblasti tsivilistiki*. St. Petersburg: Tipografiia A. G. Rozena, 1908.
Vinaver, M. M. *Nedavnee*. Paris: M. O. Volf, 1926.
Vlasov, V. I., G. B. Vlasova, and S. V. Denisenko. *Teoriia gosudarstva i prava*. Rostov-on-Don: Feniks, 2017.
Volkov, Vadim. *Violent Entrepreneurs: The Use of Force in the Making of Russian Capitalism*. Ithaca and London: Cornell University Press, 2002.
Wagner, William G. *Marriage, Property, and Law in Late Imperial Russia*. Oxford: Clarendon Press, 1994.
Walicki, Andrzej. *Legal Philosophies of Russian Liberalism*. Notre Dame and London: University of Notre Dame Press, 1992.
Weeks, Theodore. *Nation and State in Late Imperial Russia: Nationalism and Russification on the Western Frontier, 1863–1914*. DeKalb: Northern Illinois University Press, 2008.
Weickhardt, George G. "Due Process and Equal Justice in the Muscovite Codes." *Russian Review* 51, no. 4 (1992): 463–80.
Werth, Paul W. *The Tsar's Foreign Faiths: Toleration and the Fate of Religious Freedom in Imperial Russia*. Oxford: Oxford University Press, 2014.
White, H. J. "Civil Rights and the Provisional Government." In *Civil Rights in Imperial Russia*, edited by Olga Crisp and Linda Edmondson, 288–312. Oxford: Clarendon Press, 1989.
Williams, Stephen F. *The Reformer: How One Liberal Fought to Preempt the Russian Revolution*. New York and London: Encounter Books, 2017.
Wood, Elizabeth A. *Performing Justice: Agitation Trials in Early Soviet Russia*. Ithaca and London: Cornell University Press, 2005.
Wortman, Richard. *The Development of a Russian Legal Consciousness*. Chicago: University of Chicago Press, 1976.
Wortman, Richard. "The 'Integrity' (*Tselost'*) of the State in Imperial Russian Representation." *Ab Imperio* 2011, no. 2 (2011): 20–39.
Wortman, Richard. "Property Rights, Populism, and Russian Political Culture." In *Civil Rights in Imperial Russia*, edited by Olga Crisp and Linda Edmondson, 13–32. Oxford: Clarendon Press, 1989.
Wortman, Richard. "Russian Monarchy and the Rule of Law: New Considerations of the Court Reform of 1864." *Kritika: Explorations in Russian and Eurasian History* 6, no. 1 (2005): 145–70.
Yakovlev, Alexander M. *Striving for Law in a Lawless Land: Memoirs of a Russian Reformer*. Armonk, NY and London: M. E. Sharpe, 1996.
Yaney, George L. "Bureaucracy and Freedom: N. M. Korkunov's Theory of State." *The American Historical Review* 71, no. 2 (1966): 468–86.

Yaney, George L. *The Systematization of Russian Government: Social Evolution in the Domestic Administration of Imperial Russia, 1711–1905*. Urbana: University of Illinois Press, 1973.

Zorkin, V. D. *Muromtsev: Iz istorii politicheskoi i pravovoi mysli*. Moscow: Iuridicheskaia literatura, 1979.

Zviagintsev, A. G. *Istoriia prokuratury Rossii*. Moscow: Iuniti, 2010.

Zviagintsev, A. G. and I. G. Orlov. *V epokhu potriasenii i reform: Rossiiskie prokurory, 1906–1917*. Moscow: ROSSPEN, 1996.

INDEX

administration 4, 13–14, 17, 19, 22–4, 27, 34, 51, 67–8, 79, 81, 145, 151, 166
   administrative reform of 1775, 23–4
   administrative reforms under Peter the Great 4, 13, 19
   legal-administrative state 2, 33, 35–6, 40–1, 44, 67, 76, 82, 86, 166, 168
   ministerial reforms of Alexander I 28–9
advokatura
   absence of 11, 14, 17, 19, 27
   admission to 47, 97
   creation of 37
   and duality of law 56, 65
   and ethics 39, 47, 49
   "fathers and sons" 60–2
   independence of 40, 51, 63, 97, 102, 168
   and Jews 40, 102
   jury trials 45
   and legal aid 48, 102–3, 138
   Lenin on 74
   participation in political trials 41, 58–62, 77–8, 98–9, 102
   and peasantry 48
   post-Soviet 3, 133, 138–9, 149, 160, 168
   and private law 51, 103
   Soviet 75, 79–80, 82, 88, 102–3
   underground 47–8, 78
Afanas'ev, Alexander 44
Akhmatova, Anna 92
Aleksandrov, Petr A. 59, 62
Alexander I 4, 21, 28–31, 35, 37
Alexander II 4, 36–8, 41–2, 44, 84, 169
Alexander III 41

Alexei (tsar) 9
Alexei (tsarevich) 16
Alexopoulos, Golfo 83
Anchinkov, E. V. 60
Anisimov, Evgenii 17
Antonov, Sergei 34
Armenia 77, 80, 98, 111, 113
Article 87 65–7, 70–1
Assembly of the Land (1649) 9–10
Audit Chamber 145
Austria-Hungary 31, 53
Avtonomov, Aleksei 151
Azerbaijan 80, 111

Baberowski, Jörg 45–6, 60
bar. *See advokatura*
Basic Principles for the Reform of the Courts (1862) 38–9
Bastrykhin, Aleksandr 152
Batkin, Leonid 122, 128
Beccaria, Cesare 22
Beer, Daniel 41, 93
Beilis, Mendel 60, 70
Belarus 80–1, 114
Belavezha agreement 114
Belgium 38, 124
Bentham, Jeremy 28
Berezovskii, Boris 135, 138, 149
Beria, Lavrenty 91
Berman, Harold 3, 57, 109
Beslan 150
blat 104
Bludov, Dmitrii 38
Bogoliubov, Arkhip 59
Bolotnaia Square Protests 156
Bolshevik Party. *See* Communist Party
Borisova, Tatiana 33
Brezhnev, Leonid 5, 91, 96–7, 100, 104, 106, 109, 110, 115
British empire 25, 43

Brodsky, Joseph 96
Brown, Archie 112
Bukharin, Nikolai 85–6
Bukovskii, Vladimir 97–9
Burbank, Jane 49
Butler, William E. 32
Byzantium 10

Cassiday, Julie 85
Catherine the Great 4, 21–8, 34–5, 37–8, 76, 84, 167
Caucasus 21, 26, 30, 55, 131, 146, 163
Central Executive Committee 76, 82
  presidium of 82
Charter to the Nobility 24
Charter to the Towns 24
Chechnya 117–18, 130–1, 140, 147
Chernobyl 108
Chicherin, Boris 52
Civil Cassation Department 39, 44, 50
Civil Code
  1913 Draft Civil Code 50
  1922 RSFSR Civil Code 78–80, 83
  Civil Code of the Russian Federation 132–3, 146
  Digest of Laws (Volume X) 31–3, 42, 50
  and Speranskii 31
civil law. *See* private law
civil rights 53–4, 62–3, 122, 127, 139–40, 157
  differentiation of rights (tsarist) 22, 55, 87
  and dissident movement 96–9
  freedom of assembly 66, 69, 87, 100, 128, 158, 159
  freedom of press 30, 58, 66, 87, 98, 100, 111, 117, 128, 131, 140, 156
  freedom of religion 66, 69, 76, 87, 100, 117, 128, 156
  freedom of speech 60, 66, 69, 87, 98, 100, 117, 128, 156
  habeas corpus 25, 30
  property rights 27, 54–5, 66, 117, 132, 140
  qualification of (Soviet) 76–7, 79, 87, 101, 106

social rights 48, 62, 73, 83, 87, 100, 106, 128–9, 132, 147
women's rights 67, 79
codification 46, 105–6
  failed attempts at 14, 27
  Judicial Reforms of 1864 38
  1649 Law Code 10–11
  and Speranskii 31–2, 93
  under Khrushchev 93–4, 101
  and Vyshinskii 87
collectivization 73, 83–4, 88, 93
commercial law
  Higher Commercial Court 128, 137
  and New Economic Policy 78–80
  state *arbitrazh* court (Soviet) 95
  state capitalism 136, 161
  state corporations 50
  tsarist 32, 50, 93
  under Brezhnev 104
  under Gorbachev 108–9, 114
  under Nicholas I 32
  under Putin 148, 161
  under Yeltsin 118, 132–6
common law 1, 6, 11, 43, 57, 73, 95, 99, 109, 137
Communist Party 94, 107, 110–11, 115–17, 127, 140
  constitutional status of 88, 100, 109–10, 112, 114
  and legal profession 94–5
  oversight over legal institutions 102–3
  as source of law 101
Complete Collection of Laws (*Polnoe sobranie zakonov*) of the Russian Empire 31–2, 35, 41
comrade courts. *See* court system
Conception of Judicial Reform (1991) 136–7, 160
Congress of People's Deputies
  RSFSR 114, 116, 118–21, 140
  Soviet 109–10, 112, 116, 119
Congress of Soviets 76, 82
Congress of Vienna 30
Conquest, Robert 85
conscience courts. *See* court system
Constantine (brother of Nicholas I) 30
Constituent Assembly 69–71, 75–6, 120

constitution
    1906 Fundamental Laws 5, 58, 63–8, 133
    1918 RSFSR Constitution 76–7
    1924 Soviet Constitution 81–2, 89
    1936 Soviet Constitution 86–9, 97–8, 106, 110
    1977 Soviet Constitution 2, 100–2, 105–6, 109–10, 112, 114–15, 128
    1978 RSFSR Constitution 115, 117–19
    1993 Constitution 2, 5, 121–2, 123–30, 140, 145–56, 148, 150–2, 154–5, 157, 160, 168
    Finland 30
    Poland 30
    Union Republics (Soviet) 86, 88–9, 94, 102, 110, 115
    United States of America 1, 99, 124
constitutional amendments 112, 154, 160
Constitutional Court 139–40, 153–4, 160
    and appointment of governors 151–2
    and Chechnya 131, 140
    and Dadin 158–9
    and European Court of Human Rights 147, 159
    and federalism 120, 132
    implementation of decisions 132
    jurisdiction of 2, 128–9
    NGO law 158
    1992–1993 Crisis 119–20
    suspension of 122
Constitutional Supervision Committee 110
consultation bureaus. See *advokatura*
corporate raiding 148, 154
corruption
    and *blat* 104
    oligarchs 134–6, 149, 162
    organized crime (post-Soviet) 134–5
    post-Soviet 123, 133–5, 138, 140–1, 144, 146, 148, 153–5, 157, 160, 162, 164, 168
    Soviet 91, 93, 104–5, 117–18
    tsarist 12, 19, 35

Council of Europe 126, 147
Council of Ministers 65, 86, 110
court system. *See also* judiciary
    comrade courts 94, 96
    conscience courts 25
    frontier courts 26
    Muscovy 11–12
    post-Soviet 119–21, 128–9, 131–2, 137, 140–1, 147–8, 150–1, 153, 156–61
    Soviet 75, 77–8, 80, 82, 84, 87, 94–5, 102, 104, 110
    township courts 40, 47–50
    tsarist 15–17, 23–5, 34–5, 38–40, 43–6, 48–9, 51–2, 69, 71
Crimea 36, 49, 98, 114, 157
criminal law and procedure
    1649 Law Code 10–11
    1839 Rural Judicial Code 40
    1845 Penal Code 32
    1906 Fundamental Laws 66
    1922 RSFSR Criminal Code 79–80, 83
    1960 Criminal Procedure Code 95, 97, 139
    2001 Criminal Procedure Code 147, 149–50, 155, 161, 167
    accusatorial bias 90, 104, 160–1
    acquittals 80, 90, 104, 147, 160
    adversarial process 10, 39, 43, 49, 51, 60, 89, 99, 104, 136–7, 140, 147, 168
    defendant's rights 43
    de-Stalinization 92
    economic crimes (Soviet) 79, 96
    inquisitorial procedure 10, 34, 43, 46, 136
    politicization of 41, 56, 167
    post-Soviet 139, 147, 153
    preliminary investigation 43, 51, 110, 147, 151
    under Peter the Great 16, 19, 49
customary law 80, 82, 102, 127, 146
    in the Caucuses 30, 55
    Central Asia 3, 55
    Muscovy 12
    and peasantry 24, 40, 43, 45, 48–50, 65, 71, 80, 87, 93
    serfdom 24

as source of law 46, 49, 56, 166, 168
tsarist versus Soviet 87, 93–4, 102
under Peter the Great 16, 19

Dadin, Ildar 158–9
Dagestan 163
Daly, Jonathan 42
Daniel', Iulii 97
Decembrists 30
decrees
   Muscovy 22
   1993 Constitution 126, 129
   Provisional Government 69–70
   as source of law 6, 32, 35–6, 133, 166
   Soviet law 75–7, 80, 82–3, 86, 88, 101, 110, 119
   tsarist law 36, 40, 43, 64, 65–7, 70–1
   under Alexander I 29
   under Catherine the Great 27
   under Gorbachev 112–13, 115
   under Medvedev 153, 155
   under Nicholas I 32
   under Peter the Great 13–15, 19
   under Putin 145, 150, 152, 158, 164
   under Yeltsin 66, 114, 118–21, 126, 133, 140
   versus laws 123, 126, 133, 140, 166
defamation 10–11, 16, 49, 153, 156
Derzhavin, Gavriil 29
Desnitskii, Semen 25
Digest of Laws 27, 31–3, 41–2, 84
dissident trials. *See* political trials
divorce 16, 39, 44, 47, 56, 95, 103
Dobson, Miriam 92
Doctors' Plot 90–1
Dostoevskii, Fyodor 59
dual power 69, 71, 107, 112, 166
dual state 89
duality of law
   definition of 6–7
   Hendley, Kathryn 6, 105, 167
   under post-Soviet law 164, 167–8
   under Soviet law 105
   under tsarist law 50–1, 55–6, 63
Duma
   pre-revolutionary 64, 69
   Russian Federation 125–6, 140, 151, 154, 156, 166

Estonia 27, 111
European Convention on Human Rights 3, 99, 147–8, 159, 163
European Court of Human Rights 3, 99, 126, 147–8, 159
exile 10, 41, 92–3
Extraordinary Investigatory Commission (Murav'ev Commission) 70–1

family law 49, 83, 93
federalism
   post-Soviet 117, 120, 127, 130–2, 140, 145–6, 152, 169
   Soviet 77, 81, 86, 89, 113–15, 127
   tsarist 54, 64–5
Federation Council 126, 131, 138, 146, 154
Federation Treaty (1992) 117–18, 130
Feifer, George 94–5
Feofanov, Yuri 96
Finality of Judgments (*res judicata*) 103, 148, 163
Financial Action Task Force 146
Finland 29, 30, 42–3, 53, 64, 72, 77
Firestone, Thomas 148
First All Russian Congress of Workers and Soldiers Deputies 70
First World War 37, 41, 48, 68–70
Fitzpatrick, Sheila 84
five-year plan 83
Foreign Agents Law 156, 158
France 17, 22, 31, 38, 75, 124
Frierson, Cathy 49
frontier courts. *See* court system
Fundamental Laws of 1906 58, 63–70, 133

geography of law. *See also* legal pluralism; treaties
   definition of 6
   Muscovy 12
   post-Soviet 117–18, 127, 130–2, 145–6, 163
   Soviet 77, 81, 86, 93–4, 111, 113–14
   tsarist 14, 29–30, 33, 42–3, 53
Georgia 80, 111, 113
Germany 57, 77, 81, 89, 124, 143

Gessen, I. V. 60
glasnost 108, 116, 143
Gorbachev, Mikhail 5–6, 106–18, 136, 151, 169
governors
   post-Soviet 127, 132, 150, 157
   tsarist 17, 23, 27, 29, 34, 36, 40–1, 46, 59
Gruzenberg, O. O. 63
guberniia 24, 80
gulags 90, 92–3
Gusinskii, Vladimir 149

Hague Convention Respecting the Laws and Customs of War on Land (1899) 54
Hartley, Janet 30
Hellie, Richard 10–11
Helsinki Accords 98
Helsinki Watch Group 98–9
Hendley, Kathryn 6–7, 104–5, 148, 167
Hetmanate 26
hierarchy of laws
   post-Soviet 110, 123, 126, 133–4, 140, 145, 151, 164, 166, 168
   Soviet 76, 101, 110
   tsarist 16, 58, 64, 66–7
Higher Commercial Court 128, 137, 153, 159–60
Hoffman, David 134
Holy Roman Empire 15
Hughes, Lindsey 15
human rights 1–2, 5, 54, 87, 98–9, 113, 127–8, 131, 147–8, 153, 158–60, 163
Huskey, Eugene 88

industrialization 73, 83–4, 93
intellectual property 50, 132, 146, 152
investigative committee 151–2, 158
Isaev, M. A. 79, 106
Islamic law 14, 33, 49, 163

Jefferson, Thomas 28
Jordan, Pamela 102
Judicial Reforms of 1864 4, 37–56, 58, 75, 89, 128, 168–9
   and *advokatura* 37–9

Basic Principles for the Reform of the Courts 38–9
counter-reforms 40, 59
court system 39–40
customary law 40
drafting of 38–9
implementation 39, 42, 51–2
judiciary 37–8
jury 37–8
legal profession 37–40, 47
private law 49–51
procuracy 38–9, 51
Provisional Government 71
judiciary. *See also* Constitutional Court; court system; Supreme Court; justice of the peace courts
   administrative control over 19, 49
   Civil Cassation Department 39, 44, 50
   and corruption 12, 93, 104, 118
   Higher Commercial Court 128, 153, 159–60
   independence of 17, 22, 37–9, 41, 44, 46, 49, 75, 80, 110, 128, 136–7, 140, 168
   interpretation of law 43, 56, 99, 102
   post-Soviet 123, 125, 128–9, 132, 136–7, 140, 153, 158, 160, 168–9
   precedent 1, 44, 99, 132, 153, 159
   Soviet 75, 77, 95, 98, 103, 106
   tsarist 16–17, 22–3, 27, 34, 39–41
jury trials
   abolition of 75
   acquittals 45–6, 137, 161
   jury nullification 45–6
   post-Communist 128, 136–7, 140, 153–4
   tsarist 25, 44–6
justice of the peace courts
   post-Soviet 137, 148
   tsarist 39–40, 47, 75

Kadet Party 31, 61, 68–9
Kamenev, Lev 85
Kaminskaia, Dina 97–8
Karabchevskii, Nikolai P. 2, 60–2
Kazannik, Aleksei 129

Kazantsev, S. M. 26, 51
Kelsen, Hans 1
Kerenskii, Aleksandr 61
Khasbulatov, Ruslan 118–19, 121
Khmelnytsky, Bohdan 12
Khodorkovskii, Mikhail 135, 149–50, 155, 157
Khrushchev, Nikita 5, 91–4, 96, 100, 106, 108
Kirmse, Stefan 49
Kirov, Sergei 84
Kistiakovskii, Bogdan 54, 106
Kivelson, Valerie 11
Kliuchevskii, V. O. 13
Kollmann, Nancy Shields 11–13, 16, 18–19
Koni, Anatolii 46
Kononov, Anatolii 151
Konovalov, Aleksandr 158
Korkunov, Nikolai M. 13, 38, 52–6, 64, 162
Kotsonis, Yanni 42, 50
Kravchuk, Leonid 114
Kurskii, D. I. 61

labor law 83, 86, 93, 105
Land Code (2001) 146–7
Latvia 111
law-based state (*Rechtsstaat*) 10, 93, 167
   definition of 57
   Muscovy 10
   post-Soviet 164
   Provisional Government 70
   Soviet 109, 112
   tsarist 64, 66
Law Code of 1649 4, 9–12, 14, 17, 19, 21–3, 26–7
lay assessors
   Soviet 80, 95
   tsarist 16, 24
Ledeneva, Alena 104
LeDonne, John 24, 26
legal aid. *See advokatura*
legal education 4, 31, 34, 52, 74–5, 83, 86, 107
legality (*zakonnost'*) 19, 31, 53, 97–9, 148–9, 168
   bureaucratic (top-down) 21, 23, 41, 53, 56, 132, 140, 145, 150, 152, 166, 168
   definition of 7–8, 71
   socialist legality 86, 90–1, 93–4, 96, 103, 106
legal nihilism 154
legal pluralism 6, 12, 14, 19, 21, 27, 30, 33, 42–3, 55–6, 65, 71–2, 130, 146, 165
legal profession. *See advokatura*
legislative initiative
   constitutional grant of 65, 102, 110, 126, 129, 138
   judiciary 102
   procuracy 18, 102, 145, 168
   tsarist ministries 29
Lenin, Vladimir 5, 73–9, 83, 85, 93, 106
Lithuania 10, 12, 24, 98, 111, 113
Lithuanian Statute of 1588 10
Livonia 27
Loris-Melikov, M. T. 41
Luzhkov, Yurii 135

Magdeburg law 27
Magnitsky, Sergei 154–5
Maklakov, V. A. 61
Makovskii, Aleksandr 105–6
Marrese, Michelle Lamarche 35
Martens, Fyodor 54
Marx, Karl 73–4
McReynolds, Louise 46
Medvedev, Dmitry 143, 152–7
Mikhail Alexandrovich, Grand Duke 68–9
Miliukov, Pavel 69
Ministry of Internal Affairs
   Russian Federation 120, 145, 155
   Soviet 84, 92, 95
   tsarist 29, 32, 40
Ministry of Justice
   Russian Federation 139, 145, 158
   Soviet 93
   tsarist 28–9
modernization
   economic 15, 84, 134, 136, 169
   legal 4, 14–16, 20, 24, 32, 51, 84, 135–6, 164, 169

Moldova 111, 113
Montesquieu 22
Moon, David 24
Morozov, Boris 9
Morshchakova, Tamara 154
Murav'ev, Nikolai K. 61–2, 70–1, 77–8
Murav'ev Commission. *See* Extraordinary Investigatory Commission
Muromtsev, Sergei 54, 68
Myers, Steven Lee 138

Nakaz of 1767 22–3, 27
Napoleonic Code 42
Nargorno-Karabakh 111
Nathans, Benjamin 101
Navalny, Aleksei 157, 162
Nechaev, Sergei 58–9
New Economic Policy (NEP) 73, 78, 80, 82–5, 93, 109
Nicholas I 4, 21, 28, 30–7, 84, 167
Nicholas II 41–2, 61–2, 67–8, 169
Nineteenth Communist Party Conference 116
Nolde, Boris 64, 67
nongovernmental organizations (NGOs) 110, 139, 156, 158
Novgorodtsev, Pavel 52, 68

October Manifesto 64
oligarchs 134–6, 149–50, 162
organized crime 134–6
Orlov, Yuri 99
Orlovsky, Daniel 29
Orthodox Church 3, 9–11, 14–16, 39, 59, 65, 157, 165

Panin, V. N. 29
Pashin, Sergei 160
Pashukanis, E. B. 82–4, 86
Paul I 28
peasantry. *See* customary law
Pereiaslav agreement (1654) 12
perestroika 108, 116, 143
Peter the Great 2–4, 23, 26–7, 31, 34, 36, 41, 43, 66, 81, 86, 95, 145, 150, 167

law creating powers 13–14
legal system 14–17, 19–20
and procuracy 18, 79
Peter III 23
Petrazycki, Leon 52, 68
Pipes, Richard 24, 41–2, 81
plea bargaining 147, 161
Plevako, F. N. 2, 62
Plokhy, Serhii 12
Poland 29–30, 33, 41–3, 53, 72, 81
police (tsarist) 25, 41–2, 69, 75
Politburo 108, 116
political trials
    defense attorneys 58–63, 97–8
    post-Soviet 149–50, 154–7
    Soviet 77–8, 85–6, 97–100
    tsarist 46, 58–63
Politkovskaia, Anna 161
Pomorski, Stanislaw 139
Potanin, Vladimir 135
Pravilova, Ekaterina 23, 33
President's Council for Civil Society and Human Rights 153, 155
private law
    and civil society 35, 49, 54–5, 168–9
    expansion under tsarism 47–50, 56, 60
    Judicial Reforms of 1864 37, 56
    Soviet 95, 103–5
    under Catherine 27
    under Gorbachev 108–9, 118
    under Peter the Great 15, 19
    under Putin 148, 150, 152, 161, 163–4
    under Yeltsin 118, 122, 132–6, 140, 163
    versus public law 15, 35, 50–1, 56, 63, 89, 105, 150, 168
privatization 118–19, 133–6, 141, 161
procuracy
    constitutional status of 87, 102–3, 106, 129
    conflict with Yeltsin 138, 140
    creation of 3, 18
    "eyes of the sovereign" 18, 51, 158, 168

law-creating activities 87, 138, 168
legislative initiative 18, 102, 145, 168
post-Soviet 3, 138, 145, 151–2, 158, 160
Soviet 79, 87, 95–6, 103, 106
supervision (*nadzor*) 3–4, 17–18, 36, 51, 81–2, 87, 92, 95–6, 102–3, 138, 140, 168–9
and tsarist criminal law 26, 38–9, 45, 51
under Alexander I 29
under Catherine the Great 25–6
property rights 23, 33, 35, 45, 71. *See also* intellectual property
constitutional status of 76, 87, 89, 123, 127–8, 132, 150
and civil rights 54–6, 66, 105, 132, 140
Judicial Reforms of 1864 37–8, 44–5, 49, 84
Muscovy 10–11
private property (Soviet) 78–9, 87, 105, 108
state property (Soviet) 76, 78–9, 87, 89, 95, 104
property disputes (Soviet) 95, 103
under Catherine the Great 4, 23–4, 27–8
under Lenin 76, 79–80
under Peter the Great 13, 15, 19
under Putin 150, 152, 161
under Yeltsin 117, 132, 134, 136, 140–1
Provisional Government 5, 57–8, 61, 68–72, 75–7, 166
purges. *See* terror
Pussy Riot trial 157
Putin, Vladimir 2–3, 5, 135, 138, 143–64, 166–7, 169

Raeff, Marc 23, 28
Rand, Robert 103
referendum of 1992 119–20
registration (*propiska*) requirements 95, 132
Remington, Thomas 151
Revolution (1905) 41, 54–5, 58, 62–3, 68, 74, 93

Revolution (1917)
February 5, 57–8, 61, 68–9
October 5, 51, 58, 75, 112
Rodzianko, Mikhail 69
Rokotov, Ian 96
rule of law 5, 29, 37–8, 54, 93, 115, 122–3, 128, 140, 154–5, 164, 166
and *advokatura* 58, 63
definition of 7–8
Provisional Government 5, 68–9
versus law-based state 57–8, 109
versus legality 7, 168–9
Rumiantsev, Oleg 122
Russian Civil War 73, 77, 80
Russian Soviet Federative Socialist Republic (RSFSR) 76–7, 80, 113–14, 117, 120
Russification 12, 42–3, 55, 65, 82
Rutskoi, Aleksandr 118

samizdat 99
samosud 49, 80
Sazonov, Egor 60–1
secession, right of 81, 102, 110–12, 117, 130
security services 32, 40, 91, 93, 108, 134, 144, 152, 156
Cheka 77, 81
Corps of Gendarmes 42
FSB 138, 144–5
KGB 95–6, 99, 119, 143–4
NKVD 84–5
OGPU 81
Third Section 32
Senate 14, 18
as administrative body 17, 29
as judicial body 16–17, 22, 24, 29, 33–4, 39, 44–5, 50, 59
as legislative body 14
separation of powers 1, 2, 5, 115, 119, 122, 151–2, 164, 166, 169
Muscovy 10
1993 constitution 125, 129, 131, 133
Soviet 76, 79, 82
tsarist 17, 27, 29, 36, 57–8, 66–7
Sharlet, Robert 83, 112
Shcheglovitov, I. G. 70–1

show trials. *See* political trials
Siberia 10, 39, 41, 55, 74, 92–3, 139
Simis, Konstantin 105–6
Siniavskii, Andrei 97
Skuratov, Yurii 138
slander. *See* defamation
Slezkine, Yuri 89
Sliozberg, G. B. 52
Sobchak, Anatolii 143–4, 152
socialist legality. *See* legality
Socialist Revolutionary Party 75, 78, 85
social rights. *See* civil rights
Solomon, Peter 79, 84
sources of law. *See also* legal pluralism
   domestic 4, 6, 9, 11, 14, 16, 19, 27, 36, 40–4, 55, 73, 75, 101–2, 106, 115, 119, 126, 134, 166
   European Court of Human Rights 126, 147–8
   influences of foreign law 10, 14, 24, 31, 38, 108, 124, 133, 166
Spain 124
Spasovich, Vladimir D. 2, 58–9
Speranskii, Mikhail 28, 31–3, 36, 38, 84, 93
Stalin, Joseph 5, 73, 81, 83–93, 95–7, 100, 104, 106, 108, 110, 116, 124, 157, 167
state 144–5
   definition of 13
   integrity of 64–5, 111, 163
   multinational 100, 163, 168–9
   1993 constitution 124–5, 129
   and separation of ruler 13, 36, 66–7, 166
   unified 53, 56, 64, 72, 81–2, 88, 100, 111–12, 115, 129–131, 151, 163, 165–6, 169
State and Revolution (Lenin) 74–5
state capitalism 135–6
State Committee for the State of Emergency (1991) 114
State Council 28–9, 32, 66
state power 53, 114, 140, 149, 151, 158, 162
   constitutional status of 88, 100–3, 111, 124–5

and dictatorship of proletariat 88
   1992–93 crisis 121
Stolypin, Petr 42, 48, 67
striapchie 26
Suny, Ronald 102
supervision (*nadzor*). *See* procuracy
supervisory review 3, 103, 148, 153
Supreme Court
   post-Soviet 128, 131, 159–60
   Soviet 80, 82, 87, 99, 102, 104, 110
Supreme Soviet 5, 96, 103
   Estonian 111
   presidium 86–7, 101–2, 110
   RSFSR 113, 116, 118–22, 134
   USSR 86, 101–2, 110, 112
Sweden 14, 24, 29, 30
Szeftel, Marc 7, 66

Tatarstan 117–18, 130, 146, 163
telephone law 103
terror 5, 37, 41–2, 73, 75, 77, 83–6, 88–90, 93–4, 96, 106, 110, 167
terrorism 40–2, 46, 58–9, 61, 150, 154
theory of state and law 1, 3, 52–4, 86, 164–5
torture 10, 16, 34, 85–6, 154, 167
township courts. *See* court system
Transcaucasia 80–1
treaties 6, 12, 14, 29–30, 53, 77–8, 80–1, 98, 111, 113–15, 117–18, 125–7, 129–30, 132, 140, 146–7, 151, 163, 165, 169
Treaty of Brest-Litovsk 77, 81
Treaty of Fredrikshamn (1809) 30
Treaty of Nystad (1721) 14
Trudolyubov, Maxim 161
Turkey 23, 81

uezd 24
Ukraine 12, 21, 26–7, 53, 72, 80–1, 98, 112, 114–15, 157
Union Treaty (1922) 78, 80–1, 111, 113–14
United Russia Party 151
United States of America 1, 43, 94, 103, 124

Vinaver, Maxim 31, 50–1
voevoda. *See* judiciary
Volkov, Vadim 134
votchina 15
Vyborg Manifesto 68
Vyshinskii, Andrei 85–6, 90, 95, 106

Wagner, William 44
World Trade Organization 144
Wortman, Richard 7, 54–5

Yaney, George 36
Yeltsin, Boris 107, 113–24, 126–7, 130–6, 138–41, 144–7, 151–2, 160–1, 163, 166, 169
Yukos 149–50, 155, 159

Zasulich, Vera 46, 58–9
zemstvo 36, 39
Zinoviev, Grigori 85
Zorkin, Valerii 119–20, 148, 159

CPSIA information can be obtained
at www.ICGtesting.com
Printed in the USA
LVHW080302220319
611514LV00004B/21/P